*Animal Century*

ALSO BY MARK GOLD:

*Assault and Battery* (Pluto Press, 1983)
*Living Without Cruelty* (Green Print, 1988)
*Living Without Cruelty Diary* (annually since 1989)
*Animal Rights* (Jon Carpenter, 1995)

# Animal Century

A celebration of

## changing attitudes to animals

## Mark Gold

JON CARPENTER

**Our books may be ordered from bookshops or (post free) from
Jon Carpenter Publishing, 2 The Spendlove Centre, Charlbury, England OX7 3PQ
Please send for our free catalogue
Credit card orders should be phoned or faxed to 01689 870437 or 01608 811969**

*In the USA and Canada*, please order from Paul and Company, PO Box 442, Concord, MA 01742
(phone (978) 369 3049, fax (978) 369 2385)

*In Australia*, please order from Envirobook, The Gloucester Walk, 88 Cumberland Street,
Sydney, NSW 2000 (phone 02 9247 6036, fax 02 9241 1289)

*In South Africa*, please order from New Horizon Distributors, PO Box 44585, Claremont 7735
(phone 021 683 0360, fax 021 683 8666)

First published in 1998 by
Jon Carpenter Publishing
The Spendlove Centre, Charlbury, Oxfordshire OX7 3PQ
☎ 01608 811969

ISBN  1 897766 43 2

Printed in England by J. W. Arrowsmith Ltd., Bristol

# Contents

# Acknowledgements

I t *was Emily* who first came up with the thought that if we could have a fascinating television series and book chronicling the People's Century, then why not a history of the Animal Century? It is not the first time that her creativity has been the source of one of 'my' better ideas and I can only hope that this book proves worthy of the suggestion.

I am also indebted to all those who readily agreed to be interviewed — Maneka Gandhi, Jane Goodall, Celia Hammond, Ali Hassani, Kathleen Jannaway, Ronnie Lee, Virginia McKenna, Peter Roberts, Peter Singer, Antony Thomas, Dave Wetton and Irene Williams. Without their contributions, whatever is felt to be valuable in the pages that follow would have been far less so. Thanks, too, to Sir David Attenborough for supplying written answers to my questions.

I am grateful to Marjorie Sutcliffe for supplying archive material from the Captive Animals Protection Society; Sarah Kite for allowing me to quote at length from her book, *Silent Suffering*, and for additional comments; Jenny Wheadon for access to the records at Ferne Animal Sanctuary; Pat Simpson for sending me information so quickly; likewise Bronwen Humphreys at the Vegetarian Society and Tim Phillips at the National Anti-Vivisection Society. And last but not least, thanks to Ruth Iles, Mary Shephard, Becky Smith and Andrew Tyler at Animal Aid for greeting my numerous requests for addresses and information during a particularly busy period with such tolerance!

A book of this nature inevitably leans to some extent upon previously published works and I hope that those who spot their influence will accept my use of their original research as a compliment rather than an impertinence. In particular, I am indebted to two wider histories of the relationship between animals and people: *Animal Revolution* by Richard Ryder and *All Heaven in a Rage* by E. S. Turner. Jon Wynne-Tyson's marvellous 'dictionary of humane thought', *The Extended Circle*, has also proved invaluable. Other books useful to the overall concept include *Man and the Natural World* by Keith Thomas and *Who Cares For Animals — 150 Years Of The RSPCA* by Antony Brown.

In addition, I must acknowledge works that provided a wealth of source material

• • • • • • • • • • • • • • • • • • • • • • • • • • • • • • • • • • • • • • • • • •

for individual sections — *The Savour of Salt: A Henry Salt Anthology* edited by George Hendrick and Willene Hendrick; *A Dog Is For Life: Celebrating The First Hundred Years of The National Canine Defence League* by Peter Ballard, *Debt of Honour: International League For The Protection Of Horses* by Jeremy James, *The Chronicles of Ferne* by the Duchess of Hamilton, *Nature In Trust* by John Sheail, *Whale Nation* by Heathcote Williams, *The Greenpeace Story* by John May and Michael Brown, *The Hunt and the Anti-Hunt* by Phil Windeatt, *The Rose-Tinted Menagerie* by William Johnson, *A Century of Vivisection and Anti-Vivisection* by E. Westacott, *The Dark Face of Science* by John Vynan and *Against All Odds* by John Page and Jane Holgate.

Thanks, too, to both organisations and individuals who generously provided photographs, particularly Animal Aid, Born Free Foundation, British Union for Vivisection, Compassion In World Farming, Jane Goodall Institute, League Against Cruel Sports, National Canine Defence League, People for the Ethical Treatment of Animals, *Punch*, World Society for the Protection of Animals, Iain Green and Jon Wynne-Tyson.

Finally, my gratitude to Jon Carpenter for supporting the project so wholeheartedly, to Dan for being himself and to other friends, family and colleagues for their kindness, encouragement and support over many years.

Full picture credits are acknowledged at the end of the book.

# Foreword

This book was prompted by a mood of reflection which almost inevitably accompanies the imminent arrival of a new century. It deals with not only an important and largely ignored element of our social history, but also with some of the most profound of many momentous changes that have occurred in human society over the past hundred years.

Whether it be the rise in popularity of conservation issues, concern for animal welfare, or even the emergence of vegetarianism, the signs of a revolution in the way in which people respond to non-human animals are everywhere to be seen and have become crucial to any meaningful assessment of how future generations might choose to live their lives. How and why have such changes taken place? Who are the people who have campaigned so resolutely to make them happen? More importantly, what has motivated them? What have been the external social factors which have helped to establish animal protection as an issue of significant public concern? These are amongst the questions I have sought to answer.

Yet how to approach the task offered a formidable challenge. A comprehensive chronicle of every event affecting each and every species over the last hundred years, useful though it may be, might make for a very long and arduous read. Similarly, to catalogue the contribution of every single person to have played a valuable role would probably result in a book too much like an inventory to sustain attention.

What I have sought instead is to capture the *essence* of ideas which have shaped change by focusing upon a representative selection of individuals and events. I have done so in the belief that the experiences of a carefully chosen few can provide profound insights into the thoughts and emotions which have motivated impassioned advocacy by many others. Likewise, the choice of relatively few specific events offers, I feel, the most plausible method by which to reach wider conclusions about the ways in which the lives of both wild and domestic animals have been affected by shifts in human sensibility.

Such a selective scheme does, I admit, have its limitation in that the choice of what is significant is always likely to reflect the prejudices of its author. While the voices recorded in this history do, I hope, represent fully the many interests who have helped to create greater empathy for the animal kingdom, to some extent they must unavoidably reflect sentiments with which I am predisposed to sympathise. If this limits the legitimacy of the endeavour then so be it. All I can say in defence is that while every effort has been made to treat the subject fairly, in my opinion it is impossible to write any history without to some extent reflecting the pre-conceptions of the author and the age in which he or she experiences the world. Complete objectivity is impossible. I have my opinions and it would be dishonest to pretend to hide them: the ultimate judge of the validity of my case can only be the reader.

The selective method has one other major drawback. By focusing predominantly upon the efforts of relatively few individuals, I have inevitably glorified their role in relation to many others whose contribution has been at least equally important. Reading through the text, I am only too aware of the absence of names and initiatives which deserve recognition I have failed to give them. That the scheme of the book demanded such sacrifice is my only excuse, and one for which I hope I will be forgiven by all those whose noteworthy part in the *Animal Century* has been overlooked.

During my research I have interviewed or read the works and biographies of many people. About two-thirds of them are women, reflecting the dominant female influence to be found throughout the animal protection movement. Some are famous, some unknown; some are wealthy, some not; some are aristocrats; others are ordinary working people. They have been farmers, teachers, chartered surveyors, models, actors, circus performers, housewives, academics and nurses. Concern for animals apart, what they all have in common, I believe, are experiences and achievements which not only helped to instigate change in the past, but also possess the power to stir and to motivate progress in the future. As many of them have inspired me, so I hope that they may encourage others.

Although much of the text is concerned with people, it should also be remembered that individual animals have themselves inadvertently played a crucial part in dispelling misconceptions. Attitudes to non-humans might well have been very different without the lives of (say) Elsa, the lioness who befriended Joy and George Adamson in Kenya and thereby called into question our previous understanding about the capacity of wild animals to display complex emotions; Guy, the wretched gorilla whose incarceration over three decades affected profoundly many visitors to London Zoo; Digit, the first wild gorilla ever to be filmed exploring and interacting with a human being; or the little brown dog whose torture and death in the laboratories of Edwardian London led to riots in the streets against the practice of vivisection.

One other point. Responses to animals have not developed in a social vacuum. They have grown out of the same economic and social circumstances which have influenced human civilisation. World wars, developing technology, increased wealth, the growth in human population, the emergence of youth culture — these and other external factors have been as central to the experience of other species as they have been to our own. Therefore, I have endeavoured throughout to place the Animal Century within a political and social context.

As with any useful historical study, the main purpose of dwelling upon bygone events is a belief that only by understanding the past will it will be possible to create a more enlightened future. It is in that spirit that this project has been undertaken. My deepest hope is that in some small way, it might encourage a time when some of the heartless barbarities still suffered by animals at the hands of humans will be viewed with the same disgust and disbelief with which we now look back at outlawed brutalities from decades gone by.

Mark Gold, May 1998

# 1 / In the beginning

## 1  The climate at the turn of the century

A common misconception is that the animal protection movement has its origins in the same wave of environmental awareness that created radical green politics in the 1970s. This is not the case. Most of the arguments now advanced to reduce or abolish exploitation of other creatures had been well rehearsed on both sides of the Atlantic by the beginning of the twentieth century and already enjoyed organised support.

The first law to protect animals had been passed in the UK in 1822, making it an offence 'to beat, abuse, or ill-treat any horse, mare, gelding, ass, ox, cow, heifer, steer, sheep or other cattle', cruelly or wantonly. It was followed by a steady stream of new legislation which, though it left many diabolically cruel practices untouched, did at least outlaw savage activities such as cock fighting and bear and bull baiting.

The first organisations dedicated to reducing cruelty emerged soon after the introduction of the first animal welfare laws. Indeed, the primary function of the Society for the Prevention of Cruelty to Animals (SPCA), formed in 1824, was to ensure that the provisions of the 1822 Act were enforced. (It did not receive its royal patronage from Queen Victoria until 1840.) By 1900 there were also many single issue groups, including the Vegetarian Society (which claimed a highly respectable 2,000 members in 1899[1]), the first anti-vivisection societies, and organisations for the protection of horses, dogs and birds. Several other groups for the general protection of animals were also operative.

By this time there had even been the first evidence of the kind of ideological internal conflicts which have dogged the animal protection movement ever since. Then, as now, dispute was particularly bitter amongst anti-vivisectionists. Those who believed it tactically more realistic to campaign only to ban the worst excesses of experimentation soon quarrelled furiously with others who felt that any compromise was unacceptable. By 1998, a breakaway group of total abolitionists had departed from the Victoria Group (later the National Anti-Vivisection Society) to form a more hard-line second society, the British Union for the Abolition of Vivisection.

*1*

Anti-vivsection protest soon after the beginning of the century.

A similar disagreement festered within the RSPCA over whether it should adopt an anti-hunting policy, a controversy that has continued throughout the twentieth century. Right up until 1976 the pro-hunting lobby succeeded in repressing all attempts to introduce reform and it has been working with some influence ever since (though ultimately unsuccessfully) to try to reverse the Society's decision to oppose hunting.

It is not really surprising that disputes arose within animal welfare societies from their earliest days, for they simply mirrored the inconsistencies and irrationalities which characterised, and still characterise, most individual responses. Queen Victoria offers a pertinent example. She abhorred vivisection, disapproved of stag hunting and followed the activities of the RSPCA with evident interest and concern: yet she also enthusiastically attended the performances of Isaac Van Amburgh, a US animal tamer whose world-wide reputation was built around his method of subduing wild creatures through the application of crowbars and similar vicious implements.

In addition to long-established cruelties, emerging faith in and dependence upon science and technology in the nineteenth century created new forms of violence. Animal experimentation was a particularly contentious issue, debated at great length and with great vigour. In 1875, 'a widespread feeling of anxiety in the country and controversy in the Press'[2] led the government to implement the First Royal Commission on Vivisection. It took evidence from over fifty witnesses. Reading through the contributions demonstrates how little the basis of arguments either for or against has altered in more than one hundred and twenty years. Pro-vivisection interests argued that science and medicine could not progress without experiments on animals, whilst at the same time emphasising that suffering should always be kept to a minimum: opponents asserted that the practice was not only cruel and barbaric, but also 'wholly useless, and worse than useless'[3] on scientific grounds, offering data that could not be applied with any confidence to the study of human disease. Setting a precedent to be followed by every other official investigation, the commission sided with the scientific establishment, concluding that 'it is impossible altogether to prevent the practice of making experiments on living animals', but stressing that 'the infliction of any unnecessary pain is justly abhorrent to the moral sense of Your Majesty's subjects generally'.[4] It recommended the introduction of a Parliamentary Act which, it claimed, would sanction what was considered scientifically necessary, but outlaw the infliction of 'severe and protracted agony'.[5] The Cruelty to Animals Act (known as the Act to Regulate Vivisection) passed through parliament in 1876 and was to remain the principal legislation to control animal experimentation until 1986. Biting criticism of its ineffectiveness in preventing violent suffering spanned precisely the same period.

Probably the most significant scientific event of the nineteenth century was the publication of Darwin's *Origin of Species* in 1859. In one way its findings were to act as a spur to the study of biology and consequently to an increase in animal research. Additionally, some interpreted its emphasis on the competitive nature of life as further justification of the already accepted right of humans to pursue their own interests without fear of moral restraint.

Yet for others, the challenge which *Origin of Species* mounted to traditional and religious prejudices against animals had precisely the opposite effect. It was contested that Darwin's revelation of how 'there is no fundamental difference between man and the higher mammals in their mental faculties' gave new intellectual and scientific support to the campaign against animal exploitation, complementing the gut-feeling detestation of cruelty that lay at the heart of protests. If non-human and human animals were so alike where was the justification for persecution? Surely, it was pleaded, Darwin's evolutionary theories could become a basis for co-operation rather than competition.

Darwin himself was another person deeply divided on animal issues. As a scien-

• • • • • • • • • • • • • • • • • • • • • • • • • • • • • • • • • • • • • • • • •

tist, he glorified the potential of his chosen profession and defended vivisection. He told the Royal Commission that physiology 'cannot fail to confer the highest benefits on mankind'.[6] Yet only a year previously, he had offered to the RSPCA the then generous sum of £50 towards an invention that would humanely control the rabbit population — something for which humanity is still searching.[7]

It tended to be mostly the non-scientific intellectuals of the period who took evolutionary theory as a foundation for opposition to exploitation — and especially to vivisection. These included famous literary figures such as Ruskin, Carlyle, Tennyson, Browning and Hardy. They were joined by many of the early William Morris-inspired socialists, notably George Bernard Shaw and Edward Carpenter. In the US, President Abraham Lincoln was also a dedicated animal protectionist who, when he declared that 'I am in favour of animal rights as well as human rights. That is the way of a whole human being',[8] became one of the first to use a term often thought to be an invention of the late twentieth century. Lincoln was also typical of those whose re-evaluation of traditional religious attitudes resulted at least in part from dissatisfaction with attitudes to animals. 'I care not much for a man's religion whose dog and cat are not the better for it,' he wrote.[9]

## 2  Salt of the earth: the influence of Henry Salt

By far the most significant figure to emerge from this period, however, was a lesser known Englishman, Henry Salt. A self-confessed 'rationalist, socialist, pacifist, and humanitarian' who 'wholly' disbelieved in 'the present established religion',[10] Salt's criticisms of contemporary attitudes were profoundly influenced by Darwin's recognition of the kinship between people and other animals. He was a rare combination: formidable intellect, talented writer and inspired campaigner. His influence upon the campaign for the emancipation of animals was to be considerable, both in his own lifetime and in the legacy he left behind.

It takes an enormous leap of imagination to comprehend how different the world was at the beginning of the twentieth century. For the vast majority, cars, electricity, telephones, radios and many other items we now take for granted were beyond understanding. Women were still a long way from obtaining the vote. The rights of children were hardly considered. The old order of privilege and riches for the few and servitude and hardship for the rest was still largely accepted as inevitable.

At the same time, this was a period of fresh hope and advancement for new ideas. Those who did not accept the ways of the establishment rebelled against it with vigour. Amongst this growing minority there was passionate intellectual commitment to greater democracy and unprecedented questioning of established ortho-doxes, characterised by the rising influence of socialism.

In many ways the life of Henry Salt is wholly representative of this struggle for social justice. What makes him extraordinary, however, is that his plea for reform extended far beyond most of his contemporaries, so that even today his vision appears remarkably progressive.

Salt was born amongst the privileged Victorian classes in 1851. He was educated at Eton and King's College, Cambridge. His academic achievements were consider-able and after graduation he was invited to return to Eton as an assistant master — a position he took up in 1875. Soon afterwards he became a vegetarian and committed himself to socialist principles. This took him to the point where he could no longer tolerate the ways of the comfortable ruling class, prompting his departure from Eton in 1885. He and his wife then rented a labourer's cottage in Surrey, vowing to live as simple an existence as they possibly could. They had no servants — excep-tional for people of their social class in that period.

Increasingly, they devoted their time to the promotion of humanitarian causes, mixing with well-known socialists from the Fabian Society and advocating a programme of reform against injustice to both humans and animals. This activity culminated in 1891, when Salt became the driving force behind the formation of the Humanitarian League. He remained Secretary for almost thirty years, working and writing tirelessly for social equality and animal protection.

The Humanitarian League's mani-festo set out the principle that 'it is iniquitous to inflict suffering, directly or indirectly, on any sentient being, except where self-defence or absolute necessity can be justly pleaded'.[1] It set out 'to destroy the time-honoured idea of a hard-and-fast line between white man and black man, rich man and poor man, educated man and

Henry Salt (and his cat!).

uneducated man' and also to dispel 'the idea that there is any difference in kind … between human and non-human intelligence'.[2] Salt asserted that 'the emancipation of men from cruelty and injustice will bring with it in due course the emancipation of animals also'.[3] He added that 'the two reforms are inseparably connected and neither can be fully realised alone'.[4]

In support of these ideals, the League embarked on a revolutionary programme, opposing injustice wherever it found it. Hunting, vivisection, the abuse of animals for fashion, in farms, markets and slaughterhouses, were all singled out for attention, as were the inhumane treatment of human prisoners, cruel treatment of the mentally ill, corporal punishment and warfare.

Not least of Salt's astonishing talents was the way in which he was able to hold together an organisation with such a wide-ranging radical platform. He skilfully attracted support not only from the minority who were in complete agreement with *all* his ideas, but also from those with a narrower focus. He gently mocked some anti-vivisectionist colleagues at the League who 'were firm believers in the propriety of vivisecting the backs of criminals'[5] and was equally critical of others who argued 'that time spent on the rights of animals is so much taken away from the great human interests'.[6] But he inspired such great respect that he managed mostly to steer his organisation clear from destructive internal disputes. There never had been, nor has been since, a society which so successfully launched 'a systematic protest against the numerous barbarisms of the age — the cruelties inflicted by men on men, and the still more atrocious ill-treatment of the lower animals'.[7]

Salt was a prolific writer. Apart from regular articles in the League's journal, *The Humanitarian,* he produced pamphlets and books on subjects as diverse as corporal punishment, socialism, education, conservation, vegetarianism and animal protection. He also wrote literary biographies of Shelley and Thoreau. Peter Singer, the Australian philosopher whose book, *Animal Liberation,* published in 1975, is the acknowledged catalyst for the contemporary upsurge of interest in animal issues, recounts how he tracked down a copy of Salt's book, *Animals' Rights in Relation to Social Progress,* published in 1892, and found 'astonishing … the way in which he answers so many still current objections to the idea of equal rights, or equal consideration, for animals'.[8]

In part, *Animals' Rights* is a damning and harrowing exposé of many of the cruelties of the age in fashion, food, pleasure and science, but it is the philosophical basis of the protest that distinguishes it as a landmark. Although primarily inspired by a loathing of cruelty, the main argument for reform is centred upon rationalism rather than sentiment. Echoing both the words and thoughts of Darwin, Salt asserts that any differences in intelligence between animals and humans is in 'degree' rather than 'kind' and that 'evolutionary science has demonstrated beyond question the kinship of all sentient life'.[9] Consequently, he called for his fellow humans to adopt 'a consistent position towards the rights of men and of the lower animals alike and to cultivate a broad system of universal justice for all living things'.[10]

Salt's writing on vegetarianism displays a similar remarkable modernity. Incisive wit is employed as a weapon to confront what he terms 'those dear old Fallacies' which will still be familiar to those who abstain from meat. For example, the question of 'what-would-become-of-the-animals?' is mockingly summarised as a vision of 'the grievous wanderings of homeless herds who can find no kind protector to eat them'[11] and 'what-should-we-do-without-leather?' is presented as 'a lurid picture of a world left shoeless by instantaneous conversion to vegetarianism'.[12]

While the power of the pen was Salt's principal weapon, he was not simply a man of the written word. He was also a formidable campaigner. He and his fellow humanitarians achieved significant change on a wide range of issues. Despite his personal commitment to the total abolition of animal cruelty, when it came to campaigning he was a pragmatist, believing it necessary 'to push steadily *towards* the ideal by a faithful adherence to the right line of reform' rather than 'to grasp foolishly at the ideal, like a child crying for the moon'.[13] He chose his targets carefully.

In 1891, the Humanitarian League launched the first organised initiative against hunting when it made 'the Royal Buckhounds serve as a "peg" … on which to hang an exposé of the cruelty of stag hunting'. In doing so, it attacked the heart of the privileged establishment at its most vulnerable. The Buckhounds — which dated back to the twelfth century — were well-known, but very unpopular. This was partly because the hunt's mastership remained a political appointment, partly because it was funded by public taxes and also because it had a reputation for attracting social climbers. Its 'sport' consisted of chasing tame or captured deer (carted deer as they were known) which were released and hunted over and over again.

The campaign against the Royal Buckhounds represents probably the first time that an animal protection society employed what would now be called investigative journalism. In Salt's own words:

> *The doings of the Buckhounds were watched from season to season; detailed accounts of the 'runs' were published, in contradictions of the shuffling reports sent to the papers by patrons of the Hunt, and a number of horrible cases of mutilation were dragged into light. Questions were put in parliament; leaflets, articles and press letters printed in hundreds, and many lectures given at various clubs and institutions.*[14]

After ten years of persistent activity, the Humanitarian League enjoyed victory. Officially, the Buckhounds were abolished as part of cost-cutting measures in the Royal Household recommended by a Parliamentary Select Committee. Salt, however, remained convinced that it was the publication of a private letter sent to the League which revealed how Queen Victoria had been 'strongly opposed to stag hunting for many years past' which 'settled the fate of the Buckhounds'.[15] Although the letter had been written back in 1891, the League had felt obliged to keep its content secret until after the Queen's death, respecting the fact that it had been a private communication from her Secretary.

From royalty, the Humanitarian League switched its attention to a second bastion of respectable society; Salt's old public school. A campaign was launched against the hare-hunting Eton School Beagle Pack, based on the same strategy employed against the Royal Buckhounds.

> *Had humanitarians talked of the cruelty of hare-hunting in general, little attention would have been paid to them; but with concrete instances drawn from the leading public school, and quoted in the words of the boys themselves as printed in the Eton College Chronicle — a disgusting record of 'blooded' hounds and of the hare 'broken up' or crawling 'dead-beat', 'absolutely stiff', 'so done that she could not stand' — a great impression was made ...*[16]

It was during this concerted initiative against Eton that the term bloodsports was first coined. Yet despite favourable publicity, and support from notables such as the militant suffragette Christabel Pankhurst, beagling continued at Eton on the grounds that a ban 'would do more harm than good'. The one concession agreed by the headmaster was to shorten the length of the hunting season in order to reduce the risk of pregnant does being pursued and killed.

One unusual feature of the Eton beagle campaign was Salt's use of parody. In 1907, he produced a hoax publication purporting to be pro-beagling and containing what he described as 'the most idiotic balderdash and fustian that could be collected in defence of beagling'.[17] It was read avidly, though the irony of ridiculing those who supported a ban on hare coursing on the grounds that they were neither Etonians nor sportsmen appears to have been lost on some of its readers! The same satirical tactic was repeated elsewhere in the League's crusade: letters were sent to newspapers stating that pigs were indebted to meat eaters and that their cries in slaughterhouses were an expression of gratitude to those who had bred and reared them.

If the targeting of Eton failed ultimately to achieve its aims, Salt was to be more successful in an initiative against London Zoo. For many years, 'pythons and other large serpents' had been fed live prey — including ducks, fowls, rabbits and even goats — in front of visitors. Although the public exhibitions had been abandoned in 1881, the practice continued behind closed doors. Salt testifies that 'the League found the reptile-feeders at Regent's Park exceedingly slippery to deal with, and it needed long time and much patience, to bring them to book'.[18] Eventually, however, it did so. In 1907 the zoo relented in the face of mounting criticism, and, as is its policy to this day, freshly-killed animals were fed to reptiles instead.

In addition to offering a pertinent example of his persistence and fortitude, the London Zoo campaign offers a practical example of Salt's ability to override his personal long-term ambitions in order to achieve short-term improvements. He despised zoos, considering them amongst 'the saddest and dullest spots on earth',[19] but he was prepared to campaign wholeheartedly for an improvement which, in his own judgement, did no more than introduce a method 'less barbarous'. Similar pragmatism characterised his work to improve conditions on farm and in markets and slaughterhouses, despite a belief that reform of abattoirs was 'a temporary measure which will mitigate, but cannot possibly amend, the horrors of butchery'.[20]

Another of the Humanitarian League's prominent concerns was the fashion trade, particularly the use of bird feathers for ladies' hats. Salt described the plumage trade as 'murderous millinery'. Around the world, by the turn of the century birds of all species were being massacred in their millions to supply the fashion industry. Women of all classes took to wearing plumed hats, the rich preferring exotic species and the serving classes settling for the more common, such as sparrows or kingfishers. By 1894, Britain alone was importing approximately 25 million slaughtered birds, ranging from albatrosses and egrets to humming birds, parrots and canaries. Opposition to the trade was in part responsible for the formation of the Society for the Protection of Birds (later the RSPB) in 1889 and was supported by the RSPCA, *Punch* and *The Times*. The League's campaign against this 'revolting practice' included publication of a pamphlet (written by Edith Carrington) and, in 1901, a Bill drafted to outlaw the use of feathers taken from certain species. Although this failed to pass through parliament, it did provide the basis for the first effective Act against the plumage trade, introduced twenty-one years later. (Interestingly, although opposition to 'murderous millinery' was wide-ranging, the fur trade appears to have excited much less public disquiet, despite Salt's typically witty call for a programme of 'one man, one skin … if there is ever to be a civilised state'.[21] Indeed, fur was so fashionable that *The Times* carried prominent advertisements from furriers almost daily.)

"OH, YOU CRUEL BOY, TO TAKE THOSE EGGS OUT OF THE NEST! THINK OF THE POOR MOTHER BIRD WHEN SHE COMES ——" "THE MOTHER BIRD'S DEAD, MISS." "HOW DO YOU KNOW THAT?" "I SEE IT IN YOUR HAT!"

Cartoon by Arthur Hopkins, published in *Punch*, 12 June 1901.

The Humanitarian League's achievements were not confined to animal protection. Its members also played a significant part in the advancement of human rights. It was largely through their efforts that flogging with the birch was banned in the Royal Navy in 1906; it played a significant part in securing the establishment of the first Court of Criminal Appeal and revision of the laws on imprisonment for debt; and its endeavours 'to humanise both the spirit of the law and the conditions of prison life' were prominent in the campaign which led to the Prisons Act of 1898, encompassing measures which at least reduced some of the barbaric severity of penal laws.

Salt was a pioneer in the field of conservation, too. As early as 1908, he called for the provision of national parks to protect Snowdonia, the Lake District, the Scottish Highlands and the Peak District, so that they 'shall be preserved in their wildness as the cherished property of the people':[22] years before there was any society to preserve the British countryside he advocated the formation of an organisation to protect the mountains, 'the plains, the heaths, the woods, the marshes and the sea shores' from the greed of developers and the destruction of machines; he protested against the picking of wild flowers and warned of the dangers of chemical waste in rivers and streams. Humanitarianism, he declared, 'is not merely an expression of sympathy with pain: it is a protest against all tyranny and desecration', including 'the vandalism which can ruthlessly destroy the natural grace of the earth'.[23] He even managed to link his concern for conservation to his loathing of war and colonialism, arguing that 'while we are willing to spend vast sums on grabbing other people's territory, we have not, of course, a penny to spare for the preservation of our own'.[24]

Despite the limitation of its overall influence, it is a testament to the impact of radical ideas at the time that the Humanitarian League could exist and implement any change at all. All this altered, however, with the outbreak of the first world war. As an organisation dedicated to pacifism, the League was effectively destroyed by the warmongering xenophobia which gripped the country. Its work ground to a permanent halt in 1919.

A second factor in its demise was that the socialist movement from which it originally derived its inspiration was moving in different directions. Those who saw political power through the official Labour Party drawing ever nearer tended to drop radical animal protection policies from their agenda, particularly after the war. At the same time, Karl Marx was rapidly becoming the seminal influence for the younger generation of political activists. According to Marxism, animals were irrelevant. They could never be part of the all-important class struggle to control means of production, because, unlike humans, they were characterised as incapable of development. Indeed, it was considered the task of workers to progress from their pre-revolution animal-like state — defined as crude and unalterable — to become liberated and fully self-conscious human beings:

> It (the animal) produces only under the dominion of immediate physical need, while man produces even when he is free from physical need and only truly produces in freedom therefrom.[25]

When the Humanitarian League finally folded, Salt was approaching his seventieth year. With his second wife he spent the last years of his life in Brighton, writing books with great vitality until well into his eighties. While the failure of the world to respond to his message caused some bouts of depression, he never lost determination. Shortly before his death at the age of eighty-eight he wrote to a friend: 'I failed with the Humanitarian League; we were a century or two too soon and have now got to wait'.[26] But his resignation was tempered by the assertion that his organisation 'was at least a foresight, and as much ahead of the "religion" of its day as its understanding was clearer than that of the scientists'.[27] Elsewhere he described himself and his colleagues as 'a troop of venturesome pioneers … whose whim it was to open out a path by which others might eventually follow'.[28] Neither did he lose his sense of humour. Responding to a hostile journalist who referred to him as 'a compendium of the cranks', he said that he considered the remark flattering. He wrote that if 'this meant that I advocated not this or that humane reform, but all of them… that is just what I desire to do'.[29]

Assessing Salt's overall influence is difficult. In spite of his achievements, he was not widely known during his lifetime. Yet many more famous than he testified to the value of his opinion and friendship. Visitors to his cottage included influential socialists of the period, such as Ramsay MacDonald (the future first Labour Party Prime Minister), G. K. Chesterton, George Meredith, Sidney and Beatrice Webb and George Bernard Shaw. Shaw described him as 'original and in his way unique' and acknowledged that 'my pastime has been writing sermons in plays, sermons preaching what Salt practised'.[30] Mahatma Gandhi was another who paid tribute, ascribing to Salt his conversion to vegetarianism 'by choice' rather than solely as a result of Hindu religious upbringing.[31]

What of Henry Salt's long-term influence? Even today his achievements with the Humanitarian League seem astonishing. Imagine a modern day equivalent in which one organisation promotes the combined agendas of the RSPCA, Friends of the Earth, the Vegetarian Society, the Campaign for Nuclear Disarmament, the Howard

League for Penal Reform, Amnesty International, the Council for the Protection of Rural England and many others. Perhaps the nearest we have come is in the formation of the Green Party, to which Salt's political ideals are closer than to the beliefs of the modern Labour Party.

What can be said with certainty is that the programme of reform he advocated was many decades ahead of his time and created an important precedent, both for the modern animal liberation movement and for green politics in general.

A few years before his death, Henry Shakespear Salt wrote his own funeral address, summarising his hopes and beliefs:

> *I shall die as I have lived, rationalist, socialist, pacifist and humanitarian. I must make my meaning clear. I wholly disbelieve in the present established religion; but I have a very firm religious faith of my own — a creed of Kinship I call it — a belief that in years to come there will be a recognition of the brotherhood between man and man, nation and nation, human and sub-human, which will transform a state of semi-savagery, as we have it, into one of civilisation, when there will be no such barbarity as warfare, or the robbery of the poor by the rich, or the ill-usage of the lower animals by mankind.[32]*

As distant and idealistic as such a vision still seems, Salt would hopefully find it partly reassuring that, sixty years on, his views enjoy the support of steadily increasing numbers of young people — even if the vast majority are completely unaware of the initiatives he pioneered.

## The passing of legislation

Henry Salt was not alone in helping to achieve positive change in Edwardian times. The years leading up to the first world war were amongst the most vibrant in the history of animal welfare.

In particular, this period saw the passing of The Protection of Animals Act of 1911, probably the most important piece of animal protection legislation of the century. Amongst its principal architects was Sir George Greenwood, Salt's friend and colleague at the Humanitarian League. As Liberal MP for Peterborough, Greenwood skilfully manoeuvred proposals through parliament, extending legal protection from cruelty to 'any bird, beast, reptile or fish' and raising the penalties for offences.

There were two notable exclusions from the legislation. Hunting was exempt; so was vivisection. Indeed, the special licensing system under which animal experiments were governed by the Cruelty to Animals Act of 1876 gave those who conducted experiments authority to inflict suffering for which they would otherwise have faced prosecution after the introduction of the 1911 Act. This is a protection they enjoy to this day.

These omissions should not detract from the achievement of what became known as the 'Animals' Charter' of 1911. It allowed the RSPCA far greater scope to take legal action and has remained the basis of the vast majority of its prosecutions. Nor was the absence of legislation on hunting and vivisection any reflection of equivocation on the part of Sir George Greenwood himself, who remained an active and passionate supporter of initiatives against both practices. He simply recognised the need for compromise if the Bill was ever to pass on to the statute book.

# 2 / Domestic bliss?

## 1  Man's best friends?

For hundreds of years, dogs, cats and other companion animals have inspired the best and the worst of human behaviour, from extraordinary kindness to savage cruelty. Little has altered in the twentieth century.

By 1900, Battersea Dogs' Home had been providing shelter for abandoned animals for more than forty years and the National Canine Defence League (NCDL) had been in existence for almost a decade. Both were originally formed by anti-vivisectionists, their primary purpose to protect abandoned animals from sale to laboratories.

Cats were less fortunate and had to wait until 1927 for the Cats' Protection League, the first organisation concerned solely for their welfare.

The NCDL had by that time achieved some legislative success, The Dogs' Act of 1906 making it illegal to sell stray animals for experimentation. It continued to press vigorously for a ban on all vivisection of dogs right up until the second world war, but although on several occasions it seemed within sight of attaining its goal, further victories proved elusive. Indeed, the use of dogs in experiments remains legal to this day.

Other major concerns in the first decades of the century will also sound depressingly familiar to those currently concerned for the welfare of companion animals. Cats and dogs both suffered whipping, maiming, beating, poisoning, kicking, starving, muzzling, chaining and even deliberate running over.

Another difficulty to have altered only in scale over the century is stray populations. The extreme poverty of Victorian and Edwardian Britain created huge numbers of starving and homeless dogs and by 1910 Battersea Dogs' Home alone was taking in 25,000 a year from London's streets. With very few spaying and neutering programmes available the dog population expanded rapidly and the problem soon intensified. By 1924, there were a million more dogs than at the turn of the century.[1]

Had it not been for the considerable skill and enormous dedication of the British animal protection lobby, the outlook would almost certainly have been even more bleak. The NCDL became particularly active, creating kennels for strays and clinics where the poor could obtain free or cheap treatment for their pets. They offered free neutering, set up funds to pay dog licence fees for those who could not afford them and created a re-homing policy which included inspections of new homes. The subsequent reduction in the number of strays in the late 1920s and 1930s was a great achievement.

The pro-dog lobby also proved a formidable political force. This was especially vital during the first world war when desperate food shortages caused the government to consider plans to destroy at least 50% of the dog population. High taxes were threatened in an attempt to put dog-keeping out of the range of poorer people and the strays which would inevitably result were to be destroyed. Opposition was effectively mobilised and the strategy swiftly abandoned. Looking back at the end of the war, C. Rowland Johns, formidable Secretary of the NCDL, ascribed success to 'that noble sentiment which had been awakened and kept alive by the great qualities which commend themselves to all who have ever known and loved the dog'.[2]

Prominent among those who testified most enthusiastically to 'the great qualities' and 'noble sentiment' were soldiers fighting on the Western Front. Some dogs served officially in the Great War as messengers, while strays were often adopted by troops. According to the *Times* correspondent in France, canine victims of war found congenial companions amongst suffering soldiers. 'It is the dogs who enlist the men's sympathies more than anything else', he wrote in 1917. 'Like frightened children they join the ranks, nestling down by the side of the men for warmth and protection'.[3]

Further evidence of the way in which dogs can elicit intense human compassion and affection came in 1919, when compulsory muzzling was re-introduced in many areas in response to a rabies scare. Destruction notices were placed on all animals found without a muzzle. One of those picked up was Bob, a mongrel pet belonging to a London schoolgirl. Described by police as violent and uncontrollable, Bob was sentenced to death by a magistrate at Clerkenwell Court. The execution was avoided, however, when a group of schoolchildren rescued him from the court and returned him to the home of his owner. Police attempts to repossess the dog were repelled by residents and a national petition was launched by the NCDL, calling for the sentence to be revoked. 20,000 signatures were obtained. The *Daily Mail* took up the case, transforming Bob the dog into a national celebrity. A legal appeal was initiated. It was heard in front of magistrate, lawyers, public, press and the dog himself, impeccably behaved as he watched from the front of the court. Faced with such a scene what choice did the magistrate have? The appeal was upheld and the dog reunited with his young owner. In 1922, compulsory muzzling was abandoned, not to

Bob and friends after his reprieve.

be re-introduced until the 1991 Dangerous Dogs Act enforced it for pit bull breeds after a mounting number of horrific attacks on people.

Bob was one of those rare individual animals who, by a combination of circumstance and character, have not only achieved celebrity status for themselves, but also proved particularly influential in clarifying public opinion. By the time that the second world war was declared, affection for pets was recognised to the point where the possibility of the government attempting draconian measures similar to those contemplated in 1914-18 had become unthinkable. On the contrary, at the end of hostilities in 1945, it acknowledged the strong bond which many soldiers had formed with animals during service overseas by introducing a special cheap-rate scheme for transport home and quarantine.

Nevertheless, the second world war brought with it inevitable hardships. The stray population increased; dogs again served in the war effort (mostly as messengers); food was scarce and chaining became more commonplace as people found themselves pre-occupied with their own survival. Out of this adversity came new efforts to protect vulnerable animals.

Comrades in the trenches.

## 2  Shelter from the storm

At the outbreak of the second world war, animal welfare campaigners were faced with a massive problem. Evacuated families were not allowed to take their animals with them and dogs were to be barred from air raid shelters. In addition, some pets were left homeless when their human families joined the armed forces. Money was so scarce that even amongst those who remained in their homes there were many who felt that they could no longer afford to feed their animals. As soon as war became probable there was an increase in the numbers put down or abandoned.

One of those most disturbed by the situation was the aristocrat, Nina, Duchess of Hamilton and Brandon. Born into the Winterslow family, she had married the Duke of Hamilton in 1912 and was well-known for her wide-ranging humanitarian sympathies. In addition to her prominence in the animal welfare and anti-vivisection movements she also contributed generously to human charities. Amongst her many commendable acts had been to present her local town council with a completely equipped and furnished nurses home, for which she also took responsibility for day-to-day maintenance.

On August 28th 1939, Nina journeyed to the BBC in London to broadcast a radio appeal for people willing to offer a safe haven to companion animals. Leading by example, she even offered her own house as a pet sanctuary.

The response was dramatic. Within minutes animals were arriving at the Duchess' Regents Park home. It soon became evident that even though many listeners had answered the call to provide 'foster families', the number of animals in need would greatly exceed the number of homes available. That night Nina shared her own residence with twenty dogs and cats and took the decision to create an animal sanctuary at her country estate at Ferne House, near Shaftesbury.

Within weeks, two hundred written requests for accommodation for pets were arriving at her London house every day. Dogs were regularly left tied to the apple trees and railings outside. A daily procession began to wind its way down to Dorset. Most were transported at the Duchess' own expense; others were delivered personally by loving owners who wanted to view for themselves the happenings at Ferne. The newly created sanctuary became a hive of activity, with Nina insisting upon luxury quarters for all her guests:

> *Hers is not a place where animals are just tied up or caged; they must have personal attention, good food, regular exercise and all and sundry must be kept clean. To her, every animal is an individual, with a soul and must be treated as such. And she*

Dedication of the cat shelter at Ferne in 1950, by the Rev Lionel S. Lewis. The Duchess of Hamilton is on the extreme right.

*managed to find a multitude of reasons why many of her charges could not be left in kennels — even kennels with large and spacious runs — they must be near her, occupy the house and become a large family of exceedingly happy and contented refugees. The practical side of the undertaking demanded a special staff of kennel and cattery attendants and nurses. At her own expense she built rows of well-appointed new kennels with exercise runs, houses for cats, containing everything the feline species appreciates. Warmth and fresh air were both necessary. Central heating had to be installed in the kennels.[1]*

In 1940, three hundred animals were being evacuated to Ferne every week and, as German bombing activity increased, the sanctuary expanded to meet demand. Ambulances were purchased to attend to the wounded and to collect strays in London, Portsmouth, Southampton and Bath. Those beyond help were humanely destroyed; the fortunate survivors joined the rapidly growing family in Dorset. Some of the tales of how individual animals found refuge offer more touching proof of how unswerving the devotion of some people to their animals can be:

*'Nearly all the dogs have some pathetic story, or one of bravery, showing what the friendship of a dog means to his master in this time of strain. Such a story is that of Jack, a miniature collie. When Jack's master returned from work he found that a time-bomb had been dropped outside his front door and the policeman in charge would not let him go in. He begged to be allowed to pass to see if his beloved dog was within. The policeman said 'no'. But later on the policeman took a walk and Jack's master, to use his own words, 'made a run for it', got Jack and took him to the Duchess of Hamilton's private house so that he should go down to Ferne Sanctuary as soon as conveyance was available.*[2]

Later in 1940, the guest list at Ferne expanded further. As part of a scheme run in conjunction with the government, young children under five years old from the bombed areas of the East End of London were evacuated to the Sanctuary 'in batches of ten to twenty'. They joined the dogs, cats, horses, goats, cows, canaries and a monkey who were already well established.

By the end of the war the Duchess had provided refuge for 'hundreds' of small children (the government insisted that over fives were transferred to other homes offering more formal educational opportunities), dispelling further the myth that those pre-occupied with animal welfare had no interest in human suffering. On the contrary, at the heart of the astonishing practical achievements at Ferne was always Nina's personal conviction that 'by the laws of spiritual progress human welfare and animal welfare are interrelated and inseparable'.[3]

There had been many admirable animal sanctuaries for individual species before Ferne. Rest homes for horses and homes for dogs had been in existence since Victorian times and Our Dumb Friends League (which later became the Blue Cross), the PDSA and others had gone on to build an admirable network of refuges and clinics during the first part of the century. What marked the establish-

Nina, Duchess of Hamilton and Brandon.

ment of Ferne as a watershed, however, was a combination of the exceptional circumstances of its creation and the spiritual and philosophical beliefs at the core of its enterprise. Although this was still long before the term 'animal rights' was widely discussed, the insistence upon the integrity of each individual life fore-shadows much of the rhetoric of the modern animal protection movement. The Duchess insisted that no animal in need of help should ever be refused a home, whether it be old, disabled, abandoned, pensioned or ill-treated. She also ensured that different species should mix together whenever appropriate. Nina believed passionately that by observing individual animals people would learn to respect the complexity and the variety of each life:

> The diversity of character displayed by many different animal inhabitants is a matter of never failing interest. No two animals are quite alike in their reactions to life, their tastes, their friendship, their enmities — all differ. Special affinities are noticeable, between canine, feline and equine individual, but not only with their own species. Great and special friendships can be observed between dog and cat, horse and dog or cat and horse — or even between fox and dog. The same applies to their human friends. Some of the dogs at once choose which of the human atten-dants they prefer and a great many mutual friendships will spring up. Thus, individuality in preference is available in all the species of animals at Ferne — dogs, cats, horses, goats, cows etc. Each has his own way of life and likes to conduct it that way.[4]

The 'creed of Ferne' expressed a belief in the power of compassion and humane education and a further 'steadfast faith that mercy, justice, and feeling for our fellow creatures will alone make a sure foundation for civilisation'.[5] Added to these now relatively familiar sentiments was the Duchess of Hamilton's personal commitment to what she expressed as 'spiritual motherhood, with its understanding towards all who are weak and helpless'.[6]

By the time that the second world war had ended, Ferne had paid host to six thousand animals. Some were then reunited with their owners; others took up permanent residence, to be joined over the years by a constant stream of new arrivals. The innovative work continued. A new building for cows with spacious 'maternity pens' created 'a model for humane farming' and appropriate shelter was provided for injured or sick wild animals, particularly foxes.

Yet only a few years later, the death of its founder was to throw the whole future of the sanctuary into doubt. When Nina died on January 12th 1951, the death duties were so great that the Ferne estate had to be sold to meet costs. To ensure the survival of the sanctuary it was purchased by Louise Lind-af-Hageby 'at very great personal sacrifice'. Miss Lind-af-Hageby had been a close personal friend and working colleague of the Duchess for many years and may well have been the most remarkable of all animal welfare campaigners during the first half of the twentieth century. She was responsible for what was probably the most effective anti-vivisection initiative ever undertaken (see Chapter 7) and, as founder of the Animal Defence Society, had a lifetime of outstanding achievement behind her — even before she stepped in to save Ferne.

Although the Sanctuary survived, there were insufficient funds available to maintain Ferne House, which soon became derelict. In 1975, Ferne Animal Sanctuary moved to a thirty-six acre site near Chard in Somerset, where it continues its valuable work to this day. The original estate was eventually sold.

Nowadays, there are hundreds of animal sanctuaries of vastly differing sizes throughout the world. A bewildering number of individual species are catered for in specialised centres — amongst them monkeys, owls, seals, donkeys, feral cats, otters, horses and farm animals. Others, like Ferne, offer homes to any animal or species in need, however unattractive or unpopular it may be. Some UK sanctuaries — like the Donkey Sanctuary in Devon or the Redwings Horse Sanctuary in Norfolk — have become particularly successful and have grown enormously over the years. The former alone has taken seven thousand animals into expert care since its formation in 1969. Others struggle away on a few acres with only a tiny budget.

Sanctuaries are a recognition of a problem but not a solution. Their proliferation confirms that animals are mistreated and abandoned in great numbers. Moreover, the problem is of such vast proportions that however great the number established, they can hardly even scratch the surface of neglect and ill-treatment. Yet just as we cannot foresee a world where there will be no need for children's homes or refuges for women, it is impossible to imagine a time when animal sanctuaries will no longer be essential. Such, alas, are the ways of humans. At least the presence of an increasing number of homes where the neglected and abused can find shelter from suffering — some of them enthusiastically supported by public donation — is evidence of significant public sympathy. In the twenty-first century — as in the twentieth — there will no doubt be hundreds of thousands of animals who will have good reason to be grateful for that dedicated minority prepared to devote their time and money to care for the weak, injured and discarded.

## 3   From catwalk to cat rescue: the work of Celia Hammond

One modern example of the daunting workload involved in running an animal sanctuary and charity is provided by the former model, Celia Hammond. The story of her journey from early childhood in Australia, firstly to famous figure of the swinging sixties and later to devoted defender of unwanted animals, serves as a lesson in the powers of determination and dedication.

Celia's childhood could not have been easy. Born in Indonesia, she was raised mostly by her mother in Australia until, at the age of six, she was sent to England to the care of various aunts and boarding schools. She idolised her father but rarely saw him. (He served in the Australian army in Borneo and was later employed there as a tea taster). Her mother's time was divided between daughter in Europe and husband in Asia.

Sympathy for animals showed itself early in Celia's life. She can remember rescuing lizards in Australia and feeling 'terribly upset' when, at the end of one of her mother's visits to the UK, their two cats were sent away to be re-homed. At the age of fifteen she gave up eating meat after a chance meeting on a London bus with a woman armed with pictures of slaughterhouses. 'By the end of the journey I was a vegetarian,' she recalls. It was another blow to the aunts for whom Celia's stubborn and determined nature caused constant anxiety!

Yet for many years her concern for animals remained unfocused. One of her first jobs after leaving school at sixteen was in the infamous exotic pet department at Harrods, where anything from lions to panthers and monkeys could be purchased by anybody with sufficient funds. At the time, animal-loving Celia thought it near-perfect employment. 'Looking back I find it hard to believe, but I saw absolutely nothing wrong with it,' she says.

Office work followed until friends suggested she should try modelling. She was accepted for schooling at the highly regarded Lucy Clayton Agency, where Jean Shrimpton was one of her contemporaries. But whereas Jean's rise to fame was almost immediate, Celia's career began unpromisingly. She appeared to be heading nowhere fast when, in 1962, much to the surprise of her agent, she was selected for stardom by the photographer Norman Parkinson. Within a couple of weeks she was in Paris modelling collections for *Queen* magazine.

Committed vegetarian though she already was, the successful young model had not even given a thought to the slaughter of animals for the fashion trade and for the next couple of years was frequently to be seen modelling for the world's leading furriers. Yet in the mid-sixties, it was the killing of animals for fur which was to provide what was certainly one of the defining moments in her life. She saw film of the Canadian seal cull and was 'pole-axed' by what she witnessed. With typical decisiveness, she swore never to wear fur again and began a petition asking other models to join her in a boycott. She met with considerable success. 'Almost overnight the top furriers couldn't find any top models to wear their garments. It must have hurt some of those prestigious companies quite a bit.'

The publicity attracted by Celia's stand against fur created interest amongst animal welfare groups. She and Jean Le Fevre from the Beauty Without Cruelty organisation were asked to travel out to Canada to witness the seal cull for themselves. Their presence gained massive worldwide publicity for the anti-fur initiative and was to have even greater personal consequences. 'We saw animals being skinned alive. What I witnessed will stay with me for the rest of my life,' she declares.

From this time, Celia 'began to be involved in campaigns against all aspects of animal cruelty,' attending protests against fur, factory farming and other issues. By 1967, she was also heavily involved in practical cat rescue work. After having strays spayed or neutered, she either found new homes or looked after them herself in the London flat she shared with the prominent rock guitarist Jeff Beck. Already, the characteristic Hammond single-mindedness was much in evidence, for rather than work with any existing organisation she chose both to fund the work herself and to operate in her own way. 'I like to do things the way I like to do them. I don't like to do them anybody else's way,' she affirms.

In 1968, she moved to Egerton in Kent, accompanied by all her rescued cats. The animal work continued both locally and in London, becoming an increasing preoccupation. Soon the house and grounds provided a sanctuary for unwanted animals of many species. By 1971, the modelling career had come to an end and animal welfare had became a full-time commitment. 'Modelling gave me money and enabled me to see places I would not otherwise have seen. It allowed me to meet influential people, many of whom later proved helpful in supporting my animal work. It also gave me a platform from which to make people aware of what was happening, but by that time I was glad for it to be over. It was no longer what I wanted to do with my life.'

In 1975, she and her animals moved again, this time to Jeff Beck's house near Wadhurst in East Sussex. In Celia's own words, 'I filled that up with animals and drove him round the bend!' Nevertheless, it remained home until well into the 1990s, several years after the couple had ended their long-standing relationship. By this time she had set up her own charity, the Celia Hammond Animal Trust, to lend official status to the rescue work. Finally, in 1993, Celia bought a property near

Hastings in East Sussex which now operates as a sanctuary for everything from pigs to goats, rabbits, chickens, cats and dogs. 'Anything that isn't homed is ours. If they are ugly or unsuitable for rehoming they stay with us.'

Remarkable though Celia Hammond's achievements in animal rescue have been, it is her pioneering work in establishing the first permanent low-cost neutering clinic for pets that has probably been her most important contribution to animal protection. More than twenty years ago she recognised that the provision of cheap neutering clinics in the poorer areas of the country would be the single most effective method

of reducing the twin problems of cruelty and stray populations. For many years she urged the RSPCA — on whose executive committee she has served for two decades — to take on the task, but found that fervent opposition from the British Veterinary Association and Royal Veterinary College deterred the Society from action. 'Everybody wants to see low-cost neutering, but there are differences in approach. The RSPCA wants to see it carried out through private practices because they don't want confrontation with the veterinary profession.' She is openly critical of the hostility to her proposals from the veterinary establishment, though keen to differentiate between the ruling elite and the many working vets who support her views.

After many years of setbacks, Celia decided that the only answer was to set up a neutering clinic herself. 'I just realised that if it was going to be done it I would have to do it myself. I figured that if we could get the first one up and running and make it a success it would confirm that this is the best way to confront the problems *and* that it can be self-financing.' It proved to be an enormous task. 'You have to be made of steel, otherwise you'd be crushed on the way. You wouldn't believe the number of setbacks I have had with people telling me it can't be done. The more people said it, the more determined I became.' In 1995, she finally achieved her goal, opening Britain's first full-time purpose-built neutering clinic in Lewisham, south London.

Two and a half years later she feels justifiably proud of its achievements. 'We have neutered over eighteen thousand animals belonging to the poorest people — people who otherwise would never have been able to go to a private vet. That has prevented the birth of literally hundreds of thousands of puppies and kittens, because in that time several litters would have been born to those animals and some of them would have been old enough to breed themselves.'

Celia Hammond is adamant that a decrease in the population of animals is not only the key to diminishing the problem of strays, but also to reducing acts of deliberate cruelty. She cites the evidence from Canada, where, within five years of opening, a low-cost neutering clinic has achieved dramatic reductions in both destructions and reported cruelty cases. 'When you decrease the number of animals, you increase their value and people's respect for them — hence my obsession with opening this first clinic. Already the animal charities in the Lewisham area have noticed definite improvements in that they have been asked to take in fewer abandoned animals.'

Fees for neutering and vaccinations at the Lewisham clinic are roughly one third of average private veterinary costs, encouraging the poorer people of the area to use the service. Although 90% of clients are on benefit, it is open to anybody who cannot afford to pay standard charges. Celia is convinced that very few abuse the system, thus allaying the fear of local vets that their custom might be affected. 'We have a good relationship with local vets, many of whom are pleased we are here,' she says.

The work load for Celia and her colleagues can best be described as awesome. An eighteen hour working day is normal. Neutering takes place all day, five days a week. At the same time, rescue teams are out and about picking up starving or injured cats and other animals in need. After the clinic closes, the rescue work continues, usually until at least midnight and often until much later. Even then the labour is not over because the animals neutered that day and kept overnight still have to be fed. It is an all-consuming task. Celia: 'We're lucky if we get four hours sleep a night. I do get very tired, but it has become a way of life. I can't switch off.'

What about the stress that such unceasing and often distressing work creates? 'It does make you just despair of people,' she confesses. 'We get so many cruelty cases to pick up off the streets. One woman poured boiling fat over five cats — deliberate acts of cruelty like that. People get away with so much because the law has no teeth. Half of the time it simply isn't worth reporting incidents as witnesses are often too afraid to give evidence.'

And what of the urge for a life outside? After more than twenty-five years dedicated to the welfare of animals does a woman who once enjoyed a glamorous life of fame feel any sense of personal privation? 'No, I don't envy people theatre, dinners, parties and things like that, but I do envy them the luxury of actually stopping work at 5.30 pm, having a meal and putting their feet up. For me that would be just heaven.' But almost immediately she adds: 'What can I do about it? This is not something you can walk away from.'

Far from walking away, Celia Hammond is expanding her commitment. Contracts have been exchanged on a building in the East End of London for conversion into a second low-cost neutering clinic. £140,000 has to be raised swiftly. The prospect did not seem to worry her. 'If we don't take the gamble now it might never happen. I believe that if you want something badly enough you always get it.'

## 4   The century advances?

Until the early 1980s it was perfectly legal to sell pets from street market stalls, a tradition that had survived since Victorian times. Indeed, anybody wanting to gain a flavour of sordid nineteenth-century England had only to visit Club Row, a dirty animal market in London's East End. Despite its blatant squalor, it was actually defended as a quaint English 'tradition' and a 'tourist attraction'. The reality of this 'tradition' was an outdoor Sunday market packed with stalls filled with sick and diseased animals, many of which were dumped into backstreets if they could not be sold.

In 1980, a group of campaigners began a campaign to shut down Club Row. They met every Sunday to protest at conditions and to discourage customers. Enduring threats and intimidation, their message began to be heard. Numbers grew. A march was held. Slowly, public support was mobilised. After two and a half years of campaigning, Tower Hamlets Council took the decision that Club Row should cease trading. As a direct result an amendment to the Pet Animals Act of 1951 was passed through parliament in May 1983, making all street trade in animals illegal. It was one

Demonstration at Club Row in 1982.

of the first tangible signs of the strength and determination of a new generation of animal activists.

Yet despite the rise in interest in animal protection and the success of the Club Row campaign, the RSPCA annual statistics for cruelty to domestic animals are as likely to tell a tale of ill-treatment as the century draws to a close as they did one hundred years ago. Incidents of starving, beating, taunting, chaining, inappropriate housing and other forms of neglect remain all too common. The number of prosecutions has also risen, though this is due in part to the greater number of animals and an increase in inspectors. By 1997, the UK dog population was estimated at 6.5 million, with a further 7.2 million cats, 1.4 million rabbits and 0.9 million hamsters.

What has changed, perhaps, is the significance with which some observers are now likely to view offenders. For instance, there are now calls for the UK to follow the example of the US by introducing legislation which would allow animal welfare groups to exchange information with child protection agencies. According to veterinary pathologist, Helen Munro, 'if an animal is being abused in the home, the spouse and children are likely to be getting the same treatment'.[1] American studies lend credence to her views. Californian research has found 'a quarter of battered women seeking shelter had reported the killing or abuse of family pets';[2] in New Jersey figures indicate that '88% of families who had experienced physical abuse had also experienced some form of animal cruelty'.[3] It is doubtful whether brutality to animals would have merited similar concern a hundred years ago.

As great as the problems of bullying and viciousness still are, they remain secondary to overpopulation as a cause of suffering. Far too many animals are being bred and, despite the persistence and partial success of campaign slogans such as 'a dog is for life', there is a disturbingly high stray population, estimated at around 500,000 dogs and 1-2 million feral cats. Approximately 360,000 unwanted dogs are destroyed in the UK every year by vets, animal welfare associations, the police and local authorities.

New problems have also emerged, notably the rise of puppy farms churning out dogs in dirty, dark conditions by applying factory farming principles. Equally depressing has been the revival of illegal sports such as dog fighting and the deliberate breeding of aggressive dogs for badger baiting and other forms of macho entertainment — or else as guards. As a result, there has been an increase in the number of attacks on people and ill-conceived enforcement of legislation in an attempt to counteract the danger. The Dangerous Dogs Act of 1991 brought back compulsory muzzling in public for certain specified breeds, but its effectiveness is questioned by almost everybody forced to administer it. Dogs have spent up to four years in police kennels while owners contest destruction orders. The law states that pit bull type terriers must die if spotted in public without a muzzle, so legal arguments have centred upon whether or not those convicted are genuine pure breeds. The issue overlooked has been whether or not individual dogs represent a danger to people.

Dog 'lovers' themselves are not without responsibility for causing harm to animals. Tail docking and breeding of 'desirable' characteristics for pedigree show dogs (and cats) have created painful deformities. In its different way, however pampered show animals might superficially appear to be, the attitude of obsessive breeders is probably only marginally less damaging than thugs who deliberately ill-treat their pets. No less deplorable is the viciousness associated with greyhound racing — doping, untreated injuries, 'disposal' of unsuccessful dogs in the cheapest way possible and sale for vivisection.

Another pet problem to increase towards the end of the century has been the emerging popularity of exotic and designer animals. Alongside lizards, snakes and wild birds — all regularly on sale through pet shops — has developed a disturbing trade in primates, particularly marmosets, capuchins and squirrel monkeys. Some are surplus animals from zoo collections and often they spend their days dumped in small cages in suburban living rooms or garden sheds.

Against this gloomy scenario, companion animals often continue to provoke admirable human behaviour. Some people go to enormous lengths to ensure the health and happiness of their pets. There is no shortage of love and affection from many owners. The phenomenal popularity of 1990s television series such as *Animal Hospital* and *Pet Rescue* — featuring (mostly) heartwarming stories of animals recovering from illness, injury or ill-fortune — is further testament to the tenderness and passion which pets can invoke. If progress has been made in the last hundred years it is probably in that the *percentage* of animals well-treated is greater than ever before. In part this may be the result of more enlightened ideas, but it is also due to a vastly improved economy which allows far more owners to afford sufficient food and treatment for sickness and disease.

Nonetheless, some would argue that more often than not the 'love' which even many 'good owners' heap on their pets answers our own needs more than theirs. Even amongst animals who receive an abundance of food and affection, there are many who still suffer loneliness from lack of company, boredom from lack of stimulus, or lethargy from lack of adequate exercise. What percentage of the UK's 14 million dogs and cats have even their basic needs fulfilled? What of the 24 million fish, mostly kept in unstimulating small tanks? Or the rabbits and other small animals abandoned to small cages as if they were mere toys? 16,000 rabbits alone are abandoned in the UK every year.[4]

In 1996, an American computer technology company launched a new game called *Creatures*. It claimed to have created a virtual 'pet' for the family computer, setting a model for the cyberpet craze which began to grip the young in many developed nations the following summer. The game was heralded as a breakthrough in that the creatures known as 'norns' upon which it is centred are equipped with elementary artificial intelligence. Norns are able both to learn for themselves and to behave unpredictably. Once they have learnt a few basic commands they are capable of exploring the computer world without human guidance.

The key quality of the new game is that 'the creatures are designed to evoke emotional attachments in their owners, so that, like parents, they feel responsible for them. When the creatures die', asks *New Statesman* magazine, 'will children feel as sad as if their hamster died?'[5]

Scepticism is called for. It is impossible to believe that even in the sophisticated computer world of the future, a 'virtual pet in the home' will ever provide anything approaching the complex physical and emotional responses of a living and breathing animal? Nevertheless, given the enormous scale of suffering which so many companion animals continue to experience, the idea does have its attraction. In the doubtful event that computer technology does ever replace the family cat or dog, in many cases might not our loss be their gain?

## 5  Imperfect companions: humans and horses

Throughout the Victorian period and early part of the twentieth century, horses probably suffered more from the hand of human tyranny than any other species. Civilisation depended upon them and they were exploited ruthlessly. Cab horses were routinely overworked, underfed, beaten, overloaded and badly driven. Animals employed to draw trams and buses fared little better — hundreds were destroyed every year, maimed or exhausted. Pit ponies presented another massive welfare problem. 100,000 animals worked below the surface, rarely emerging from mines until they were worn out from their labour. Records show that the RSPCA obtained more convictions for cruelty to horses and donkeys than for any other species until well after the first world war.

Even the horrific suffering endured during working life often paled into insignificance compared to their fate when it was over. Worn out pit ponies joined discarded horses from farms, cabs, hunts, the military and elsewhere on the pitiful trail to Belgian and French slaughterhouses, most of them to be killed for sausage meat. One observer described the trade in the period leading up to the first world war as follows:

> *The horses were required to walk — crawl might be a better term — four and a half miles from the docks at Antwerp to the abattoirs. Whilst these ghastly processions were passing, many Belgians pulled down their blinds and closed their shutters as a protest against the iniquity.*[1]

Outbreak of the first world war brought a welcome cessation of the trade for butchery, but brought fresh burdens in its place. Every available horse was 'conscripted' to join the war effort. Although the RSPCA did what it could to protect them by setting up special shelters and horse ambulances which helped to treat more than 700,000 animals,[2] the death toll ran into millions. According to some estimates as many as 8 million horses died before the war was over.[3] Often corpses were hastily devoured by starving troops.

Louise Lind-af-Hageby actually visited the battlegrounds of the Marne in September 1914 to witness conditions:

> *She saw horses, wounded, exhausted, straying along the roads, abandoned. There could be no doubt, she said, as to the enormous amount of suffering which was inflicted on horses in war. It was computed in October 1914 that by that time every French cavalryman and German Uhlan had 'ridden through' three horses since the*

*beginning of the war. The wastage of horses was terrific. There were always the conditions caused by bad food, little or no water etc. and the lesser, but neverthe-less potent suffering of the millions of horses called for war service who had to leave their comfortable stables and all the care they had received.*[4]

Other horses and donkeys were employed to help the wartime economy on home soil, drawing loads of munitions. As described by an RSPCA inspector of the time, their lot was similarly hard:

*The horses were rationed and they were overloaded; to make matters worse, there was the inexperience of young drivers. That was because of the war: what happened was that the boy at the back of the van took the reins, when the driver joined the army... They used to have a steel-lined whip with the end bent, so it'd cut into the horse like a fish-hook. You'd get mouth soreness from the bits tugging, and you'd get cases of over-driving sores, or lameness. And a lot of those animals were suffering from malnutrition.*[5]

War also brought suffering to some of the principal defenders of horses. Back in 1911, Ada Cole had witnessed a pathetic procession of horses on their way to a slaughterhouse during a visit to her sister in Belgium. She had vowed 'to make people listen' to what was happening and had formed the International League for the Protection of Horses to carry out her mission. When the war came she stayed in Belgium and towards its end was imprisoned and sentenced to death by the occu-pying German authorities for helping patriots to escape across the border. She was saved by the armistice and released after three and a half months in jail. She was later honoured for her bravery by the King of Belgium.

In 1919, at the age of fifty-eight, Ada Cole returned to England and worked briefly as a nurse in Norwich. But after witnessing animals loaded for transport to the conti-nent from King's Lynn docks she realised that the war had changed nothing and that vast numbers of British animals were still facing brutal journeys to barbaric European slaughterhouses. She returned to campaigning and remained at the forefront of the fight against live exports until her death in 1930.

In the 1920s, graphic descriptions of both the processions of exhausted animals to the slaughterhouses and the hellish conditions of the abattoirs themselves helped to create a strong force for change. Particularly disturbing were several eye witness accounts from the massive Vaugirard horse abattoir in the suburbs of Paris, from where it emerged that blows from hammers and poleaxes were often inaccurately

## THE OUTCAST.

Bernard Partridge's cartoon highlights *Punch*'s opposition to the trade in worn-out horses. 'Have you anything to declare?' asks the Belgian customs officer. 'Only this, that I'm ashamed of my country,' replies the horse. From *Punch*, 18 August, 1909.

33

delivered, causing slow and painful deaths upon 'blood-covered floors'.[6]

One reason for the massive scale of the live export trade in the early part of the century was the sheer number of unwanted animals. Developing nations were fast weaning themselves away from their economic dependence on equine labour. Cars, buses and mechanical haulage systems were replacing horse-drawn vehicles and pit ponies, while the first tractors were reducing the burden of farm horses.

Eventually, this technical revolution would save millions from a life of hardship and drudgery, but in the short-term it created the impetus for massive suffering. The most profitable solution was to sell redundant horses to the continental butchery trade. Relatively healthy animals who were no longer needed simply joined the worn out, whipped and exhausted on the death journeys to Europe.

Given the economic logic, it is little wonder that successive governments resisted mounting pressure for an outright ban, introducing instead a series of unenforceable safeguards which were supposed to ensure welfare during transport and slaughter. (This is strikingly reminiscent of the response of authority to the current public protests against the live export of farm animals — a succession of ineffective directives rather than decisive action.)

In the end, however, the campaign for legislative protection did succeed in preventing much of the suffering. In 1937, the Conservative MP Sir George Cockerill, a champion of horses throughout his political career, steered The Exportation of Horses Act through parliament. This effectively put a stop to the trade in the live export of horses for butchery by introducing a minimum value of £25 on each animal to be sent abroad. Any animal fetching less — and worn out horses would inevitably be worth less — could not be exported. The only limitation to Cockerill's Bill was that ponies were excluded, a loophole which remained until The Ponies Act of 1969.

The 1937 Act formed the basis on which British horses have been protected from live export ever since. From time to time it has been amended to ensure that the minimum value has kept pace with inflation and, in the early 1990s, found itself threatened by European Community objections that it impinged unfairly upon free trade between member states. It is a testament to the high level of sympathy for horses amongst British people that in 1991, the Conservative government chose to introduce the Retention of Minimum Values Order and to do battle with EC authorities rather than to risk alienation from the UK pro-horse lobby. No species enjoys such widespread support, particularly from those in high places with power and influence.

That the live export trade should have been banned back in 1937 demonstrates how attitudes had already progressed from the beginning of the century. This was confirmed during the second world war when the International League for the Protection of Horses (ILPH) were able to gain 'absolute assurances' from the War Office in response to 'acute anxiety in the minds of the public' that horses used by the military might afterwards be sold overseas. This was in marked contrast to the Great War, after which some survivors were shamefully exported to Egypt, often to endure a life of neglect and deprivation as working animals. (Their unhappy fate caused Dorothy Brooke to create the Brooke Hospital for Horses in Egypt in 1930.) Another fortunate development was that advances in military technology ensured that the role of horses in 1939-45 was less pivotal than in 1914-18, though huge numbers were still used by both sides.

A further problem to emerge during the second world war was that the UK human population — faced with meat rationing — suddenly acquired a taste for horse flesh. The Duchess of Hamilton recalls how, 'at the end of the war, but not the end of rationing... a new and un-British trade sprang into existence and grew with rapidity, like a mushroom in the night. Within two years thousands upon thousands of horses were being slaughtered'.[7]

Fortunately, the gradual easing of austerity measures ensured that this 'un-British' craze died out fairly swiftly and with machines continuing to oust them from traditional working roles, horses soon began to enjoy improved status. In the 1950s — an unremarkable decade for most animal welfare groups — horse protection organisations were financially well supported and able to set up considerable numbers of rest homes and sanctuaries. The ILPH even goes so far as to consider it 'a golden age'[8] for its work.

As the century draws to a close, horses in the UK undoubtedly enjoy a privileged status compared to most other domesticated species. Legislation protects them from wanton cruelty and neglect; export for butchery is still outlawed (though this will no doubt come under further threat from the EC in coming years); and stables which keep them commercially are licensed and reasonably well regulated. There has been a proliferation of sanctuaries to ensure that many animals live out a contented old age and those who work with horses often show great dedication, compassion and affection.

Yet all is relative. Inhospitable pony fairs where animals are bought and sold for a pittance offer a distressing reminder that the fate of many animals is far from rosy. The increased affluence which has seen so many more teenage girls presented with a 'dream' pony may have had some beneficial impact in developing understanding amongst young people, but it has also led to many creatures being discarded when the 'horsy' phase is short-lived. Many are sold at market for slaughter. The housing of pet horses in unsuitable conditions is another difficulty created by the pony boom — as is the fact that many animals live lonely lives deprived of companionship.

Cases of outright cruelty also remain depressingly common, ranging from deliberate ill-treatment to neglect. Grossly overgrown hooves and other signs of absence of care and understanding remain all too familiar. RSPCA convictions for cruelty to horses and donkeys reached record levels in 1995.

As with cats and dogs, other misery is created by so-called 'animal lovers'. In particular, the increasing competitiveness and high finance of the racing industry is leading to many discarded thoroughbreds ending their days in the meat factories of Belgium, Italy and France; some via the continental race circuit and others through a legal loophole by which licensed racehorses are taken out of the country and sent to abattoirs under the pretext that they are travelling abroad to take part in races.[9]

Competitiveness in show jumping, eventing, flat and National Hunt racing is also responsible for its share of suffering, causing high levels of stress and injury. In 1996, ten horses died during the National Hunt's premier event — the Cheltenham Festival Meeting — and the famous Grand National continues to claim lives. Approximately 250 horses die on Britain's race tracks every year.

Equally disturbing is the use of low value ponies in animal experiments. Many are funded by the racing industry in its desire to reduce the considerable financial cost of injuries and illnesses which are a direct consequence of the 'sport' itself.[10]

For all the problems which still exist, most of the UK equine population enjoy an enormously improved quality of life compared both to their forebears and to their relatives abroad. Around the globe the story is far more disheartening. The use of horses and donkeys in fiestas, rodeos, bullfights and other dubious entertainment; the brutal trade in live animals for meat from South America and Eastern Europe to Western Europe; the life of perpetual grinding hardship which is still the lot of thousands of working animals in every continent of the globe — all these are stark reminders of the widespread suffering which remains commonplace.

What progress can be expected in forthcoming years? Most of those concerned specifically with the welfare of horses are happy to see them used by humans, believing that 'the best future for the horse in this increasingly overcrowded world is in his close association with mankind, for the mutual benefit of both species'.[11] The major task, as they see it, is to try to wipe out *abuse* of animals worldwide, whilst still supporting responsible *use* for work and entertainment.

A smaller minority is less convinced of 'mutual benefit'. It believes that suffering will continue on a massive scale for as long as people domesticate horses and perceive them as 'chattels' to be purchased, sold, castrated, mated, moved or killed according to the whims of their human owners. It is an idealistic position which probably contains ultimate logic.

Nevertheless, given the sad state of servitude endured by hundreds of thousands of horses and donkeys in the 'real world' at the end of the twentieth century, abolition of the worst abuses seems a massive enough goal to work towards — for the next century at least.

# 3 / Born to be wild

## 1 Cruelty or conservation?

Inspired primarily by the Romantic writers of the late eighteenth century, the nineteenth century witnessed a steady stream of authors who asserted passionately the power and beauty of the natural world. Some expressed beliefs which even now appear extraordinarily modern, pleading for the preservation of wild places or the right of animals to live free from persecution. For instance, the Anglo-Catholic Gerard Manley Hopkins wrote:

> What would the world be,
> once bereft
> Of wet and of wildness?
> Let them be left,
> O let them be left, wildness and wet;
> Long live the weeds and
> the wilderness yet.[1]

Or the charming sentiments of Christina Rossetti's poem in defence of creatures considered small and insignificant:

> The tiniest little thing
> That soars on feathered wing
> Or crawls among the long grass
> out of sight
> Has just as good a right
> To its appointed portion of delight
> As any king.[2]

For all its literary allies, however, wildlife enjoyed precious little legislative protection before the year 1900. Almost all animal welfare laws applied only to domestic animals. Birds were granted limited protection under the Wild Birds Protection Act of 1880 and it was illegal to bait wild animals or place them in 'pitted combat', but other than that it was more or less a case of anything goes.

For the most part conquering nature was the dominant ethos rather than protecting it. Amongst the ruling classes hunting and shooting were major pastimes, so much so that male members of the aristocracy would have been thought unconventional if they *did not* indulge. Interest in wildlife was confined predominantly to killing for sport, obtaining trophies from hunting expeditions at home or in colonial lands, or collecting live species either for zoos or for increasingly popular private collections. Wild animals were shot, stuffed and displayed as trophies; or else captured alive and shipped back as bounty from the Empire. It was a fashion which fitted perfectly Britain's confidence in its colonial role, taming and ruling savages whether they be human or non-human!

Nor did emerging interest in natural science do much to advance respect for animals. The vast majority of the new breed of professional scientists were more interested in examining dead creatures under laboratory microscopes than learning from the splendour of the living natural world. Their thirst for specimens to dissect simply gave fresh impetus to the killing.

Amongst opponents of the prevailing spirit, two who stood out were converts from the entrenched belief in human dominance over nature. The ex-hunter and gamekeeper Richard Jefferies (1848-1887) became an outspoken defender of animals and the natural world, disseminating a passionate message of respect and reverence for nature. He spent his days walking the countryside, writing with enormous energy, joy and sensitivity about the sky, water, flowers, trees and animals he observed. W. H. Hudson (1841-1922) was equally influential. Having once made his living by capturing birds on the Pampas of Argentina to sell to the scientists of London, he became vehement in his advocacy of wildlife protection after coming to England and comparing the beauty of creatures he had left behind with mounted specimens in dusty UK laboratories.[3] Birds were his great love and he was to play a leading part in the early development of the RSPB.

By 1900, white hunters had already decimated the world's wildlife sufficiently for some of the most powerful nations to meet in London and sign a Convention for the Preservation of Animals, Birds and Fish in Africa. The aim was to prevent African wildlife from being wiped out, though the main motivation was to preserve sport for future hunters rather than to protect the lives of animals. Nonetheless, it is significant in that it marks the first international agreement on conservation grounds. It was followed three years later by the formation of the Society for the Preservation

• • • • • • • • • • • • • • • • • • • • • • • • • • • • • • • • • • • • • • • • • • • • • • •

of the Wild Fauna of the Empire (later the Fauna Preservation Society), the first organisation with a primary purpose to conserve threatened species.

Closer to home, the Society for the Protection of Nature Reserves was established as early as 1912, campaigning for the creation of sanctuaries to counter the perceived menace of spreading urbanisation. Its objectives were welcomed by *The Times*, which warned in an editorial of the countryside being turned into 'a sort of universal suburb… Lovers of nature will have to act resolutely and quickly', it stated, 'if the last unspoilt relics of wild nature in Britain are to be preserved for the interest and inspiration of generations to come'. Others, though, dismissed its aspirations as alarmist.

The latter reaction typifies the considerable problem faced by those who called for measures to encourage nature conservation and wildlife protection in the period up until the first world war. The UK human population was little more than half its current size at only 31 million, and so habitat loss from human development was not universally considered an urgent problem. The late twentieth-century menace of the motor car was only in its early infancy; food production was labour intensive and not dependent upon poisonous chemicals. In the words of famous social historian G. M. Trevelyan, the general consensus was that 'natural beauty needed no conservation. Man was camped in the middle of it and could not get outside it, still less destroy it'.[4]

In the period between the two world wars, the threat to the natural world gained far wider acceptance. Cars, factories, towns, electricity pylons, agricultural development and massive house building programmes began to alter radically the face of the countryside. The call for conservation measures began to enjoy significant support, alongside declarations of the emotional value of nature to an increasingly urbanised population. Some, wrote J. S. Huxley, require 'the wildness of nature, the contact with wild animals living their own lives in their own surroundings' to ensure their spiritual health and happiness.[5]

In 1926, the Council for the Protection of Rural England was formed, serving as a focus for an increasingly popular campaign to establish national parks. Four years later a committee set up by government supported the call. In a more advantageous political climate its recommendations may well have been implemented, but faced by economic depression at the beginning of the decade and a massive rearmament programme at the end, successive governments failed to find necessary resources. Plans were shelved.

Although the need to set aside areas for native flora and fauna was a far more popular concept by 1939 than it had been at the time of The Great War, it still remained surprisingly 'outside the mainstream of the nature preservation movement'.[6] Unlike today, it was considered less important than initiatives to prevent deliberate acts of cruelty to animals and birds. Wildlife protectionists pinned their faith largely in the power of education, believing that therein rested their best opportunity of discouraging all-too-common practices such as ill-treatment of wild mammals or collecting of bird eggs.

In this policy they were more successful than in attempts to promote new legislation. Grey seals were the only wild mammals to be protected by law in the period up until the second world war. The Grey Seals (Protection) Act (1914) prohibited slaughter during the breeding season, establishing the basis of laws to protect the species for the rest of the century. Its introduction resulted from merciless cubbing by sealers and fisherman on the islands and rocks off the coastlines of Scotland, Ireland and the Scillies. In Scottish waters numbers were reduced to below five hundred, creating the danger of extinction. It was the first time that a parliamentary act to protect any mammal from cruelty had been introduced partly on conservation grounds.

By the time of the second world war, the need for careful future planning to protect the countryside had been officially recognised. Even during wartime itself the government found time to instigate a committee to recommend a national strategy; the first of several reviews during the 1940s which eventually led to legislation. Tighter controls on development were introduced in the Town and Country Planning Act (1947) and the National Parks and Access to the Countryside Act (1949) was eventually implemented in the 1950s. Conservation was also granted its own official statutory body — the Nature Conservancy — with a mandate to supply government with 'scientific advice on the conservation and control of the natural flora and fauna of Great Britain'. The emphasis on science was typical of the changing times: as in most other areas of life, decisions upon the preservation of nature were, in future, to be justified almost exclusively upon scientific assessments.

The introduction of these measures shows that environmental protectionists had by this time established influence and legitimacy, but the problem was that the scale of destruction they confronted had also escalated rapidly. All the threats identified by conservationists before 1939 had intensified, particularly from agricultural development.

During the war, increasing areas of land had been brought under cultivation — a trend which continued apace after 1945. Clement Attlee's Labour government was determined to reverse the pre-war conditions where Britain had imported 70% of its own food. Accordingly, farmers were granted massive tax incentives to stimulate self-sufficiency. Heavy machinery soon became commonplace; traditional crop rotation was abandoned. Liberal application of artificial fertilisers, pesticides, insecticides and other chemicals became the norm. Hedges and woodlands were decimated, destroying habitat. Wildlife suffered unprecedented damage. Far from enjoying their traditional reputation as custodians of the countryside, farmers were soon identified by many naturalists as a major threat to its survival.

Throughout the 1950s and 1960s the industrialisation of agriculture advanced without concerted challenge. Old grasslands were ploughed up, drainage systems introduced, pollution incidents became more commonplace. Populations of hares, partridges, dormice, voles, hedgehogs, shrews, many species of birds and other small mammals declined alarmingly. Increasingly, the policy of acquiring land to conserve in managed sanctuaries gained credence as the only effective method of saving species from destruction. The number of declared nature reserves rose spectacularly from 61 in 1942 to more than 1000 by 1975.[7]

By this time the conservation movement had in many ways separated itself from those wildlife organisations whose primary concern was to oppose cruelty. By doing so it had established itself as a considerably more powerful force for change. For one thing, it could appeal to forces who were more concerned with preserving a traditional notion of Britain as 'a green and pleasant land' than any reform to prevent cruelty. Furthermore, it could call upon the unequivocal support of influential elements of society — particularly the hunting and shooting community — that anti-cruelty campaigners were opposing with renewed vigour. The royal family offer an obvious example. George V, Edward VIII and George VI had all been devoted to hunting and shooting — a passion inherited by the present Queen, the Duke of Edinburgh and Prince Charles. Deer stalking, fox hunting, wild fowling, game, duck and wild boar shooting were all popular pursuits. Yet at the same time the Royals were only too willing to offer patronage to organisations concerned only with endangered species or threatened habitat. Both for financial and political reasons, it was, therefore, in the obvious interest of conservationists to divorce their activities as far as they possibly could from the sometimes more controversial aims of animal protectionists.

This is not to say that individual wild animals did not benefit from growth in support for conservation. On the contrary, the proliferation of well-managed reserves protected millions from extermination. But what became more clearly defined than ever before was a philosophical difference at the heart of the two interests. Whereas conservationists were essentially concerned with preserving *species* in order to maintain a traditionally perceived order in nature, animal protectionists were motivated primarily by a desire to protect *individual* animals from pain and suffering.

George V indulging his passion for shooting in India in 1911. For details of his kill, see page 96.

From the end of the 1960s onwards the efforts of conservationists were augmented by a new style of crusade for environmental protection. This was inspired in part by Rachel Carson's groundbreaking book, *Silent Spring* (1962), in which the author exposed the potentially catastrophic effects of chemical farming world-wide for both humans and animals. Hers was the most influential of several widely publicised exposés of the polluting and unsustainable consequences of agriculture polices based upon maximum production without care for long-term damage. Not only were the policies themselves denounced as deeply flawed; they were also shown to be manipulated ruthlessly to their own ends by big business interests. By the end of the decade, corruption, incompetence and greed were implicated extensively in the decimation of the countryside. The young rebelled. Radical groups were formed. Greenpeace (1969) was followed closely by Friends of the Earth (established in the US in 1969 and the UK in 1971).

'Holistic' was the term often used to describe the ethos of the new movement. There was a philosophical freshness in that young environmentalists emphasised a more overt spiritual concern for the preservation of the earth and its inhabitants than had been heard from the conservative and scientific world of traditional nature protection. They also tended to be idealistically anti-establishment. For the first time polluting big business interests, greedy landowners, corruption and inept government policies found themselves under sustained attack, opening the way for the emergence of green politics.

Yet although many supporters of the new organisations expressed deep sympathy with animal protection issues, officially, they, too, were more concerned with threatened species than individual animal welfare. 'Save the whales' campaigns were acceptable because whales were in danger of extinction, but issues such as hunting and factory farming were either not on the agenda or considered to be of secondary importance.

Indeed, when a radical environmental organisation did eventually choose to become involved in an exclusively anti-cruelty to animals campaign, it only served to provide spectacular evidence of an ultimate philosophical difference. In 1985, Greenpeace abandoned its then one-year-old campaign against the fur trade on the grounds that it threatened the livelihood of a small number of indigenous Canadian and American Indians who relied upon trapping for economic survival. The decision infuriated animal protectionists both within and outside the organisation and caused Mark Glover, co-ordinator of the Greenpeace fur initiative, to quit. Taking the campaign plan with him, he launched his own organisation, Lynx.

In the following few years, the innovative methods employed by Glover and his colleagues were to make a massive impact upon an anti-fur movement already gathering in strength through the work of the RSPCA, Beauty Without Cruelty and others. Utilising the creative talents of sympathetic designers, artists and film makers, Lynx destroyed the idea of fur as fashionable. The photographer David Bailey made a hard hitting anti-fur commercial which received far more attention than it might otherwise have enjoyed when it was banned from cinemas. Controversial billboard posters also took effect. The poster slogan 'it takes up to forty dumb animals to make a fur coat but only one to wear it' inspired the wrath of a few feminist groups, but its powerful message struck an influential note with the public. Lynx also popularised its own fashion counter culture. Towards the end of the 1980s it became chic to be seen wearing a Lynx T-shirt, featuring attractive animal images created by well-known designers.

Until the 1970s, it was the aspiration of many women to own a fur coat. Less than twenty years later the UK fur trade was in a state of collapse and fur was the last thing that most young people would want to be seen wearing. Most factory fur farms closed; the Hudson Bay Company quit Britain after centuries of profitable trading; shops went out of business and department stores closed their fur departments. Based on the success of methods employed by Lynx, protests also gathered momentum in many other countries. After a legal challenge brought about the demise of Lynx in 1991, Mark Glover formed the organisation Respect For Animals to continue the work.

As the years pass by the fur trade does claim to be making a comeback — though it seems highly unlikely that it could ever regain its former popularity in the UK. Yet

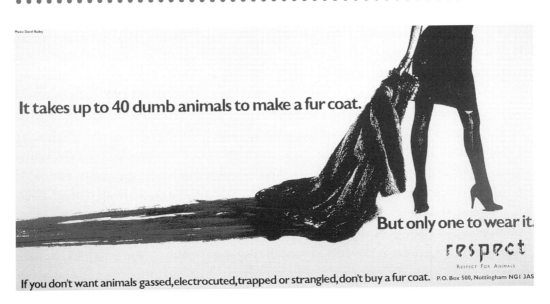

Photo: David Bailey

It takes up to 40 dumb animals to make a fur coat.

But only one to wear it.

re/pect

RESPECT FOR ANIMALS

If you don't want animals gassed, electrocuted, trapped or strangled, don't buy a fur coat. P.O. Box 500, Nottingham NG1 3AS

world-wide it remains a powerful industry. There are still an estimated thirty million plus animals slaughtered every year and the fur trade can still boast global sales of over $1 billion dollars.[8] Wild animal trappers in the US and Canada and factory farmers in Eastern Europe are amongst the chief suppliers.

As the century draws to a close, the considerable influence of both environmentalists and animal protectionists is unmistakable. If membership of the National Trust is included, an estimated six million British people now belong to conservation groups, mostly helping to fund the purchase and expert management of an increasing number of sanctuaries. Influenced by the success of the more radical environmental movement, there has also been a willingness amongst some conservationists to become more openly critical of politicians and polluting big business, though criticism has sometimes been tempered by the availability of funds from industry and government for non-controversial schemes. Polluting multinationals who associate themselves unashamedly with campaigns to save wildlife have become a regular feature of late twentieth-century life.

The more radical green movement has also enjoyed its successes, even if support declined from the extraordinarily high levels at the end of the 1980s. It has prospered to the point where no political party would dare now to enter an election without at least paying lip service to its commitment to protect the environment. Policies instigated by the Green Party have fairly commonly found themselves adopted by mainstream politicians, albeit often in weakened form.

Campaigns to protect domestic wildlife from cruelty have made some progress, too, though change has proved slow and difficult to accomplish. In 1958 — some seven years after recommendation by a government instigated committee — the infamous gin trap was outlawed as a trapping instrument. Deer (1959 and 1963), badgers (1973 and 1982), seals (1970) and otters (1978) have all benefited from specific parliamentary acts to safeguard their welfare. Eventually in 1995, all wild mammals were at last granted limited protection, ending a previously deplorable situation under which it was legal (say) to pull the legs off a hedgehog for amusement. The Wild Mammals (Protection) Act makes it an offence 'to mutilate, kick, beat, nail or otherwise impale, stab, burn, crush, drown, drag or asphyxiate' any wild mammal.

Perhaps the most depressing aspect of the new legislation is that it was still so desperately needed, for it was introduced in the wake of an alarming increase in incidents of cruelty and a renaissance of illegal 'sports' like badger baiting and digging.

Despite the new protections, snaring, poisoning, trapping or shooting of many species of wildlife remains legal.

## 2   Birds fly ahead

Wild birds were granted legal protection before any other wild animal and efforts to defend them have continued to achieve swifter progress. Does the comparatively enlightened treatment they receive offer significant evidence of how attitudes to other wildlife might develop? Or is the campaign to help birds symptomatic of the kind of inconsistencies only too obvious in our treatment of other animals?

As we saw earlier, it was largely to oppose cruelty for the fashion trade that the Society for the Protection of Birds (later the RSPB) was formed back in 1889. By that time British birds already enjoyed some safeguards under an 1880 act of parliament which established a close season when killing was prohibited, but this had proved inadequate to the task of preventing their wholesale slaughter for the millinery trade. The massacre was so unremitting that urgent concern was voiced for the survival of some species. Conservation and anti-cruelty interests went hand in hand. Both *Punch* and *The Times* were outspoken in their contempt, their scathing articles helping to transform the women who wore feathered headgear from figures of fashion to figures of fun.

Legislation ensued. Firstly, a ban on the export of bird-skins from British India in 1904 and six years later an end to the trafficking of birds of paradise from New Guinea. In 1922 came the clinching victory of a ban on the import to the UK of all foreign plumage. This legislation more or less put an end to 'murderous millinery', though the trade did stage a couple of brief revivals in the 1930s and early 1950s respectively.

By the 1920s, the RSPB had established a broad network of support and could turn its attention to another crisis. Waste oil from vessels of increasing size was drifting onto British shores, polluting waters and creating havoc for sea birds. For probably the first time environmental pollution became central to a campaign for wildlife protection. A 1922 act of parliament made it an offence to discharge oil within three miles of the coastline and this was followed by various international conferences which attempted to provide more comprehensive solutions. How dismally they failed was to be demonstrated tragically in later decades by the pitiful sight of thousands of seabirds caked in sticky and filthy oil, particularly after the *Torrey Canyon* slick off Land's End in 1967 and the *Exxon Valdez* spill in Alaska in 1988. Few environmental disasters have stimulated either such massive anger against polluters, sympathy for victims or voluntary help with the respective rescue missions. Nevertheless, the oil menace goes with us into the next century.

Efforts against oil pollution apart, bird protectionists followed up their victory over the feathered hat trade by embarking upon a fruitful twin strategy comparable to that employed by other wildlife groups. Firstly, they prioritised education, and secondly, they purchased land in order to establish sanctuaries for threatened species.

In the former programme, they were assisted greatly by W. H. Hudson, who died in 1922 having played an important role in the fight against fashion. Horrified by the ignorance towards nature amongst an increasingly urbanised population, he left most of his by then considerable estate to the RSPB, with a specific mandate to pursue an educational campaign which would promote greater respect for wild birds.[1] It was a legacy that contributed significantly towards the fascination and sense of wonder which has developed so strongly as part of our national consciousness. Popular traditional childhood pastimes such as egg collecting and trapping gradually lost much of their appeal and were eventually regulated by legislation. For the vast majority of the population, watching, feeding or encouraging birds to nest became far more appealing than destroying. As a consequence, the RSPB has gone from strength to strength, its membership rising from 71,000 in 1970 to over 1 million in 1997. It is now reputedly the largest single conservation organisation in Europe.

The RSPB's sanctuary programme has proved equally rewarding, saving many species from the dual threat of habitat destruction and poisoning from agricultural chemicals. By 1997, it owned and managed 148 reserves, covering more than a quarter of a million acres.[2] Even though many species continue to dwindle alarmingly in number, it is a testament to the skill of the pro-bird lobby that so few have been lost completely. Some conservation programmes have proved spectacularly successful, most famously the high-profile Operation Osprey to re-establish a bird of prey that collectors had exterminated from UK shores during the previous century.

For all these advances, birds do, inevitably, remain under threat from precisely the same factors which endanger all wildlife. In 1997, an investigation commissioned by the RSPB reported that 'the growing use of poisonous sprays' is turning the British countryside into a 'tragic wasteland', causing a 'dramatic decline' in songbirds. It also claimed that the use of herbicides has practically doubled since 1970 and that there has been a massive increase in areas of land sprayed with insecticides. 'The grubbing up of thousands of miles of hedgerows' is identified as another major menace.

Internationally, birds face not only the perils of chemicals, habitat loss and 'sportsmen', but also a ruthless pet industry. Millions of exotic species are trafficked around the globe every year. Leaving aside the miserable lives to which caged birds are ultimately subjected, up to 50% of those originally caught die during trapping and transport.[3] Despite the introduction of bans on the *export* of their own native species, both the EC and the US still permit the *import* of wild caught species, primarily from Africa, South America and Asia.

As such double standards indicate, love of birds has not exempted the campaign to protect them from the kind of contradictions which characterise almost all human relationships with other creatures. We still make up the rules to suit ourselves rather than out of any consistent philosophical position. Not even the RSPB is immune, combining its zeal to defend many species with a deafening silence on controversial issues such as the rearing of game birds. Almost certainly the reasons are largely pragmatic, many landowners and other sportsman combining their love for song birds and rarities with a passion for blasting game or 'pests' out of the sky.

Birds bred for food highlight another contradiction. The Protection of Birds Act of 1954 makes it an offence to keep any bird in a cage where it cannot spread its wings, but includes a subsection which excludes poultry from the provision. On what rational grounds — other than commercial exploitation — can it be considered cruel to keep a robin crammed tightly in a cage and yet perfectly acceptable to inflict the same on a battery chicken?

Other controversies highlight wider ethical questions. Exactly what are we trying to conserve and why? In 1996 — in a policy supported by the RSPB — the British government gave its backing to the shooting of ruddy ducks in the East Midlands. The bird is an American native, brought to Britain in captivity. Some individuals escaped and adapted successfully, spreading throughout Europe. Males began to mate with the increasingly rare white headed duck (rare because of destruction of habitat and shooting), producing a hybrid and threatening the survival of the pure white headed bird. To the RSPB and other traditional conservationists the situation justifies extreme measures to preserve the white headed duck in its pure form. This means attempting to control the ruddy duck population through a culling programme.

Opponents see such interference as both inept and immoral. Inept because controls over nature are exceedingly difficult to achieve once a group has become as firmly established as the ruddy duck now is: immoral because interference demands the death of thousands of individuals in an attempt to conserve one species. According to Andrew Tyler of Animal Aid, 'the white headed duck has already worked out its survival strategy by copulating with the ruddy duck for a fresh input of DNA. It is essentially the same species, otherwise it could not possibly produce healthy offspring'. Why, he asks, should the ruddy duck become 'the scapegoat for what is essentially a problem caused by our reckless and polluting behaviour?'[4]

Those against the cull temporarily won the day, the proposed initial kill being cancelled by the Department of the Environment in the face of mounting criticism. Long-term resistance is less assured, particularly as the influential Berne Convention favours culling. But possibly more important than the particular dispute itself is its wider implication — pivotal to implementation of future wildlife protection policies. How far should humans interfere with nature in an attempt to compensate for the problems almost invariably created by ourselves? Should rarity be the measure of compassion? Does protection of threatened species justify the slaughter of the common? Should we scapegoat creatures whose crime is only to disobey our human perception of how the natural world should be? How far can nature be left to follow its own course? And what exactly is 'natural'?

Support for the massacre of ruddy ducks is an example of how ruthlessly hostile humans can be to species which upset our conventional notion of what constitutes a balance in nature. A further example is the war declared upon Canada geese. There is currently a massive population causing high levels of crop damage, but this is clearly the effect of the way in which the shooting fraternity distributed them around the countryside in the 1950s and 1960s. Are we right to denigrate them as pests simply because they have proved smart enough to adapt and to thrive? Or should we accept the consequences of our folly and leave nature to make its own adjustments?

Magpies offer yet another illustration. For decades they have been condemned as partly responsible for the decrease in songbirds. As the leading ornithologist Chris Mead puts it, 'read many bird books and you get the feeling that the magpie is Satan personified'. Recent evidence, however, 'shows it is simply not the case'. While they may take chicks, 'they are certainly not responsible for the wholesale demise of

Britain's songbirds'. Rather, they have become the scapegoat for the real cause — modern farming methods. Herbicides have decimated seed-bearing weeds from crops and winter stubble is rarely available for birds to feed upon.

Vilification is not confined to bird conservation. Grey squirrels (introduced by humans in the last century) and mink (escapees from fur factory farms) are amongst wild mammals whom some accuse of causing a decline in numbers of native species. Is it right to persecute them in a (usually) vain attempt to redress a problem that humans have created? Or in time will they, too, be accepted as 'natural' and others classified as 'unwanted pests'?

## 3  Capturing the wild

Exotic wildlife in remote areas remained outside the experience of most people until well after the second world war. Apart from circuses, stuffed specimens in museums, or adventure books written by naturalists and explorers, it was zoos alone which offered the possibility of contact.

For the most part menageries meant animals kept in inadequate and unstimulating pens and cages, perpetuating a prevailing message of savage and dangerous nature subjugated by human superiority. True, the opening of Whipsnade in 1931 had marked the then revolutionary provision of more 'naturalistic' enclosures in larger areas, but by and large welfare was not a priority. There was widespread ignorance about the psychological needs of animals. Conservation did not feature much on the agenda.

Only a tiny minority presented a more sympathetic view. Of these, Konrad Lorenz — usually described as the first ethologist — was particularly significant and won many admirers from the 1930s onwards for his loving and sympathetic observations of animal behaviour.

More than any other factor, however, it was the evolution of film technology which led to a wider understanding of the sophisticated emotional lives of wild animals. In the 1950s, a generation of young people became familiar with wildlife through watching Walt Disney nature movies, usually shown in cinemas as the support programme to one of his hugely popular animated cartoon classics. A few years later came the first television programmes and the formation in 1957 of the now world-renowned BBC Natural History Unit.

One of the first producers to become involved was David Attenborough, who, as a young producer at the BBC, was responsible for a series 'explaining the meaning of the shape and pattern of animals'. It was not illustrated by film taken in the wild, but by showing the inhabitants of London Zoo. The programmes were 'relatively successful' and prompted Attenborough to realise how much more powerful they might have been 'if we had first shown on film an animal in the wild state'. Consequently, he and his colleagues created plans for a television series to include film of animals in their natural surroundings.[1]

What followed was a long way from the wildlife documentaries of today. Funded jointly by the BBC and London Zoo, David Attenborough and crew set out on a series of trips, firstly to Sierra Leone and later to the South American countries, British Guinea and Central New Guinea. There, they not only filmed animals and birds, but also *captured* them for transportation back to London Zoo. Broadcast under the title of *Zoo Quest*, both the nature of the programmes and their popularity offer an extraordinary reminder of how faith in human beings as the great adventurers and rulers of the natural world remained largely unquestioned. Nature was still there to be tamed, even by those who were fascinated and excited by it. Creatures brought back to the zoo from South America, for instance, included a tamandua, a capybara, a snake, three macaus, five parrots, two parakeets, a capuchin monkey and, 'best of all' — according to David Attenborough at the time — a pair of red-billed toucans.[2]

One of the principal catalysts for change came in 1960 with the publication of Joy Adamson's book, *Born Free*. It described how she and her husband, George, had raised an orphaned lion cub named Elsa in a remote area of Kenya. The bond that developed was so close that the lioness continued to visit her surrogate human parents regularly, even after she had been successfully returned to the wild and had bred young.

Within months, *Born Free* had been read by millions and was soon translated into twenty-five languages, creating unprecedented popular interest in wildlife and its conservation. Here were dangerous mammals represented in a new light, as intelligent and sensitive individuals and not simply as cold, automated killers or specimens to be captured, caged or hunted.

Joy Adamson spent the next few years touring the world, promoting her own books (*Born Free* was followed by the story of Elsa's cubs in *Living Free* and a third publication, *Forever Free*) and raising support and money for wildlife preservation. From South Africa to the UK and the USA she was greeted by massive audiences, helping to establish conservation as an issue of international concern.

Nor did her influence end there. In 1964, the story of the relationship between Elsa the lioness and Joy and George Adamson became the subject of a feature film starring the young English couple, Virginia McKenna and Bill Travers. (By this time, Elsa had died and a mixture of trained and circus animals were employed during filming.) The experience was to have such a profound effect upon the two actors that the seeds were sown for the popularisation of a fresh approach to wildlife and eventually to the establishment of the first organisation set up specifically to oppose zoos.

## 4  Virginia McKenna and the legacy of *Born Free*

It was purely by chance that Virginia McKenna and Bill Travers found themselves in Kenya starring in the film of Joy Adamson's book.

Virginia explains: 'It started in 1962 when Bill was rung by the first director — he left early on in filming — who told us that they were going to make the film. Bill said it sounded absolutely fascinating, but that he would be acting in Stratford for the next year and was therefore unavailable.'

After his Shakespeare season, Bill went to New York to take part in a play which lasted only one night. It was at that point that he wondered if there had been any developments with the planned film? He asked his agent to get in touch and when he and Virginia returned to England they met with the director and one of the producers. 'They said "it is going to be a semi-documentary real life type thing, but we need actors. Will you do it?" … Well, we didn't hesitate for a second. We were so excited. It was an adventure and we both liked challenges,' recalls Virginia.

Neither had worked with animals before, nor did they know anything about lions, though Virginia herself 'can't remember a time when we didn't have pets at home.' Her parents had separated when she was four and she had spent the next five years living with her father in London. Apart from dogs and cats, he kept several wild species in their maisonette in Hampstead. He had a snake, bush babies and a parrot — a collection Virginia would heartily disapprove of now. 'I don't think we should ever keep wild animals in domesticity. When I eventually saw bush babies in the wild in Kenya, I realised how terrible it was to keep them in captivity.'

It took ten and a half months to film *Born Free* and Virginia describes it as 'a life changing experience… We only had Sundays off, but in fact on Sundays we used to go down to the lions and help feed them because the safety factor was constant contact, doing lots of things with them and not being separated for very long.'

The Adamsons were both on site throughout. Joy was there primarily for press and publicity, but Virginia describes her as 'incredibly generous towards me when I was interpreting her. It couldn't have been easy.' George, she remembers as 'the best teacher we could possibly have had. He never told us how to behave, but he taught

Virginia McKenna with Boy during the filming of *Born Free* in 1964.

by example. In fact, we couldn't have made the film without him, not in the way that it was done. It wasn't made with tricks and trainers, but with a genuine relationship between people and animals.' She believes that this is the main reason that its popularity has lasted. 'I doubt whether they could ever make films in that way now. It takes so long and would cost too much.'

As the film progressed it became clear that something new and exciting was emerging. 'It was a small scale film to begin with,' recalls Virginia. 'As time went past, I think things were happening that they never imagined. Suddenly it escalated to Panavision and became *the* big film. In 1966 it was chosen for the Royal Command performance.'

Summarising the impact of the experience on both her own life and the wider public, Virginia recalls how Joy Adamson used to stress the significance of 'the spirit of Elsa'. 'Of course one can be cynical and say what a load of nonsense, but in a funny way I think she was quite right, because it is that dimension of an animal/human relationship which isn't anything to do with humans dominating animals that made an impression.'

According to Virginia, *Born Free* also emphasises the depth of understanding which can develop between people and individual animals. 'This is how we worked in the film, how we viewed things ever after and how I think those who were affected by the story came to see it. It probably is the spirit of Elsa that has carried through and anyone sensitive to the issue will have picked that up. It has changed the way a lot of people think about wild animals.'

At the end of filming Virginia, Bill and the Adamsons did their best to obtain the release of some of the lions who had starred in *Born Free*. 'George had always said that it would be possible, so we wanted to rehabilitate them, as Elsa had been. We managed to obtain three out of the twenty-four and the others went to zoos and safari parks. Subsequently we managed to obtain four more.'

At the beginning of the production the thought of what would happen to the animals when their role was over had not occurred to the eager young actors, but as time passed and relationships developed it became a source of deep anxiety. They felt 'dreadful' about the lions that were returned to captivity. 'We felt we had absolutely betrayed them,' says Virginia.

A year later, Bill embarked upon a new career, writing and producing wildlife films. The first was a documentary, *The Lions Are Free* — the story of what happened to some of the lions who had appeared as Elsa in *Born Free*. In 1968 he followed up with the script for *Ring of Bright Water*, based on Gavin Maxwell's book. He also acted in the film, which featured both Virginia and a cast of otters! In the same year he and James Hill (who had eventually directed *Born Free*) travelled to Kenya to make a film entitled *An Elephant Called Slowly*, featuring a young elephant named Pole Pole.

Pole Pole was destined to become not only 'the other catalyst' besides Elsa in the lives of Virginia and Bill, but also another potent example of how the close relationship which can develop between people and an individual animal can have wider consequences. Unlike the inspiring story of the lioness, however, Pole Pole was to become a haunting tragedy. Virginia explains: 'Basically the story of *An Elephant Called Slowly* was of a young couple who had been asked to caretake a house for a friend in the bush while he had an operation. They also had to look after some friends of his. The friends turned out to be elephants and through all the funny things that happened or the mistakes the couple made you learned a little bit about how elephants live in the wild. It was all very light-hearted.'

Virginia and Pole Pole in 1968.

The plan was to work with the orphan elephants of Daphne and David Sheldrick, by then well-known for their work in rehabilitating animals whose families had been torn apart by poachers. Unfortunately, however, when the film crew arrived in Kenya, they found that the Sheldricks did not have any young elephants in their orphanage suitable for the film.

'We needed a little two-year-old,' recalls Virginia. 'David knew that there was one in the trappers yard in Nairobi which had been captured as a gift to London Zoo. So we went to see her and she was really crazy, rushing around and banging her head on the side. David said to us, "Look, if they let us have her, I will be with her for two or three days and she will be fine."'

The trappers agreed to release Pole Pole to make the film and the Sheldricks were as good as their word. 'We shared an amazing six weeks with her. She was a friend. She'd follow us around and we developed such a lovely trusting relationship.'

When filming was over Virginia and Bill asked if they could buy her so that the Sheldricks could keep her with their other elephants for eventual return to the wild. But they were told that if Pole Pole was released another elephant would have to be trapped, so they reluctantly decided that they had to let her go to London Zoo. 'We couldn't allow another to be captured, because that doesn't just affect that individual animal, but the whole elephant family.'

Bill went once to visit Pole Pole in London and fed her oranges. She remembered him, of course, but he concluded that there was no point in going back again because it was probably as unhappy an experience for the elephant as it certainly was for him. He decided that she had to form new relationships and make new friends.

Fourteen years passed until Virginia and Bill received a letter from Daphne Sheldrick informing them that Pole Pole was about to be destroyed. They were asked to find out the circumstances. It emerged that the elephant had become difficult to handle after a series of companions had either died or been sent to other zoos. Virginia went to visit her and found 'a pathetic looking creature… A solitary female elephant in captivity is a very sad sight,' she adds.

The Travers managed to find a home for Pole Pole in a safe South African reserve, but the zoo would not even discuss it. Eventually, they did at least agree to send her to Whipsnade, where she would enjoy improved conditions. They even put in special electric doors in preparation for the move because they said that she was so difficult and dangerous.

Virginia concludes the sad story: 'Before the move even started, she collapsed in the travelling crate because they kept her standing for so long. When she recovered they heaved her up with a jack and she hobbled around indoors for a week. They put her under anaesthetic to look at one of her legs which had been damaged when she collapsed. We were told that she came around, but couldn't get up. They claimed that she had lost the will to live. So they put her down.'

Pole Pole died in 1983. The following year Virginia and Bill formed Zoo Check (now the Born Free Foundation). It was a natural progression, since even during the years of the elephant's captivity their interest in wild animals had developed steadily. Bill had continued to make visionary documentaries, including a film with Simon Trevor about the elephant ivory trade and another on the remarkable story of Christian the lion. As a young cub, Christian had been rescued from the pet department at Harrods by two young Australians. (The same pet department where Celia Hammond had worked as a young woman — see Chapter 2.) After spending some months living in a pine furniture shop in Chelsea, the lion went with her two owners to live at the Travers' home in Surrey. Christian spent four months in a specially built enclosure in the garden while — with assistance from both the Kenyan government and George Adamson — Bill arranged for his rehabilitation. The eventual film followed Christian from Surrey to Kenya, ending with his introduction to the wild and to the big male named Boy, one of the rescued lions from *Born Free*.

Virginia's involvement had been less prominent, mostly contributing voice-overs for Bill's films, but she, too, had become deeply concerned about the treatment of wild animals in captivity. 'We used to go to zoos whenever we travelled to look at the conditions. Slowly this interest became all-absorbing. When Pole Pole died everything fell into place. We formed Zoo Check and after that I was working on the zoo issue every possible moment. Eventually, there was little time left for acting!'

By the time that Zoo Check was set up, disquiet about the incarceration of animals had progressed significantly. More than any other factor (in the UK at least), feeling had been stimulated by the condition of Guy the Gorilla from London Zoo. Often slumped in the corner of his solitary cage, Guy stared out at visitors from behind bars with a haunting look which seemed to convey such intense misery and despair that it could not fail to disturb many of those who saw him. Until his death in 1978, his suffering probably prompted deeper concern about menageries than any other individual animal.

Nonetheless, the formation of Zoo Check was received dismissively by the zoo community. Virginia and Bill were accused of ignorance and of seeking personal publicity for their careers. 'At first we were treated like an irritating fly to be brushed away — a nine day wonder. Then, when they realised that we weren't going to disappear they became angry. That was followed by a long period of shut down. They wouldn't talk to us, refused to debate with us on television and some even banned our son Will (now Director of the Born Free Foundation) from entering their premises. That attitude has sort of ended now and we have a relationship with them on a level where we can discuss topics of mutual concern, such as the implementation of a Zoo Directive throughout Europe. It is in everyone's interest to see legal safeguards which would raise all zoos to a higher standard.'

As time has passed there can be no doubt that the Born Free Foundation and others have made an impact. Zoos have admitted what most once denied; that wild animals kept in captivity can be affected psychologically. They have also become much more conscious of the need to justify their existence on conservation rather than entertainment grounds. And even though poor conditions are far too commonplace, many have made considerable efforts to enrich the environment in which their animals are confined.

Yet Virginia and her colleagues remain largely unimpressed. 'I think that there are some genuine conservation projects, but I just wish they would be more selective. Unfortunately there is a role for captivity because you only have to see how the forests are disappearing to know that we are destroying our natural environment. But I don't think there is a role for collections. I think the whole captive wildlife "industry" should be much more specialised; ideally offering protection in the animals' own country, like the rhino sanctuaries in Kenya. Or at the very least in a similar climate. Rhinos on a pad in London Zoo shouldn't be allowed — it denies the nature of the animal.'

She accepts that the best zoos are a big improvement on the worst, but guards against acceptance of improved conditions as a permanent answer. 'You can go to the Far East or parts of Europe, look at some terrible pictures, or hear about a lion dying of starvation in a zoo in Spain. Then you go to a safari park or to a better zoo and at first you almost breathe a sigh of relief. You see they've got bushes and trees and ropes and you're almost conned into thinking that if it was all like this it would be OK. But would it? When you see a lot of awful things you are enchanted to see something where at least the animal can hop about a bit. You can start to get it out of proportion. You can easily forget that it is still a menagerie and that animals are still being exploited in one way or another. You have to look further and ask where the animals go when they are not wanted — when they are "surplus"? Where do the dealers come in? Who really cares about the individual?'

The dilemma of how to protect wild animals in a world where their natural habitat is disappearing fast will continue to loom large in the next century. That there is now some informed debate as to whether zoos have a suitable role to play is due in no small measure to the campaigning efforts of Virginia McKenna, the late Bill Travers (Bill died in March 1994) and their colleagues. Yet Virginia is modest about her own achievement. 'I am just pleased we weren't a one-day wonder. We launched Zoo Check at a time when many things were beginning to change and I think that we have developed and expanded because what we believe in is needed. I am just so pleased that we've been able to use our experience as actors in a film to do something about real life.'

The influence of the Adamsons is not universally accepted. Sir David Attenborough — one of several people who visited Kenya to make documentary films about their work — does not believe that 'they played such an important part in interesting the public in wildlife'.[1] Moreover, he is of the opinion that 'from some points of view, they had rather an unfortunate effect. The result of treating lions in that way was that habituated lions with no fear of human beings killed several people and had to be shot'.[2]

Whilst paying tribute to the influence of the Adamsons, others stress that their success was very much dependent upon the timing of Joy's book. As one critic put it, 'a few years earlier and *Born Free* would have escaped publication: a few years later and it would have been derided as naive in the climate of the Swinging Sixties'.[3]

## The right moment had arrived

The same surge in interest also led to other initiatives. Most important was the formation of the World Wildlife Fund in 1961, partly through the efforts of Peter Scott, another who had been responsible for some of the early BBC wildlife documentaries. With its well-respected patrons and influential supporters (notably the Duke of Edinburgh), the organisation was soon attracting unprecedented media attention for conservation issues.

A further sign of a fresh approach to the wild was the slowly evolving interest in studying animals in their natural environment. At around this time, several animal behaviourists began to travel to distant areas of Africa. One of the first was Jane Goodall who, in 1960, set out for Tanzania to begin the life-long project which has so dramatically revised our understanding of chimpanzees.

## 5 Jane Goodall's African dream

Why Jane Goodall should always have been fascinated by animals is unclear. Born in Central London in 1934, her family kept a pet dog but had no special affinities. The first few years of her life were spent with little access to wild places. Yet for as long as she can remember, Jane delighted in the company of other creatures. From earliest childhood her greatest pleasure was both to be with them and to observe their ways.

It was during the war years that Jane's passion first found true expression. At the age of five she sat patiently crouched inside a hen house for more than four hours to see how a hen laid an egg: at a similar age she recalls long periods watching frogs in a pond. A few years later she met Rusty, a black mongrel dog who was to convince her definitively of the unique individuality of every animal. 'More than any other animal I have ever met, Rusty influenced my understanding. My very strong belief in animal personality, rationality and emotion was established by the time I was eight or nine,' she confirms.

Rusty lived at a hotel near to Jane's home in Bournemouth and took to tagging along whenever she took another neighbour's dog on its daily walk. In her book, *My*

*Life With The Chimpanzees*, she describes his significance in more detail:

> *Rusty taught me so much about animal behaviour, lessons I have remembered all my life. He taught me that dogs can think things out — that they can reason. If, for example, I threw a ball from an upstairs window, he would watch where it landed, then bark for the door to be opened, rush downstairs, bark for an outside door to be opened, then go and find the ball. He could plan, too. When it was very hot he sometimes took himself off along the street to the sea, had a swim, then trotted back, wet and cool.*[1]

As a young child, Jane was also an avid reader. Unsurprisingly, books with an animal theme were her favourites. Hugh Lofting's *The Story of Dr Dolittle* made a particular impact. She read it when she was seven years old and from that time determined to visit Africa when she was older. The Tarzan stories and *The Jungle Book* added to her resolve.

Despite a fairly successful academic school career, Jane narrowly failed to gain a scholarship to university. Since her parents could not afford to pay for her admission, she went instead to secretarial college. She obtained a diploma and found employment as a secretary in Oxford. This was followed by a 'fascinating' position working for a documentary film company in London. But all the time the African dream stayed with her. As often as she could she spent time in the Natural History Museum, learning more about the continent's wildlife.

The opportunity to visit Africa came sooner than expected. Out of the blue an old schoolfriend invited Jane to stay on her parents' farm in Kenya. After a period working as a waitress to save money for her passage, Jane set sail on a passenger liner bound for Mombasa in 1957. She was twenty-three years old.

Within two months of her arrival in Kenya, she landed a job as secretary to the man who eventually 'made all my dreams come true' — the anthropologist Louis Leakey. 'I made an appointment to see him and I was able to impress him with my knowledge of Africa's natural history. He offered me a position as his secretary there and then,' she recalls.

Leakey was to prove a seminal influence, providing the young naturalist with a privileged education in natural history over the next two years. They visited Nairobi National Park and the then remote area of the Oldivai Gorge, where for the first time she saw a wild rhino and a lion. 'Although Louis is famous for his work with fossils and skeletons he also had a passionate interest in modern African wildlife,' Jane asserts.

She also learnt much from her routine work in Leakey's museum in Nairobi, where — in addition to valuable knowledge — she gathered a growing family of orphan animals, including a vervet monkey, bush baby, dwarf mongoose, black and white rat and hedgehog.

It was in 1959 that Louis Leakey first told Jane about his plan to study a group of chimpanzees living on the Gombe Nature Park, 'on the shores of a far-off lake in Tanganyika' (now Tanzania). He believed that an understanding of chimpanzee behaviour might provide important insight into the life of Stone Age humans. Aware of Jane's passionate desire to live amongst wild animals, he invited her to run the project. He wanted, he said, 'a mind uncluttered by theories.'[2]

It took a further year to find sufficient funds, during which time there was also considerable controversy over the appointment of Jane Goodall. Leakey was condemned as 'amoral' for proposing to send a young woman alone into the bush. The British government in Tanganyika (still under colonial rule) was reluctant to allow the scheme, considering it too dangerous. It eventually agreed to do so only on the condition that a companion was appointed. (This task was undertaken by Jane's mother, who stayed for the first three months before it was agreed that Jane could live there alone, with support from her cook and boatman.)

They arrived at Gombe in July 1960. Jane describes it as 'a magical time. I was so excited that my dream had come to pass. All I had ever wanted was to be with animals and to write about them.' The well-publicised dangers of the bush held no terror, her one great fear being 'that the chimps kept running away and the money would run out. I was terrified of letting Louis down. He had given me my opportunity and shown such faith in me.'

She need not have worried. The first year was one of 'gradual discovery', learning about the animals and slowly gaining their acceptance. To begin with they were often belligerent and 'quite scary', but in time this mostly gave way to 'mutual trust and respect'. She also grew quickly to love the 'aloneness' of the forest, so much so that when visitors came she often hid with the chimpanzees rather than seek human company.

As little as she seemed to need other people, one of the strengths of Jane Goodall's work has always been her ability to relate to the local community. From the beginning she established good relations, involving it in her work as much as she could. Today, much of the project work at Gombe is undertaken by the native population, ensuring that they share concern and fascination for the chimps.

The Gombe project soon ran into scientific controversy. In reports, Jane insisted on naming the animals she observed — David Graybeard, Fifi, Faban and so on —

a practice alien to the then narrow and statistically-obsessed world of natural history. The mere suggestion that animals might have individual personalities was ridiculed. In the next few years, Jane compounded her 'crime' by using such words as 'childhood', 'adolescence', 'excitement' and 'mood' to describe chimpanzee behaviour, constantly implying similarities to human behaviour. She responded to criticism with characteristic resolve. 'I knew I was right,' she says confidently.

Whatever reservations existed about Jane's insistence upon the emotional capacities of chimps, two important new discoveries within the first year ensured that the study established credibility. Firstly, she found that the chimps sometimes ate meat when it was assumed previously that they were totally vegetarian; and secondly — and most significantly — she observed that they made and used tools. This indicated a degree of planning and intellectual sophistication previously thought impossible in non-humans.

These successes secured continued funding for the Gombe project. Its reputation grew. Others came to help with the work. An influential film was made by National Geographic, bringing the inventive and sophisticated emotional lives of the chimp

Jane with Flossi, granddaughter of one of the original visitors to the Gombe project.

family alive for viewers all around the world. They were shown playing, planning, holding hands, embracing, kissing, patting one another on the back, caring for their young, being gentle with their brothers and sisters. Above all, it established the vastly differing individual characters of each animal — then a revolutionary breakthrough.

Until 1986, Gombe remained Jane's principal home, punctuated by periods of absence for a variety of reasons — studying for a PhD, researching the behaviour of hyenas in Ngorongoro Crater, fund raising, writing and lecturing. In 1967, she gave the chimpanzee study greater long-term stability by establishing the Gombe Wildlife Research Centre, which persists with its pioneering work to this day. The important discoveries have also continued, establishing ever more dramatically the parallels between chimpanzee and human life. In 1970, animals were observed performing a 'spontaneous dance-like display' in awe of the sight of a waterfall; in 1974 they conducted a vicious war between groups of rival males; twenty years later they were shown to have the ability to transfer the use of tools (twigs to catch carpenter ants) from one community to another; and in 1995, it was found that chimps probably use medicinal plants to relieve stomach pains or reduce internal parasites.[3] Like us, they have been shown to possess qualities ranging from gentleness and compassion to brutal cruelty.

Life changed dramatically for Jane Goodall in 1986. A scientific conference entitled Understanding Chimpanzees was organised at Chicago Academy of Science to mark the publication of her award-winning scientific study, *The Chimpanzees of Gombe: Patterns of Behaviour*. Sessions were held on issues ranging from conservation to laboratory welfare. Both the threat to animals in the wild and the 'horrible conditions' endured by captive chimpanzees became abundantly clear. Buoyed by a 'new self-confidence' inspired by the completion of her book, Jane vowed to campaign forcefully on issues which had always concerned her. 'The time had come when I had to speak out,' she says. She describes it as her 'paying-back time' for all the wonderful years spent with the animals.

The Jane Goodall Institute had been set up almost a decade earlier, principally to raise funds for the Gombe project. Now its agenda became much wider. Jane protested about the use of chimpanzees in research and, in particular, the barren conditions in which they were housed; she became involved in campaigns to conserve the rainforests of Africa; she protested against the hunting of chimps for the pet trade, circuses and zoos; she helped to set up sanctuaries for orphan animals in the Congo, Uganda, Tanzania, Kenya and Burundi (once again involving the local population); and she initiated an innovative education programme for young people called Roots and Shoots, with the aim 'to integrate educational goals, environmental awareness and community involvement.'

In support of these campaigns Jane follows a punishing schedule. Now well into her sixties, she travels the world constantly — lecturing, overseeing projects and attracting funds. She still visits the Gombe Research Centre whenever she can, though less often than she would like. Once there, she not only oversees the research, but also observes the fourth generation of the chimp family she first brought to the attention of the world in the early 1960s. The wildness itself still possesses a strengthening quality for her. 'Out in the forest there is a timeless quality,' she says. 'It enables me to shut away all the horror and be connected to a great spiritual power. I try to keep a piece of the forest with me wherever I go.'

There is no apparent impulse to relax her campaigning. The urgency drives her on. 'It is the look I have seen in the eyes of so many suffering animals, and in the eyes of the little children whose parents were killed in Burundi, and in the eyes of inner-city kids, terrified by gang violence, not knowing how to escape. I see the look, I hear the message, I *have* to try to help.'[4]

The need to preserve land for wild creatures also remains a priority. 'In 1960 chimpanzee habitat stretched as far as I could see at Gombe,' she says. 'Today the chimpanzees are imprisoned as if they were on an island.'[5]

In the face of so much horror Jane remains optimistic. 'I hope that we are slowly moving towards a time where we shall extend certain basic rights to chimpanzees — life, liberty within reason and freedom from torture. There is a new surge of interest, but we still need to move people away from apathy. We have to stop thinking that there is nothing we can do.'

She is also heartened by what she describes as a 'softening of science… When I started my work ethology tried to be hard-edged. Statistics were considered more important than feelings. Now scientists are far more willing to accept complexities. Studying the minds of animals has become popular: when I began they argued that animals didn't even have minds!'

## 6  Life on earth

Jane Goodall can provide no conclusive reason why the late 1950s and early 1960s should have witnessed a sudden upsurge of interest in studying the behaviour of animals in their natural habitat. 'I've often wondered why,' she says. 'I think that one reason is that in Europe we were struggling to pick ourselves up after the war. It took a long time, but at the end of the 1950s there was a general expanding of horizons. Also, people like Louis (Leakey) were an influence. He inspired many people.'[1]

Further evidence of this growing interest in wild animals was provided by the dramatic increase in the exodus of film crews to remote and exotic parts. Wildlife documentaries were soon established as a regular and much-loved feature of television schedules. Film technology became ever more sophisticated, able to reveal much more of the secret world of animal behaviour than could previously have been imagined. In the 1960s the big breakthrough was colour television; by the 1990s this had progressed to the electronic wizardry of remote-controlled cameras, time-lapse photography, live satellite animal watches and cameras with the capacity to see in the dark without artificial light. A new sense of respect and wonder was awakened. The ability of film makers to capture for television audiences the knowledge obtained from pioneering field studies became irresistible. Proof that chimpanzees could make tools, that whales were able to communicate over long distances and that elephants perform something akin to grieving rituals for their dead were only three of numerous thought-provoking discoveries which forced a re-evaluation of long-held scientific misconceptions about a lack of complex thought and emotion in non-humans. Perhaps even more dramatic was the moment when Dian Fossey — another protégée of Louis Leakey — became the first person to demonstrate the potential kinship between people and wild gorillas:

> *Digit (as the gorilla was later named) became involved with Fossey. He didn't just touch her and then run away. First he took her glove in his hand and sniffed it, and then her pencil, and then he put that down and picked up her notebook and put it back down. Then, nestling in beside her, he rolled over and went to sleep.*
>
> *Both Fossey and Campbell (the cameraman) instantly realised what they had captured. Without prompting, without encouragement, a wild mountain gorilla had proved what Fossey had been trying to show the rest of the world. He had demonstrated the gentleness and empathy of the species. He had shown his kinship to human beings. In 1973, this strip of film would be the centrepiece of a National Geographic television special. The special,* The Search for the Great Apes, *would ultimately be shown on television screens around the world, seen by tens of millions of people who were startled and beguiled as for the first time they saw what they had never imagined possible.* [2]

Fossey, whose work (and violent death) was later to become the subject of the successful feature film, *Gorillas In The Mist*, also played a less recognised part in what has so far probably been the most remarkable and influential incident of all in the history of wildlife films. In the late 1970s, a curious but gentle silverback gorilla explored and slumped down upon the reclining body of Sir David Attenborough during a BBC documentary made in Uganda. 'The encounter was only possible,' explains Sir David, 'because Dian Fossey had accustomed that particular group to the presence of human beings.'[3] The impact of the meeting was enormous. For Sir David the principal response was one of 'great privilege that such intelligent animals should accept a human being in that way':[4] for the estimated 500 million or more viewers world-wide it not only further destroyed time-honoured myths about the uncouth and savage nature of gorillas, but also helped to create a thriving tourist industry. Organised trips to view them at close quarters provide much-needed funding for protection and conservation.

Attenborough was also responsible for the most ambitious natural history series of the century. His 'huge trawl through the vast diversity of animal life' in *Life On Earth* (1979) achieved for his subject the kind of in-depth treatment previously reserved only for long-established academic disciplines such as art and science. Yet in spite of his evident respect for passionate conservationists such as Fossey and Goodall and the unrivalled contribution of his own work in demonstrating the subtle complexities of animal life, Attenborough himself has largely avoided the role of campaigner. 'I'm in natural history film-making because it is so deeply enjoyable,' he maintains. 'I don't send messages. I don't recognise the distinction between entertainment and education.'[5]

Nothing illustrates this apparent detachment more significantly than his insistence that 'on my part there is no difference in attitude to animals between *Zooquest* and *Life On Earth*. They were two very different series with very different objectives.' He adds further that 'it would not have been possible to have made *Life On Earth* in the 1950s — neither the technology nor the budgets were there at that time.'[6] This may well be so, but to many observers — the present writer included — there is a difference in concept and underlying message which appears far greater than can be explained simply by the availability of greater resources or technological progress. Notwithstanding Sir David's obvious personal appreciation of 'the splendour and fecundity of the natural world'[7] in both series, to watch *Life On Earth* after viewing *Zooquest* is to witness an extraordinary leap forward in our understanding and sympathy.

It was not only conservationists who grasped the potential power of film to disseminate their message. Campaigners against specific cruelties were also keen to use the abilities of cameramen and women, often finding it easier to gain public and media

interest in the problems faced by exotic wildlife overseas than for more common species nearer to home. Whales and seals became a particular focus.

The fate of the latter was brought to global attention initially by the innovative efforts of a Canadian, Brian Davies, who eventually founded the International Fund for Animal Welfare (IFAW) in 1969. With a genius both for fund-raising and for obtaining publicity, Davies ensured that the barbaric Canadian seal cull reached massive television and newspaper audiences. Graphic photographs and films of the slaughter of baby seals for the fur trade stimulated a ground swell of disgust, culminating in a European ban on the import of seal skins in 1983.

Regrettably, however, Europe's stance failed to prevent the killing permanently since new markets opened up for the sealers. In 1996 the Canadian government sanctioned the largest seal hunt for over a quarter of a century.

As for whales, their rise in status from the ranks of the most brutally exploited species to the most revered and respected offers one the most heartening developments so far for those who yearn for a less abusive relationship between people and animals.

## 7  Beyond conservation: saving the whales

Humans have hunted whales for centuries. In the middle ages they were a source of food: between the seventeenth and nineteenth centuries they were killed mainly for oil. Indeed, by the early part of the nineteenth century, civilisation was almost totally dependent on the whale industry for soap, oil lamp lighting and fashion. Whalebone adorned the corsets of many 'fine ladies' and was commonly used in other products, too. As one recent commentator put it, it had become 'the plastic of the eighteenth and nineteenth century'.[1]

By the beginning of the twentieth century, whaling was in decline. The causes were twofold. Overfishing had greatly diminished the number of grey and right whales and the discovery of petroleum in 1859 had led to a gradual reduction in dependence on whale oil. Even though it was as late as 1860 when the Norwegian, Sverd Foyd, invented the cannon for firing grenades which was to become the key to the development of the modern whaling industry, many of the traditional fleets were disappearing. The Americans, who had dominated, were worst hit, but the demise was general and affected British ports such as Hull and Dundee.

Decline was reversed by a series of events in the early part of the century. In 1903

Opposite: Newspapers began to pay more attention to animal issues in the 1960s. In 1968, the *Daily Mirror* played a big part in awakening public revulsion against the seal cull. Kent Gavin was the photographer whose image shocked the world.

the first 'floating factories' appeared; ships able to haul whales on board and to begin processing instantly. This was followed in 1908 by the key commercial breakthrough; the discovery of the process by which oil can be hydrogenated. This enabled fishy-tasting liquid whale oil to be processed into an odourless solid suitable for margarine production. These innovations led to a massive escalation of whaling in Antarctica and the killing of a staggering two million animals between 1924 and 1974.[2]

One of the many who spotted the commercial potential of hydrogenisation was Lord Leverhulme. In 1919 he purchased the South African Southern Whaling and Sealing Company, laying the foundations for the amalgamation ten years later with Margarine Unie and the creation of the Unilever multinational company. Enjoying a virtual monopoly over the margarine trade, Unilever set about hunting whales from its station in the Hebrides with renewed vigour. Overfishing soon became an even greater problem than it had been in the previous century.

War brought fresh demand for killing. Glycerine in whale oil was a vital ingredient in the manufacture of explosive nitro-glycerine for the arms industry in both world wars. Soon after coming to power in 1933, one of the first steps taken by Hitler in building up his military capability was to create a powerful German whaling fleet, both for armaments and to ensure adequate supplies of fat for food supplies. (Interestingly, much of the new German fleet was built with capital provided by Unilever, an Anglo-Dutch company.) These factors contributed to whale production reaching a peak at 3 million tonnes in 1938.[3]

Although the war itself decimated the industry again, it recovered successfully for a second time. Production remained constant at the extremely high level of around 2.3 million tonnes well into the 1960s.[4] New uses were found. When food was scarce in the late 1940s, whalesteaks were introduced by the UK government (they never really caught on); sperm oil became invaluable to manufacturing industry; bonemeal went into fertiliser and meat meal into animal feed. In the 1960s whalemeat was tried in petfood and was commonly used as an industrial oil in products such as antifreeze. Even the space race brought fresh demands with whale oil used as a lubricant in the production of rocket engines.

Whereas the whole fabric of the nineteenth century depended upon the hunting of whales, as the twentieth wore on it became simply a case of advances in technology enabling merciless commercial exploitation. Numbers dwindled. As early as 1910, the Zoological Congress was expressing concern about levels of 'stocks' and this was in some ways a prelude to the eventual formation of the International Whaling Commission (IWC) in 1948 to control the number of animals who could be slaughtered.

Orca pod.

Although the IWC was ostensibly set up as a conservation organisation, it was motivated solely by self-interest. It represented the whaling nations and existed to promote and to safeguard the future of their industry by ensuring that there remained enough whales to hunt. In this it was not altogether successful. Despite the stream of controls it introduced, whales continued to be slaughtered at a rate of one every twenty minutes during the first thirty years of its existence.

Outside the IWC, public attitudes were changing rapidly. For as long as humans had hunted whales, there had always existed a strange veneration of the magnificence of these creatures alongside the brutality and carnage — a recognition of powers incomprehensible to our own species. Hidden amongst written accounts of daring adventure and chilling slaughter, many whalers had themselves testified to moments in the presence of whales that can best be described as spiritually uplifting. For instance, in the most famous account of them all, *Moby Dick*, Herman Melville writes:

> *I once saw a large herd of whales in the east, all heading towards the sun, and for a moment vibrating in concert with peaked flukes. As it seemed to me then, such a great embodiment of adoration of the gods was never beheld.*[5]

Similar descriptions were augmented by a series of modern ecological studies which provided further evidence of both the dwindling numbers and the extraordinary behaviour of some species of whales: their complex and melodic songs; their ability to communicate over hundreds of miles; the awesome size of their bodies and brains; the apparently playful beauty of their lovemaking.

In the 1950s, the indefatigable Dr Harry Lillie ran a lone campaign, filming the horrors of whaling and showing the results to whoever would watch. Opposition increased. In 1972, the United Nations Conference on the Human Environment in Stockholm passed a resolution calling for a ten-year moratorium on conservation grounds. It was ignored by the IWC.

Then, in the mid-nineteen seventies, anti-whaling sentiments were given the focus that was soon to lift the slogan 'save the whales' to the centre of public consciousness in many areas of the world. The catalyst was the involvement of Greenpeace.

Greenpeace had been formed in 1970 as an anti-nuclear organisation. Daring protests against the French nuclear tests in the Pacific Ocean soon earned the organisation international recognition and admiration as members risked their lives by sailing directly into excluded areas where bombs were due to be exploded. Their boat was rammed and their crew beaten up by French forces. This served to increase public sympathy and to create unparalleled support for a ban on nuclear testing.

By 1973, some of its members had decided that they would diversify activities and launch a campaign against whaling. They began to plot 'Project Ahab' (Ahab the whaler was the principal character in Moby Dick) independently of Greenpeace, some of whose anti-nuclear members opposed the change of emphasis. By the time it was officially launched in 1975, however, an internal revolution ensured that the new campaign did take place under the Greenpeace banner. The two leading figures were Robert Hunter, a journalist and veteran of the first Greenpeace anti-nuclear voyage, and Paul Spong, a marine scientist who had spent a year studying the behaviour of a captive orca in Vancouver Aquarium. They were joined by what Hunter described as 'a fine, if unconventional, blend of human talents and skills… for every mystic there was at least one mechanic, and salty old West Coast experts on diesel engines and boat hulls showed up at the meetings to sit next to young vegetarian women. Hippies and psychologists mixed freely with animal lovers, poets, marine surveyors, housewives, dancers, computer programmers, and photographers'.[6]

The campaign was to be conducted on two fronts. Spong's stories of the wonderful communication skills of whales would be the basis of attempts to enhance public respect for the magnificence of the creatures and the barbaric nature of whaling would be exposed by direct action. Protesters in small inflatable boats (known as zodiacs) were to be positioned between the whaling ships and the whales and film would be taken and rushed back to the world's media. One of the methods used to locate whales would be to utilise their love of music by broadcasting sounds from underground speakers. Subsequently, it emerged that raucous rock music actually drove some whales to flee the area, whereas classical recordings evoked a more enthusiastic response!

The first confrontation between the crew of the Greenpeace boat, the *Phyllis Cormack*, and the whalers was to prove highly significant. Eighty kilometres west of the Californian coast, protesters encountered the Soviet whaling fleet and took to their small inflatable boats, placing themselves between the harpoon guns and the whales. Undeterred, the Soviets fired, narrowly missing the boat manned by Jim Hunter and his Czechoslovakian colleague, George Korotva, and exploding into the back of one of the whales. The incident was filmed from another of the zodiacs. Meanwhile, other members of the Greenpeace team pulled alongside the Soviet factory ship, the *Dalniy Vostock*, and sang anti-whaling songs while filming and photographing dead whales being loaded aboard and a waste outlet from which blood was gushing into the water.[7]

These images were broadcast on news bulletins and in newspapers across the world, making enormous impact. The appeal of a group of unarmed volunteers in tiny boats risking their lives to protect defenceless animals from the mighty weapons of huge whaling ships (Russian, too!) was irresistible. The Save the Whales campaign was alive and kicking with almost incontestable momentum.

In the following few years it seemed that the world was inundated with whale T-shirts, stickers, petitions, leaflets, posters, records, documentaries and poems; Greenpeace support groups were formed around the world; both animal protection and conservation organisations took up the cause of whales with renewed vigour; popular recordings of the plaintive songs of humpback whales became a potent symbol of growing human empathy for the rest of the natural world, particularly amongst young people; anti-whaling demonstrations were organised with increasing public support.

Other Greenpeace missions were equally successful in hardening public opposition. In 1976, its ship the *James Bay* spent ten days pursuing and confronting the Soviet fleet, saving — in the estimate of Paul Spong — 100 whales directly and 1300 others by keeping the whalers from their traditional hunting grounds; a year later the now famous *Rainbow Warrior* was launched on its first ever journey from London to

Images like this became familiar as Greenpeace won international support for its Save the Whales campaign.

challenge the Icelandic fleet. On this mission, Greenpeace not only saved more animals from slaughter, but also raised a serious public debate on whaling in Iceland for the first time. Film taken of eight sperm whales being killed by Russian harpoons during another mission created such an outcry in the USA that President Jimmy Carter personally requested a copy.[8]

Equally important was the initiative against the Cheyn Beech Whaling Company in Western Australia in August 1977. This was the last trader from an English speaking nation still engaged in whaling and was responsible for 600 deaths every year. The type of images obtained by Greenpeace were by now powerfully familiar: protesters in inflatable boats risking their lives as harpoons were fired over them and seas turned red with the blood of dying whales. Broadcast on Australian television, the film created an immediate national outcry. Opinion polls showed 70% of Australians were opposed to the trade, causing the Prime Minister to set up a Royal Commission to investigate.

When its report was finally published in 1979 it called unequivocally for a ban on all whaling within Australia's 200 mile fishing exclusion zone and the closing down of the last whaling station. The government not only accepted the recommendations in full, but also committed itself to campaigning for a world-wide ban on both scientific and ethical grounds. Thus, within a couple of years, Australia was transformed from the main villain of the English speaking nations to the first to state its opposition to whaling on *moral* grounds. For the first time the right of individual whales to be free from persecution by humans was recognised by the government of an influential state.[9]

By the beginning of the 1980s, a ban on whaling seemed inevitable. On the eve of the 1981 International Whaling Commission annual conference in Brighton, England, an estimated 15,000 attended a rally in London, followed by large scale demonstrations at the conference itself. The general feeling was that the campaign was already won with everybody other than the IWC. Campaigners could hardly believe that they could go resisting overwhelming public hostility.

Delaying the inevitable, however, was precisely what the International Whaling Commission attempted to do. It announced new smaller quotas and a ban only on the killing of sperm whales. It was to take another twelve months of equally emphatic protests to achieve the victory of a ten year moratorium on the killing of all whales and even then enforcement was to be delayed for a further three years. Four of the main whaling nations — Japan, USSR, Norway and Peru — lodged objections.

As momentous as this decision was, it was only a partial victory. The moratorium still allowed whalers to kill a limited number of animals for 'scientific purposes'. This measure was implemented partly under the specious argument that it was for the benefit of the whales themselves in that it would help conservationists to collate important information on diet, health and stock numbers. In practice, it was an excuse for some countries — notably Japan and Norway — to continue whaling activities legally, albeit on a smaller scale. Whalemeat continued to appear on the menus of Japanese restaurants, as it does to this day. According to official figures, 13,000 whales were slaughtered in the name of science in the period 1986-1991, though many environmentalists believe that this is a serious underestimate.

Pirate whaling crews (ships staffed by workers from non-whaling nations which make profits by supplying whale products, usually to those with an established industry) have also remained a problem, as have the traditional kills by native communities exempt from the IWC ban. Amongst these were the Faroe Isles, which prompted a world-wide boycott campaign on all their products after brutally killing 21,000 pilot whales during the 1980s — more than any other nation.

Nevertheless, any hopes the pro-whaling nations might have entertained that public interest would disappear over the ten years of the first moratorium proved ill-founded. On the contrary, hostility to whaling strengthened. One incident above all others exemplifies the remarkable revolution in attitudes which had taken place. In the severe winter of 1988, three Californian grey whales became trapped under ice in a bay near Barrow, an Eskimo town in Alaska. They became the subject of a rescue bid which gripped the world for almost three weeks. Initially, a local wildlife ranger persuaded the native population to keep the whales alive by cutting breathing holes in the ice with axes, ice poles and chainsaws. Film was distributed far and wide and voluntary help poured in from all across America. An enormous bulldozer was employed to try to break through the ice, as was a sky-crane helicopter. Both failed. One of the whales died.

Then the Russians also sent help. Their giant ice breaker, the *Admiral Makarov*, was despatched to Alaska. Twenty days after the whales had first become trapped, a wide channel was created for them to escape to the open waters. As they watched the whales swim to safety from the bay, the crew of the Russian ship, Eskimos and Americans all cheered and hugged each other. The world looked on, sharing their pleasure. Three individual whales — members of species which humans had decimated almost to extinction — had inspired an international rescue effort which symbolised both a crack in the cold war between Russia and the USA and some distant possibility of a world where humans might derive peace and joy from protecting rather than persecuting other animals.

With Greenpeace and other organisations continuing their newsworthy activities, most western governments by now felt confident in adopting a strong anti-whaling stance in the sure knowledge that public opinion was behind them and that conflicts of economic interest no longer existed. Led by lobbying from France, Australia, the UK, USA and New Zealand, the moratorium was renewed by the IWC at its 1993 annual conference; an event which also marked an agreement in principle to declare the whole of Antarctica a whale sanctuary.

The significance of the 1993 decision cannot be overestimated. As we have seen, the original intention of the IWC was to act as a self-interested conservation group, ensuring sufficient 'stocks' of whales for future hunters. On these grounds there was no longer any real justification for re-imposing a total ban: it was conceded by most conservationists that some species — minke whales, for example — were no longer under threat. By now, however, the criteria had moved beyond conservation to ethics. The vote against whaling was based largely on a recognition of the moral right of individual whales to be free from persecution by human beings. Implicitly, whales had become the first non-human animals to be granted rights by people.

The liberation of whales is far from complete. Iceland and Norway have both left the IWC in protest against the 1993 decision and continue to hunt them, as does Japan, under the 'scientific purposes' banner. Russia is also threatening a return. Native customs which involve slaughter and pirates there will probably always be. Captive orcas are still to be found performing for zoo audiences. Nonetheless, there now exists a general consensus of world opinion that there is no human justification for exploitation. The reduction in the numbers slaughtered from 50,00 per year in the 1970s to 1200 in 1997 is remarkable. To kill whales is considered morally wrong by many nations.

What does the success of the whale campaign tell us about our relationship to animals? On the positive side, it clearly demonstrates that on some deep-seated level we recognise that we do not have a right to destroy for our own benefit. In denouncing the suffering we have inflicted, we also affirm that non-humans are fellow-feeling creatures, sometimes possessing powers beyond our own understanding. Rather than kill, nowadays we seek the company of whales on tourist packages, hoping to lift our spirits or even to cure our diseases by absorbing healing gifts which some attribute to their presence. They encourage our humility.

Less optimistically, opposition to whaling could never have been motivated so successfully had it not been that the perceived economic dependence upon slaughter had already waned. Aside from the wonderful qualities which whales possess, perhaps the main lesson to be learnt is that even when we know in our hearts that killing other animals for our own benefit is unworthy of our highest aspirations, acting upon that instinct often appears too difficult and too frightening.

## 7 Conservation, cruelty and contradiction

In wildlife protection — as in all our relationships with animals — there are often sharply contrasting interests at work. Contradictions are legion. In the early days these tended to be particularly blatant, as when Joy Adamson appeared wearing a leopard-skin coat during a world tour to promote conservation. The Duke of Edinburgh offered another classic example, when in 1961 — soon after he had been photographed alongside the Queen proudly displaying the tiger he had shot in India for processing into a rug for Buckingham Palace — he accepted an invitation to become British President of the World Wildlife Fund. On an earlier visit to Australia, he had killed a crocodile and ordered it to be skinned for handbags.

Nowadays, concern for wild animals tends to have become more sophisticated and inconsistencies are normally at least a little less obvious. In part this is due to the constant new discoveries which have ensured that the study of animal behaviour and intelligence has steadily gained impetus and respectability. The words that Michael Bright chose in the foreword to a book which accompanied the 1984 BBC television documentary, *Animal Language*, summarise succinctly the speed of change. 'Almost every week', he wrote, 'scientific journals report new and ever more astonishing abilities of animals, abilities which we never suspected'.[1]

For all the emerging knowledge, however, there remains little consensus either on the methods by which we should study animals or on how we should respond to growing awareness of their sophistication. Those concerned primarily with the conservation of species are sometimes less than sympathetic to the argument that the emotions of individual animals are of overriding importance. For the former, captive breeding in well-managed zoos is likely to be acceptable; to those believing in the sanctity of every life, invariably it is not. Once again one of the key questions is whether those species threatened with extinction should always be given priority. Or should opposition to abuse be the main motivation for reform, regardless of rarity or aesthetic attractiveness?

Even in the relatively small academic world of animal behaviour there are enormously contrasting approaches. Some believe strongly that only non-intrusive studies of animals in their natural habitat should be sanctioned. Others advocate laboratory research. Whilst it is easy to condemn the more extreme examples of the latter method — such as the deafening of hand-reared birds to examine whether song is affected[2] — it has also undeniably produced some exciting discoveries. Without it we would have been unlikely to find out how (say) primates are capable of learning and communicating through human sign language. Some laboratory investigations have added considerably to an appreciation of our kinship to non-humans: but at what cost to the individual? Great apes such as Washoe the chimpanzee or Koko the gorilla have endured an unnatural existence on an American university campus in order to prove the hidden potential of their species to communicate and to express a wide range of emotions. Can such conditions ever provide a suitable home, even when their human captors are as benign and sympathetic as many of those who work on animal language projects clearly are? Or should the legitimacy of such projects be accepted, given that there are numerous captive primates for whom a caring and stimulating environment is probably the best alternative available? Jane Goodall is one expert who feels that 'provided it is done right with choice and no punishment', language research may be the best choice for chimpanzees who are 'out of the wild and can't be put back… Captive chimps need to be intellectually challenged,' she believes.[3]

While it is easy to find conflict and contradiction between different interests, all of those working for the animal kingdom can at least lay claim to have had some positive impact. Even at its least radical, conservation has helped to gain support for the now widely accepted belief that survival of a wide variety of species is vital to the long-term future of both humans and the planet. Muddled messages there may have been, but the insistent call for action did relatively quickly achieve the desired effect of stimulating international governmental action to protect species threatened with extinction. In Washington DC in 1973, twenty-one states signed the historic agreement at the Convention on International Trade in Endangered Species of Wild Flora and Fauna (CITES) to control the trade in animals and plants. CITES laid down lists of species threatened with extinction and a further list of those whose decline is causing concern, even though short-term safety is assured. Any traffic in listed species requires a special permit from the permanent offices of the organisation in Switzerland. It is an imperfect agreement and one that has been too easily flouted; nonetheless, wildlife in many areas of the world would clearly be in a more desperate state had CITES never existed. Moreover — even leaving aside its practical impact — the organisation is important in the principle it has established. The Washington agreement marked not only the beginning of global recognition of the enormous threat faced by wild creatures, but also the first time that nations had cooperated in any meaningful way in their protection. By 1997, 138 states had become members of CITES.

Further evidence of the growing influence of conservationists has been the establishment of 'biodiversity' as a popular concept for the 1990s. True, this has been motivated by the threat posed to the human population by unsustainable growth rather than by disinterested concern for the wild, but the overall effect has been to push ecological issues swiftly up the political ladder. This culminated in the 1992 Earth Summit in Rio attended by leaders from all over the world. In some ways it was more show than substance, but the conference did achieve an international agreement that nations should implement 'a comprehensive programme of action needed throughout the world to achieve a sustainable pattern of development for the next century' — an obligation which by implication includes a pledge to conserve endangered species.

As in the UK, the conservation ethic now enjoys far greater influence world-wide than the anti-cruelty campaigns which preceded it — a matter of obvious frustration and regret for those who believe in the sanctity of every individual animal life. Yet despite the ultimate philosophical differences, the interests of the two movements do often go hand in hand. At its best, conservation does enhance respect for individual animal lives, as exemplified by the work of such people as Jane Goodall or

Claudio Sillero-Zubiri — the latter a specialist who has worked in recent years to protect the dwindling Ethiopian wolf population:

> *Ecosystems, communities, populations, individuals, they are just different lenses we may use to watch and understand nature. We will fail in our quest to conserve Nature if we do not protect the ecosystems as whole, or preserve the critical processes that bind different species together, but we would be poorer in spirit without the ability to mourn the death of an old wolf friend or laugh with joy when a new pup emerges from the den.*[4]

Is not this the kind of outlook — combining acknowledgement of the urgency of conservation measures with a warm sympathy and respect for individual life — which can best carry the cause of wildlife protection forward into the next century?

As communication technology continues to make the world seem a smaller place, concern both for the animals of distant regions and those closer to home has been largely united under the influence of the 'green' maxim, 'think globally, act locally'. These sentiments are now being supported on an unprecedented scale as millions demonstrate their desire to encourage wild creatures. On a local level, nest boxes are built, hungry birds and hedgehogs fed, ponds for toads and frogs dug out, flowers sown to attract butterflies and trees planted. Globally, thousands give their financial support to organisations dedicated to defend threatened or abused animals. Even in areas of the world where wildlife protection is a relatively new concept, there is greater recognition than ever before of the need to preserve natural habitat, often through the establishment of guarded and fenced sanctuaries.

Yet sadly, even though wild animals enjoy the goodwill of so many people ready to campaign on their behalf, never before have they been confronted by such powerful or dangerous foes. The white trophy hunters may have mostly disappeared, but the modern twin destroyers — heartless poachers and developers — have proved far more ruthless. A quarter of the world's mammals — approximately 6000 species in all — are threatened with extinction according to the International Union for the Conservation of Nature.[5] In addition, the rising human population creates ever increasing demands upon space and resources.

Nothing highlights the scale of the threat more than the dwindling world tiger population. At the beginning of the twentieth century there were an estimated 100,000 animals. Hunting was so careless that George V personally killed twenty-one during a two week visit to India in 1911 (see photograph on page 43). By 1997, the total number of tigers in the world had been reduced to an estimated 5000. Despite the creation of sanctuaries and patrols to protect shrinking habitat, ruthless poaching — inspired by the high prices paid for skin, meat and body parts for oriental medicine — is rampant. Whether or not tigers will survive far into the next millennium remains far from certain.

# 4 / The hunt is up?

## 1   A changing country

Even allowing for the achievement of Henry Salt and his fellow humanitarians in raising limited anti-hunt sentiments, hunting with hounds remained an established and largely accepted part of British life in the early years of the century. It was one thing to have banned working-class bloodsports such as cock fighting and bear baiting, but 'country sports' enjoyed by the privileged and the less affluent alike were another matter.

The first world war did put a temporary end to hunting when all fit horses were conscripted to experience the horrors of the front line, but it was revived with renewed vigour when peace returned. There was a prevailing national desire to regain the perceived order and stability of pre-war rural Britain and hunting activities were central to the vision. All country sports enjoyed enormous support. In the 1920s, the Waterloo Cup — highlight of the hare coursing calendar — reputedly attracted amongst the highest crowds of any sporting event world-wide and in 1927 more than 8000 people were reported to have attended the opening meet of the Quorn Hunt in Leicestershire, at which the Prince of Wales himself rode to hounds.[1]

The enormous popularity of hunting in rural circles failed to deter opponents. In 1924, the League for the Prohibition of Cruel Sports (later to become the League Against Cruel Sports) was formed out of the ashes of the Humanitarian League, causing outrage amongst hunt supporters. Its inaugural meeting was invaded by hecklers and similar treatment was afforded to speakers at a series of meetings against stag hunting organised in the west country in 1928.[2] Nonetheless, by 1930 the hunting community was sufficiently concerned about the growing strength of opposition to create its own official lobby group, the British Field Sports Society (BFSS). The two organisations have been at the core of uncompromising dispute ever since.

By the mid-1930s, anti-hunting sentiments had developed steadily, as indicated by a 1936 public opinion poll conducted in the *Daily Express*. Of 5000 people asked the question, 'Are you in favour of bloodsports like hunting?' 55% answered 'No'.[3] In part the change in attitude was probably due to the immense shift towards urban living that had taken place since 1918, though it was also encouraged significantly by powerful crusades in popular newspapers. Then — as now — the *Daily Mirror* led the way in indicting the hunting community.

Yet there was still little prospect of successful legislation. A 1938 Bill to ban carted deer hunting and rabbit coursing met the same fate as earlier twentieth-century attempts to change the law, failing dismally. Parliament — representing mostly the ruling elite — remained resolute in its support for hunting.

With the outbreak of the second world war all campaigning came to a halt once again. The League Against Cruel Sports closed its offices and very few hunts continued to operate.

When hostilities ceased in 1945, the atmosphere in the country was very different from that which prevailed at the end of the first world war. Rather than looking back sentimentally to an idealised past, the principal sentiment was a desire to move forward to create a fairer and more egalitarian society. All traditions based on privilege and class were open to challenge. Supporters of hunting found themselves under increasing pressure. The newly elected Labour government contained many who were passionately opposed and who sought a ban through legislation as part of their sweeping plans for the reform of Britain. In 1948, two MPs launched Private Member's Bills — one to prevent the hunting of deer, badgers and otters and the coursing of hares and rabbits; the other to abolish fox hunting. The former was introduced into the House of Commons by Mr F. Seymour Cocks, MP for Broxtowe.

The proposals drew a swift and effective response from pro-hunt interests. The British Field Sports Society (BFSS) organised demonstrations in which mounted huntsman blew their horns in Piccadilly, Regent Street and Soho. Larger scale protests were held in Kent. Miners (many of whom enjoyed coursing) and farmers lobbied parliament, obtaining more than a million signatures for a BFSS petition. 'Freedom of choice for the individual' was the main sentiment on which the campaign was conducted — a principle particularly powerful in a nation which had sacrificed so much in a war fought in the name of liberty and democracy. It won the backing of the influential *Times* newspaper: 'to maintain that hunting should be stopped because it is bad for man to kill for sport is to invade the sphere of individual conscience', the paper argued.[4]

Concern over the potential loss of rural support led the government to choose political expediency as its best policy. It was particularly worried by the threat of farmers to withdraw their commitment to the great post-war drive for self-sufficiency in food production if hunting were banned. Not only did it fail to support the Bill for abolition, its spokesmen actively opposed it in parliament. Tom Williams,

Minister of Agriculture, argued that 'we should risk the loss of willing co-operation in a great national effort'.

Although Seymour Cocks' anti-hunting Bill was defeated by 214 votes to 101, the Prime Minister, Clement Attlee, was still worried about the possibility of further attempts to legislate from the backbenches. Therefore, as a sop to the strong anti-hunting sentiments within the Labour Party, he set up a committee to investigate all cruelty to wild animals (the Committee of Enquiry on Cruelty to Wild Animals). The eight man committee was chaired by Mr John Scott Henderson K. C. and weighted significantly in favour of the hunting community. Its members included a master of foxhounds and a veterinary surgeon to two packs of hounds. There were no comparable animal welfare interests.

When its final report was published in 1951, the committee carried little comfort for those who opposed hunting. It did recommend that in future all wild mammals should be afforded the same protection by law as domestic and captive animals, but it also concluded that the hunting of deer, foxes, hares and otters should be exempt from legislative control, governed only by statutory rules laid down for each sport. Other proposals included the banning of certain practices which have remained common to this day, particularly 'bolting the fox and hunting it'. This was considered 'needlessly cruel'. Henderson also recommended that the brutal gin-trap should be prohibited (which it was in England and Wales in 1958 and in Scotland in 1972) and that snaring of deer should become illegal (eventually enshrined in legislation through the Deer Act of 1963).

As ineffectual as it now seems, the Scott Henderson Report remains a significant document. Forty-five years after its publication, the British Field Sports Society still claimed that it 'is as relevant today as when it was written' and 'should remain the policy of any future Government'.[5] In fact, current knowledge of wildlife and conservation make many of its conclusions seem hopelessly outdated. For example, on otter hunting, Scott Henderson did 'not think that the degree of suffering involved is sufficient for us to recommend that this sport, which does make a useful contribution to *the control of otters*, should be prohibited'; yet when otter hunting was abolished in 1978, it was actually *to protect otters from the threat of extinction*. On badger baiting, the committee optimistically concluded that 'very few people are willing to spend the time and energy involved' and that 'provided the badger is killed quickly and humanely when it is reached, badger-digging need not involve any excessive suffering'. Badger digging was eventually outlawed by a series of Badgers' Acts, the first in 1973.[6]

Elsewhere, Scott Henderson made 'no specific recommendations' about coursing

The well-known pacifist and preacher Lord (Donald) Soper addressing a League Against Cruel Sports rally in about 1960.

of hares, despite acknowledging that organised coursing events 'come within the definition of cruelty which we have adopted'; and asserted that the hunting of red deer to the point of exhaustion does not involve 'any additional suffering and should therefore be allowed to continue'. Other controversial practices were simply ignored, such as the digging out of foxes and the use of snares and caged traps.[7]

To be fair to the Henderson Committee, it is little wonder that some of its proposals now seem to have been based on ignorance. This is particularly true of fox hunting, for the perception of the fox as a vicious predator in need of ruthless control was still commonplace. Scientific studies of animals in their natural habitat were non-existent and the misapprehension that the only way to control fox populations was through unremitting human interference was an inevitable consequence. Scott Henderson could not have been expected to know that fox numbers are largely self-limiting, controlled predominantly by the availability of food and safe territory.[8]

One unexpected source of support for the Scott Henderson view of wildlife came from the RSPCA. Over the decades, many of the Society's influential supporters had combined their declared opposition to cruelty to animals with a love of chasing them in the field. It was not until 1957 that it came out with a statement of unequivocal opposition to coursing and the hunting of wild deer, otters and badgers. Foxes had to wait almost another twenty years before they were to enjoy similar support, the RSPCA finally declaring official opposition in February 1976.

Failure to achieve legislation in the years following the second world war was a blow from which the anti-hunting movement took many years to recover. Although political campaigning continued, understandably it lacked vigour. Passionate opposition to country sports remained, exemplified by the enduring commitment of respected figures such as the life-long pacifist and methodist preacher, Donald (later Lord) Soper, but new directions were needed. Foreshadowing the launch of the Hunt Saboteurs, the League Against Cruel Sports briefly tried direct action in 1958, spraying aniseed in an attempt to put hounds off the scent. The tactic was soon abandoned. In 1959, the Society bought its first piece of land in the middle of hunting territory on Exmoor; the birth of its successful policy of setting up sanctuaries in strategic areas in order to curtail hunt activities.

The fresh boost sought by the campaign came with the formation of the Hunt Saboteurs Association in 1963 by Devon journalist John Prestige. Assigned to cover a story in which the Devon and Somerset Staghounds had driven a pregnant deer into a village and killed it, Prestige was so disgusted that he decided to sabotage hunting activities. The initiative was launched on Boxing Day of 1963 when he and his colleagues fed meat to hounds belonging to the South Devon Foxhounds, effectively destroying their appetite for the day ahead.

For the next three years, Prestige and friends took regular action against hunts in the west country, undeterred by an often violent reaction which led — amongst other injuries — to one of his friends having his jaw broken with an otter hunting stave. Media reaction was generally supportive, enthusing the formation of a second Saboteur group in London to confront hunts in the south-east of England.

John Prestige eventually decided to quit the Saboteurs in 1967, 'disillusioned by the strength of the entrenched system'.[9] He was soon replaced as main spokesman by Dave Wetton from the London group, who was to guide the Society through the next decade.

## 2  Rebels with a cause: Dave Wetton and the Hunt Saboteurs

Dave Wetton had joined the Hunt Saboteurs in April 1964, only a few months after its formation. It seemed like a natural progression for a working class lad from a radical left-wing family in Tooting, who had already discovered vegetarianism in his teens through involvement in a school rock band.

He had been brought up by his mother and grandmother after his parents divorced when he was two years old. His mother was fiercely anti-monarchy; so much so that during the war she 'wore a hammer and sickle on her WRAF uniform'. Their family included a dog and cat, but there was no particular interest in animal causes until Dave was 'fourteen or fifteen' and was introduced to vegetarianism by grammar school friend and fellow guitarist, Tony McPhee. (McPhee went on to find

commercial and critical acclaim with his band, The Groundhogs.) 'My grandmother did most of the cooking in our house and she was horrified,' he recalls.

After he left school, Dave embarked on a career as a quantity surveyor. He joined the RSPCA and later the League Against Cruel Sports, taking part in Boxing Day demonstrations against hunting. 'We used to meet in South London, take a coach to Enfield Chase and get our banners out. There would be a bit of jostling by the hunt and then they would go on their way. Once they had left we would board the bus and go back home. It was satisfying to a point because you felt you had done your bit, but then in 1964 the news started breaking that there was a more radical group formed and that really appealed.'

He joined with a few others from Weybridge and they began to sabotage hunts with 'half a dozen people — ten maximum. We blew the hunting horn, sprayed aniseed concoctions and let off tame smoke bombs. We also used to drag rags doused in creosote to put the hounds off the scent, until we were taught the environmental damage it could cause.'

According to Dave Wetton, the Saboteurs were very much a product of their age. 'It was a very radical period to be in, that part of the sixties — anti-Vietnam war, The Beatles and so on. We were very much part of that questioning, anti-establishment spirit.'

In the mid-sixties the London group was officially formed. It raised money for a 'dormobile called Doris' and travelled 'all around' — including the Midlands, Dorset and East Anglia — to oppose the hunt.

In 1968, the administration of the national group switched from Devon to London and Dave became General Secretary. He recalls the period with affection: 'It was a good time when the hippy period came along. You could more or less set your own agenda. There was this feeling too that the young had much more of a say in things — a sense that if you feel it is the right thing to do you should go and do it.'

In those days the Hunt Saboteurs Association consisted of only a few small groups of half a dozen people who spurred each other on and met up occasionally for bigger demonstrations. They were astonishingly active, travelling the country to protest against hare coursing events and otter, fox and stag hunts. They also organised peaceful demonstrations in churches, interrupting the sermons of vicars who supported hunting.

The Saboteurs attracted widespread media coverage. As Dave Wetton explains, 'the press were interested in the novelty aspect. It was peaceful, "hey man, here we are looking after the animals" type stuff. The attitude of the hunters was basically one of tolerance, but of course each hunt had its nasty personality who used to threaten to do things like wrap us in barbed wire and put us in a tub of creosote! There were some attacks, but I was never involved in fighting. We just used to have to run. We kept our noses clean somehow.'

Even though by this time the Hunt Saboteurs were well known nationally, there were still very few groups and only about 200 members. A national committee was formed and regular adverts placed in *Private Eye* and university magazines in an attempt to expand interest. Slowly numbers increased.

In 1972 the first significant breakthrough came when the well-known journalist Jill Tweedie wrote an influential piece in *The Guardian* newspaper. She had accompanied saboteurs on an otter hunt in Dorset and contrasted them sympathetically with what Dave describes as 'the throwback to the eighteenth century — same old clothes out of the same old wardrobe' of the hunters.

Jill Tweedie's half-page article led to the formation of groups as far afield as Scotland and the arrival of a new breed of campaigner. 'Between 1972-75 more hard line radicals came in. We'd set the trend and got the ball rolling, but then you had this younger element. It was much more like the beginning of the animal rights movement as we know it.' Amongst the fresh intake were people such as Ronnie Lee, later to help in the formation of the Animal Liberation Front.

In 1975, the organisation enjoyed its most successful moment to date. It was offered a slot on the BBC2 television 'Open Door' series in which the chosen organisation was more or less invited to make its own thirty minute documentary. A week before transmission, 'as luck would have it', the London Saboteurs went to protest against the Tickham Fox Hunt in Kent. According to Dave, the hunt 'went bananas — it was bloody mayhem. They just decided to go berserk — there had never been violence to that extent before. We all ended up at Maidstone Hospital.'

The violence was covered extensively in the Sunday newspapers and film of the event was added to the television documentary. Two saboteurs who had been horse-whipped (in the ill-chosen words of one hunt master, 'horse whipping a hunt saboteur is rather like beating a wife — they're both private matters'[1]) made a huge impression when interviewed and the organisation received more than 3000 letters in response. Membership grew rapidly to 2000 and new groups were set up nation-wide.

Inevitably, the nature of the organisation changed. While most groups still consisted of only a few people who carried on in much the same old way, there were also larger scale demonstrations which tended to end in confrontation. 'Many of the new Sabs were prepared to stand their ground. Some members of the newly elected

Committee even called for self-defence training, whereas we always thought that the best means of defence was to run like hell!'

Despite his peaceful nature, Dave Wetton himself was involved in a violent fracas in 1979.

'There was a bit of a scuffle and as I was going across the field a horse barged into me. I didn't realise it at the time, but it was ridden by a woman — she just pushed me down. She ended up further down the field, hitting another group of Sabs with her horse whip. I picked myself up and had a go at her with a stave I had picked up. I genuinely thought she was a bloke — just her demeanour struck me that way. At the same time there was another member of the hunt who had left his horse and was whipping people from his side of a gate. He eventually found himself outnumbered and was attacked.

'When it was all over, the other Saboteurs went off and I found myself having a philosophical conversation on the morality of field sports with the hunter with the blooded nose! As I walked off, a policeman grabbed me and accused me of hitting him in the face with a stick, which I hadn't done.

'I was taken to Worcester Police Station and left to stew in a cell for a while. When they eventually questioned me and asked me if I had hit him, I came up with the honest but not very bright defence that I couldn't have done so because at the time I was hitting somebody else! I ended up facing two assault charges.

'When the case came to court there were six witnesses from the hunt lined up to say that I had hit the man and I had twenty-four to say that I hadn't. The case looked likely to last a week and the judge wasn't happy. He told my solicitor that if I was found guilty I would face one year in prison. I didn't fancy that, but at the same time I wasn't going to admit to hitting this bloke when I hadn't done so. In the end the judge offered a deal: if I pleaded guilty to assaulting the woman they would put the main charge on the shelf. So, I was fined £150 for hitting her and a further £150 for possessing the stick.'

Soon after the case Dave resigned as General Secretary, concluding 'that the Secretary of the Hunt Saboteurs — a non-violent organisation — could not have a conviction for aggravated assault against him.'

There were other reasons for his resignation. 'When I left in 1979/80 we had 7000 members and no office. It was all done from home in the evenings. My enthusiasm had begun to wane.' He accepted an invitation to sit on the council of the League Against Cruel Sports and continued to take part in 'sabs' at weekends.

Despite the controversial end to his time as General Secretary, it is for his prowess on the hunting horn that Dave is most often remembered by his contemporaries.

Dave was renowned for his skill on the hunting horn.

'I didn't know what I was blowing particularly,' he explains, 'but it was a lovely feeling if you were on one side of the wood blowing the horn effectively and you got the pack to go with you. We did it once on the South Downs. The hunt were on the other side of the hill and we started on the hunting horns and you could see all the hounds working their way down through the heather to the valley bottom and straight up towards and past us. It was wonderful.'

During the 1980s violence increased. Dave believes that the main reason was that 'the hunts realised we weren't going to go away and grew more desperate.' At the same time he accepts that on the Saboteurs' side there were also 'one or two groups you could point to and say they were ready for a punch up' — in addition to those who would always fight back when attacked. Nevertheless, he maintains that for the vast majority of the new generation of Saboteurs 'the commitment is just the same as ours was — the basic desire to stop the foxhunt killing the fox on that day'.

He realises, however, that many people find this hard to believe. 'The hunters used to claim that we were paid by the Kremlin, £1 a day plus all your sandwiches,' he adds jokingly. 'Then when the Berlin Wall came down it was supposed to be Linda

91

McCartney who bought the sandwiches! They definitely couldn't believe that anybody would go sabbing for free.'

Confrontations and violence have escalated further in the last decade. Split lips, bruises and broken bones turned to more serious injuries, such as a fractured skull. Eventually tragedy struck. In 1991, Mike Hill became the first saboteur to lose his life during a protest in Cheshire. Two years later, 15-year-old Thomas Worby was also killed, run over by a hunt vehicle during a 'sab' of the Cambridgeshire Hunt. Provocation increased on both sides, with the decision of some hunts to employ private security guards a particularly worrying and dangerous development.

Now in his fifties, Dave Wetton is still a quantity surveyor and though no longer involved regularly, he continues to take part in the occasional 'sab'. He remains admirably willing to assess the activities of the organisation he helped to develop without either glamorising its function or underestimating its impact on the lives of many ordinary country people. With typical humour he recalls a recent demonstration which exemplifies the changing world he has helped to create:

'I was in this ride in the wood and I saw a redcoat trot by, followed by a punk with a Red Indian haircut from the Saboteurs. Then came a policeman and finally, a hunt security guard wearing a brown suit with swastikas.

'I thought to myself — what has this got to do with hunting? The old boys who support the hunt know that, too. They just want to follow along on their bicycles as it was in the 1940s and 1950s, watching the hunt master take the hounds. On this particular day, I even felt a bit sorry for them because we'd ruined what they thought of as their idyllic lifestyle. All of a sudden you've got guys with orange haircuts, coppers and brown jacketed thugs wandering round the woods and none of them should really be there. But then I thought to myself, this is the way it has to be. Hunting has to stop.'

What can be said of the overall influence of the Hunt Saboteurs? Over the years they have succeeded in saving hundreds and probably thousands of animals from death at the hands of the hunt. Moreover — while their methods are not universally popular — they have helped considerably in raising media profile of the hunting issue.

Perhaps the greatest testament to their impact, however, is the draconian change in the law that they provoked from the last Conservative government. In 1995, the pro-hunting Home Secretary, Michael Howard, added an offence of 'aggravated trespass' to his Criminal Justice Bill, principally to deter what he referred to as the 'nonsense' of hunt protests. The new offence allows senior police officers to order individuals to leave an area if it is considered that they are 'seeking to deter by intimidation to disrupt persons engaged in lawful activity'. This provision effectively empowers police to disband any peaceful attempt by the Saboteurs to obstruct the hunt, though in practice many police forces are still ready to allow some level of demonstration.

According to Dave Wetton the new law is a measure both of how far government was prepared to go 'to protect its own kind' and of how difficult it is to achieve a total ban on hunting. Nonetheless, he remains cautiously optimistic. 'You soon realise that nothing gets changed overnight,' he says, 'but the Saboteurs have kept going for over thirty years and now there is real hope that hunting will be banned within the next few years. That is something I desperately want.'

If and when hunting is eventually abolished Dave predicts that the Saboteurs might continue in a new role as law enforcers! He envisages them working in a similar way to badger protection groups, carrying out a vigilante role to save animals from illegal hunting.

'What a great change that would be,' he concludes.

## 3  The hunt is up ?

The political campaign against hunting has also gathered pace in the last couple of decades, led by the League Against Cruel Sports (LACS) and strengthened by the eventual involvement of the RSPCA and the International Fund For Animal Welfare. It has also created a degree of controversy. In 1982, LACS was widely criticised when it gave a £75,000 donation to the Labour Party. By 1996, the stakes had been raised considerably and the Political Animal Lobby (an offshoot of the International Fund for Animal Welfare) donated £1 million towards Labour's election coffers — mostly, it seems, as a result of the party's commitment to allow a free vote on hunting in the House of Commons if elected. Some considered such inducements as a sign of political maturity, justified on the grounds that they encourage legislative progress: others argued that the task of pressure groups is to raise public support and that large-scale financial gifts to individual parties are inappropriate, amounting to little more than the type of glorified bribe associated with big business interests.

By the early part of the last decade of the twentieth century there were sure signs that legislative success for the anti-hunting lobby was becoming a distinct possibility. On St. Valentine's Day 1992, the Labour MP Kevin McNamara introduced a Private Member's Bill which included a special provision to end hunting. It was allowed a free vote by the Conservative government and failed its second reading in the House of Commons by only 12 votes.

The closeness inspired a second MP, John McFall, to introduce his own Private Member's Bill in 1995 to outlaw fox hunting, stag hunting and hare coursing. Once again the government allowed a free vote in the Commons and this time it became clear that the anti-hunt lobby would win. Significantly, the Bill enjoyed the backing of 30 Conservative Party MPs, traditionally staunch supporters of hunting. It was passed by 253 votes to nil, opponents deciding it was better not to take part at all rather than to reveal an accurate measure of their defeat.

Despite its success in the House of Commons, John McFall's Wild Mammals (Protection) Bill failed to reach the statute book because it did not enjoy government backing. It did achieve some legislative action, however, when — in the following year — provisions *other* than those relating to hunting were passed through parliament, making it an offence to 'mutilate, kick, beat, nail or otherwise impale, stab, burn, crush, drown, drag or asphyxiate any wild mammal'. As discussed in Chapter 2, this gave all wild mammals legal protection for the first time.

Political events at local level have also reflected the growth of anti-hunt sentiments. At some stage more than half the county councils in the UK have voted to ban hunting with hounds on land which they control. While these measures have had only limited practical effect, they have played a part in adding to the image of hunting as socially unacceptable.

Deer protected on a League Against Cruel Sports sanctuary.

A more telling blow was delivered by the National Trust in 1997. After several years of fierce internal conflict, it banned stag hunting from its land, effectively curtailing activity on Exmoor and the New Forest, the traditional homes of the 'sport'. The decision was reached after a scientific study commissioned by the Trust had confirmed that deer suffer excessive stress during the chase.

With the Labour Party returned to power in May 1997, the anti-hunt lobby looked towards the new century with unprecedented confidence that coursing and mink, stag and fox hunting might soon be abolished. When Michael Foster MP's Wild Mammals (Hunting With Dogs) Bill gained a large majority in the House of Commons at its second reading in November of the same year (411 MPs voted to abolish hunting against 151 in favour), it could point impressively to widespread parliamentary backing to add to overwhelming public opinion on its side.

Yet success was still far from assured. The hunting community remains a powerful and well-organised minority. In an event that echoed its effective response to the threat of a ban back in 1945, it staged an impressive rally supported by an estimated 80,000 people in Hyde Park in July 1997. Once again its defence on the grounds of freedom of the individual won considerable media support, as did its claim to be a 'countryside movement' defending a traditional way of life against an increasingly urbanised society (though, in fact, opinion polls show that even in rural areas there is now a majority opposed). In March 1998, it followed up with the highly effective Countryside March in London, attended by approximately 200,000.

Affected by the strength of pro-hunt protests, Tony Blair's government proved unwilling to support Michael Foster's anti-hunting proposals. Without it, the Bill was doomed to fail because of a lack of parliamentary time.

Torn between the massive majority in favour of a ban amongst both MPs and the larger population and the powerful and vociferous minority who demand the right to continue their 'sport', the government decided that the most politically expedient short-term policy was to do nothing. It remains to be seen whether it still entertains any long-term plan to put an end to the hunt.

History, however, warns that optimism would be premature. In 1975, the then Labour government gave its backing to a Bill to end hare coursing. It passed through all stages of the House of Commons, but in 1976 it was rejected by a House of Lords Select Committee. Rather than risk a full-scale conflict with the Lords, the government accepted the recommendation. Defending coursing in the Lords, Lord Denham stated that abolition would make the law 'a gibbering lunatic'.[1] There can be few more potent examples of the way in which the old English traditions of privilege and minority interest can still conspire to defeat the forces of democracy.

## 4  Hunting, shooting and the royal family

Public reaction to the love of the royal family for hunting and shooting summarises perfectly the way that anti-hunting sentiments have strengthened as the decades have passed.

Since the death of Queen Victoria many male (and some female) members of the royal family have been enthusiastic in their support of field sports.

In 1913, King George V was invited to what was billed as the biggest shoot in history. More than 10,000 birds were killed over four days at Sandringham, the King himself bagging more than 1000. Even the gun-happy George himself told the then Duke of Windsor, 'I think we overdid it a bit today'.[1] Yet there was comparatively little public condemnation.

Nor had his hunting expedition in India two years earlier provoked too much negative comment, though Lord Crewe — newly appointed Secretary of State for India — did remark that 'it is a misfortune for a public personage to have any taste so strongly developed as the craze for shooting is in our beloved Ruler'.[2] For the most part, however, the King's personal kill of twenty-one tigers, eight rhinoceros and one bear was praised lavishly for its skill. The *Sphere* described how 'his majesty on one occasion secured a tiger and a bear with his right and left barrel and shot splendidly throughout the whole tour'.[3] In this context, it is little wonder that his fox hunting activities raised few complaints.

George VI continued the family tradition. As a young man he also loved chasing

foxes and he referred to shooting as 'the great passion of his life'. He kept records of his scores assiduously, killing 1055 woodcock before his retirement in old age.[4]

When, at the age of thirteen, Prince Charles joined his father and shot his first stag at Balmoral in

Prince Charles out hunting in Cheshire.

1962, times had changed sufficiently for some concern to be voiced in the press. Not that the morality of killing itself attracted a great deal of condemnation: it was rather that doubts were expressed about whether Charles was old and experienced enough to be entrusted with carrying out the task 'humanely'.[5]

By the 1990s, the royal family's support for hunting and shooting had become a subject of mounting public disapproval. In an opinion poll conducted in 1992, 78% of those questioned voiced displeasure at royal participation in hunting. A further 69% were opposed to their shooting of game birds.[6] Newspapers even began to hint that the continuing participation of Prince Charles in hunting was a cause of dispute with Princess Diana. She was reported to be particularly upset when her husband insisted on introducing their sons to bloodsports.

This was followed in 1996 by the remarkable outburst of the Labour MP and then shadow Welsh Secretary, Ron Davies. He stated that Prince Charles was not fit to be king because of his involvement in hunting. 'We're told that he spends his time talking to trees, flowers and vegetables and so on and yet we know that he encourages his young sons to go out into the countryside to kill wild animals and birds just for fun, for sport,' Davies told a television audience in Wales. Even though pressure from Tony Blair led to an apology, the Welsh MP claimed to have been inundated with letters in support of his remarks.[7]

A year later that bastion of English respectability, *The Times*, irreverently named the Duke of Edinburgh 'the firm's most tireless killer', implying disapproval of a record that has seen him shoot 'one tiger, two crocodiles, sixty wild boar, innumerable stags, rabbits and ducks and 30,000 pheasants' over the years.[8]

Mounting public criticism is, of course, a measure of a general decline in deference to the royal family and not simply an expression of changing perceptions of bloodsports. Nonetheless, the readiness of all elements of society to declare their distaste so forcibly is further evidence of a prevailing impression that hunting and (to a lesser extent) shooting are no longer felt to be compatible with civilised behaviour.

# 5 / That's entertainment?

## 1   The circus comes to town

The introduction of performing wild animal acts into the circus arena began to gain popularity in Victorian times. During the 1850s, George Sanger became the first British impresario to build up a circus empire, with amphitheatres in ten major cities stretching from Plymouth to Aberdeen. It was a trend that had originated in the US earlier in the century and became such an accepted part of American life that by 1900 there were over one hundred established travelling menageries there.

The chief inspiration for the wild beast show on both sides of the Atlantic had been the New Yorker, Isaac Van Amburgh, who won international fame for his subjugation of wild beasts. As mentioned in Chapter 1, Queen Victoria was amongst many who were fascinated by Van Amburgh's ability to bully dangerous animals, attending six performances when his travelling show visited London in 1838. In his book *The Rose Tainted Menagerie*, William Johnson describes the performance as follows.

> *Dressed in jungle fatigues, wielding a whip and firing blanks from his pistol, he would stride into the cage, deliberately baiting and taunting the animals to bring out as much ferocity and jungle savagery as he could, whereupon he would proceed to bully them into submission. His pièce de résistance was forcing the lions to approach and lick his boots as the ultimate sign of his conquest.*[1]

Although the basis of Van Amburgh's act was to inspire many future animal tamers, in Europe there was soon to be a partial reaction against the severity of his methods. Carl Hagenbeck, also characterised as the 'father of the modern zoo' for his design of enclosures to replace cages, is credited with the establishment of deprivation and reward (usually food) as the principal training regime for circus animals. How far the new 'kind' methods were implemented, or indeed how benevolent they actually are, has remained a matter of contention throughout the twentieth century. There are those who continue to find it difficult to believe that fear and punishment do not play a significant part in the 'schooling' process.

By the turn of the century (in Britain at least) disquiet about the treatment of circus animals was sufficiently intense to create legislation to protect them. The Cruelty to Wild Animals in Captivity Act 1900 made it an offence to abuse, infuriate or tease any captive animal. This was followed in 1914 by the formation of the Performing Animals' Defence League, the first organisation with a specific mandate to oppose animal acts.

In 1919, consistent allegations of cruelties pressurised government into the establishment of a select committee to investigate. Several ex-circus employees offered damning evidence and — according to *The Times* — produced 'more than sufficient grounds for immediate legislation'. While conceding that 'the time has not yet come for total prohibition of this particular form of exploitation of animals for the pleasure of men', the newspaper did so only 'with reluctance'.[2]

Although the final report of the select committee maintained that some improvements in training methods had occurred, it did, nevertheless, make several recommendations for change. These included a ban on the use of chimpanzees. Unfortunately, however, by the time that the ensuing Performing Animals (Regulations) Act found its way on to the statute book in 1925, this and many other of its strongest proposals were omitted. Notably, the Act weakened the Committee's suggestion that access to the RSPCA should be granted 'without previous notice' to 'at reasonable times' (in other words by prior arrangement), though it did compel circus trainers to register and grant access to training areas for local authorities.

In spite of opposition, circuses with animal menageries continued to expand in both number and size. In the 1930s, Bertram Mills established the biggest circus dynasty, followed by John Sanger and Sons. The potential for wider audiences escalated with the increased possibility of relatively speedy long-distance travel. By the 1950s, Billy Smart, Chipperfields, Roberts Brothers and Fossetts were also thriving.

Throughout the 1950s, 1960s and into the 1970s, the circus was an integral part of British family life. In particular, in the austere decade following the second world war — before most people owned a television — the appearance of a circus in town was an event anticipated with great excitement. At Christmas, taking the children was as much a family tradition as a trip to the pantomime is today. Elephants begging or performing balancing tricks, tigers jumping through hoops of fire or chimpanzee tea parties were amongst the most common 'highlights' of such entertainment. On television, too, the Christmas circus established itself as an annual event in the schedules as certain as the Queen's speech. It was a tradition that survived until the mid 1980s.

Meanwhile, animal welfare campaigners ploughed on with their struggle. In 1954, they were given a boost by the publication of a book called *Wild Circus Animals* by Alfred Court, a well-known trainer. Without any apparent twinges of doubt or regret, he described in glorified tones how he had violently subjugated errant animals. 'The stick and the whip are as necessary as the reward of meat, the soft voice and the caresses', Court wrote.[3] A parliamentary debate ensued in 1956, but failed to produce any changes in legislation.

The Circus Animal Protection Society (CAPS) was formed in 1957 and in the early 1960s the RSPCA launched a fresh press campaign calling for a public boycott. While much of the criticism of animal acts continued to be based upon doubts about training methods, it was the conditions in which animals were kept *outside* the ring — together with the humiliating nature of the tricks they were forced to perform — on which anti-circus campaigns were increasingly centred. As a 1963 advertisement from the RSPCA put it: 'To be made to perform unnatural antics just to raise a laugh … to spend dreary days in captivity and to be jolted on dark journeys from town to town'.

Even amidst performers dedicated to the romantic circus life, there always seemed to be some unease about the suffering of animals. Over the decades a few individuals spoke out after their employment had come to an end, while others silently witnessed. Closet dissenters included the famous Coco the Clown, whose comic routines with Bertram Mills Circus made him a household name and earned him the honour of an O.B.E. Although Coco loved circus life, he was unhappy about the use of performing animals and for many years nurtured an ambition to establish a troupe based entirely upon human skills. It was a goal which remained unfulfilled during his own lifetime, though it did lead eventually to the creation of the first non-animal circus in Western Europe by his daughter Tamara and her husband Ali.

## 2   Circus Hassani and Coco the Clown

The background to the formation of Circus Hassani reads like a tale spawned in the far-fetched imagination of some fanciful storyteller. Its themes include child abduction and exploitation, teenage rebellion, romantic love causing and eventually conquering family divisions, religious conflict and resolution, attempted sabotage, and finally, the last gasp triumph of fortitude and perseverance over what seemed like overwhelming adversity. Its locations span from Russia, Spain and remote areas of Morocco to suburban England — all of this set against the exotic lives of circus acrobats, clowns and ballerinas at the peak of their popularity.

Ali Hassani was born in Marrakech in 1927, one of fourteen surviving children of a labouring father. His mother was a laundry woman. At an early age he took to missing school and making for the main market square, Jamaa Al Fna, where he became fascinated by the acrobat troupes who performed and begged for money.

The troupe leaders were always on the look out for potential young recruits and soon spotted young Ali. They asked if he would like to join. He agreed and at the age of 'seven or eight' found himself whisked away to Ousda on the Algerian border of Morocco, far from the reach of his parents. He has not seen any members of his family since.

Fortunately for Ali, he proved to be a naturally talented acrobat so the back-bending training was not too much of a problem. Nevertheless, the troupe regime was gruelling and the rewards very small.

'We would get up first thing in the morning and go and do our acrobatics outside shops and houses. By midday we would be performing in the market square. After a short rest it was out to the cafés and restaurants. It was the same routine day after day — we had no choice. It didn't matter how much money you made, it was the boss who put it all in his pocket and as long as they did not give you a good hiding you were happy. A cup of tea and a piece of bread was all the reward you got.'

Escape was practically impossible since all the children were taken long distances from their homes and any attempt at running away was punished by severe beating. 'It was rough, but it was even harder in Morocco for other children who had nowhere to go and nobody to look after them.'

Life as a travelling acrobat-cum-beggar lasted several years, until 'luckily' the boss decided to move the troupe to Europe and to join a circus. In 1941, Ali was taken to Spain. Although life was a bit easier than in Morocco, arrival coincided with the end of the Spanish Civil War and there was strict rationing and hardly any food. For the next seven years he was part of an enterprise which, interestingly, contained no animal acts.

In 1948, the Moroccan acrobat troupe moved on again, this time to England.

Once again it was the end of a war and the period of rationing and austerity, but to Ali it seemed like relative luxury. 'We could get bread and potatoes,' he remembers. 'It was quite something for us.'

His troupe became the acrobats in Billy Smart's Circus. He was introduced to Tamara, daughter of Coco the Clown, by her brother, Sasha. (Three of Coco's children were working at Billy Smart's.) They fell in love. Her family disapproved. Leaving aside his humble origins, Ali was a Muslim; Coco was Jewish. A feud ensued. Ali: 'The father disowned her and the brothers ran around the circus trying to bash me in. I had bodyguards whilst I did my show. Everybody said it wasn't going to work out and that I would disown her after a few weeks or months, but we stayed together for thirty-six years until she died.'

As a teenager, Tamara had already displayed the strong-willed determination which was to ensure that young love would persevere. At the age of thirteen or fourteen she had run away from her convent boarding school three or four times to join the circus life she had been accustomed to as a young child. On each occasion her father came and fetched her back. 'We fought a lot,' she told *The Guardian* in an interview published in 1980.[1]

The family crisis over her relationship with Ali slowly thawed. After about a year the eldest brother left for America and the younger called a truce. Tamara began to visit her parents again. Another year or so later, Ali, too, began to be accepted, firstly by Tamara's mother and latterly by Coco himself. Eventually father and son-in-law became close friends, so much so that when Coco died, Ali was left in charge of his estate. 'I treated him like a father, with great respect. He was a very good man.' In his later years the famous clown even lived with the couple at their home in Northamptonshire, though he could never adjust to staying in houses and had his own caravan parked in the garden.

Coco was born in Russia, real name Nikolai Polokov. An experience he shared with his son-in-law was that in his youth he, too, had been part of an enterprise which did not use animals. As a twenty-three-year-old he had even owned his own circus based upon clowns, acrobats, fire eaters and magicians. In his late thirties he moved on to England, joined Bertram Mills and began to establish himself as probably the most popular British circus act of all time. His fame was built partly upon his skills as a clown, but also on his genuine love for children. Wherever the circus was booked, he would visit schools and hospitals, taking sweets, teaching road safety and creating joyous laughter. He took no fee. According to Ali, he lived to entertain and without it 'he didn't feel he was a full person.'

With family harmony restored, the Hassanis' careers blossomed. They formed their

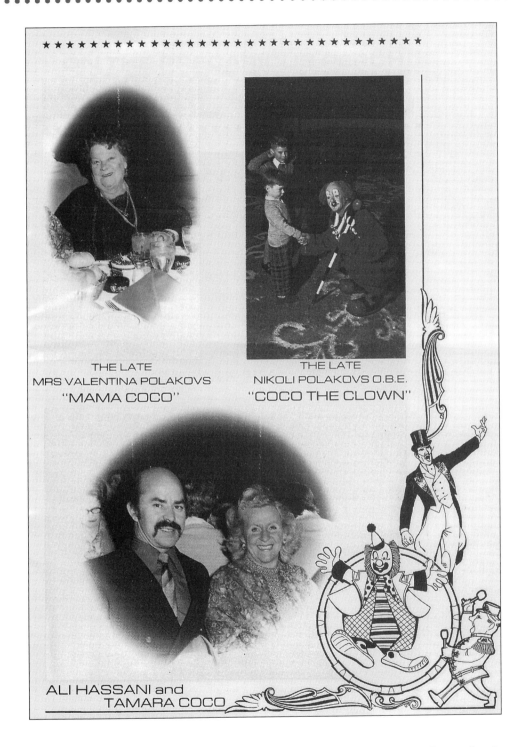

THE LATE
MRS VALENTINA POLAKOVS
"MAMA COCO"

THE LATE
NIKOLI POLAKOVS O.B.E.
"COCO THE CLOWN"

ALI HASSANI and
TAMARA COCO

Programme at Chessington Zoo in 1983, when Circus Hassani was known as Tamara Coco's.

own highly-rated acrobat troupe and enjoyed the circus heydays to their full. 'The circus was magic. The whole town used to shake when we would visit.'

In his forties, Ali returned to Morocco to try to trace his family and was told that they had all been killed for their part in trying to overthrow the Sultan. He is unsure to this day whether it is true. Nor does he know whether his parents tried to find him when he left as a young child, or whether instead his disappearance was viewed mainly with relief at having one less mouth to feed.

By the early 1970s, Ali and Tamara had built sufficient savings and reputation for them to consider that one day they might be able to launch their own circus. They discussed it with Coco, who had harboured similar ambitions. It was then that Coco first expressed his desire that they should try to establish a non-animal show. Although nothing was to materialise at the time, it was a wish that he repeated just before his death in 1975. According to Ali, there were three reasons for his request. Firstly, he sensed that public opinion was beginning to turn against performing animals; secondly, he came from a tradition where circus based solely upon human skills was 'no mystery'; and lastly and most importantly, 'he had seen some terrible cruelty — some very primitive ways of training animals — and he didn't like it.'

It took until December 1979 before the Hassanis were able to gather together sufficient funds to put their circus on the road. Its debut was set for Southend, one of forty towns where local councils had followed the example set by Bath earlier in the decade by banning circuses with animals from their land. Launch date was four days before Christmas. But it seems that the heavens were against them. A few days before opening night a force eleven gale smashed the king poles. Their expensive purpose-built Big Top had to be dismantled twice and a third time it was shored up by staff as it was in danger of being torn to ribbons. No sooner had they survived the gales than the heaviest snow that the area had encountered for many years hit them. The outcome was a near-empty arena on their opening nights.

Although the Coco legacy (as well as Tamara, the circus had Sasha as its chief clown) and the novel nature of the enterprise ensured widespread publicity in national and local newspapers, the audiences did not follow. The severe winter weather pursued Circus Hassani relentlessly around the south of England, as did the hostility of conventional circus interests, determined to see them fail. Press reports were issued insinuating that the absence of animals was a consequence of lack of funds rather than a principled decision; the diesel tanks of their lorries were filled with paraffin; cancelled signs were added to their advance notices and publicity was sabotaged. Ali: 'One of our staff was being paid by other circuses to take us the wrong way and to the wrong places. We would print 300 posters for each town and yet there would be only a few put up. When I eventually sacked him, I found them all stored under the bed in his caravan.'

Animal welfare organisations did their best to help. Both the Captive Animals Protection Society (CAPS) and the RSPCA rallied their members. Virginia McKenna sponsored an appeal for financial help in newspapers; CAPS opened up a rescue fund with an initial donation of £1500; the RSPCA gave £10,000 — a generous sum, but still only enough to pay wages for three or four weeks. Within a year, all of the £43,000 that the Hassanis had invested was gone and the bank was threatening to repossess their Northamptonshire home to cover further debts. 'It was distressing. We had lost all of our gold, all our money, all our savings. People in this country were simply not awake to a circus without animals and we needed more resources than we had available to prove to them how good it could be. Not only were our pockets empty, but our hearts were down.'

One of the big circuses stepped in with a take-over package. The offer was to buy the name Hassani on the condition that Ali and Tamara went to the press and stated that a circus without animals was not viable. Animal acts would then be added to performances. With characteristic determination, Ali and Tamara refused to comply. Instead, they planned to form a new acrobat troupe and to seek work abroad. 'We figured it was not the end of the world; just the end of our dream.'

Last ditch rescue came from an unexpected source. By a great irony, Western Europe's first non-animal circus was to be saved by an organisation which was itself condemned by some animal welfare supporters. Out of the blue, Chessington Zoo rang and offered a summer season residency for 1981. Ali believes that they did so partly because they had received complaints about animal acts in the small family enterprise which preceded them and also because it was seen as a way to allay some of the general criticism of zoos which was increasing at the time. It was the big break-through that Circus Hassani needed. It offered them security and the chance to prove that it was possible to produce an entertaining show with only human acts.

Eighteen summers on, the Hassani circus is still performing at Chessington. Since Tamara's death in November 1988, Ali runs the business alone from a caravan housed on site. Now into his seventies, he has no plans to retire from the life he loves. 'Thirty years ago I tried to go and do other things, but it didn't work out. I missed it too much.'

The intervening years have seen the path they opened up followed by many others. In particular, the French Canadian Cirque de Soleil and Australian Circus Oz have won international acclaim for their daring shows. Moscow State Circus also often tours without animals; the US has Circus Smirkus and others; Zippos became one of the first of several smaller British circuses to abandon performing animal acts (other than horses) as opposition to their use intensified.

While no modern circus enjoys the mass appeal of the 1950s and 1960s, Ali Hassani is convinced that there is still a popular role for those with sufficient innovation and funds. He believes that decline was mostly self-inflicted, caused by a lazy failure to move with the times. 'After the war you could put people in a cold and uncomfortable arena and they were glad to be entertained. Now you need good seating, comfortable conditions and a good atmosphere. You need an elaborate show with nice music, developed lighting, stage effects and dance — as well as the traditional human talents. And it definitely has to be a non-animal circus. People are waking up to that.'

For Ali though, the circus is much more than an entertainment. It is a way of life and at its best, a model of community living from which humanity has much to learn. 'We have no borders in circus life — that Big Top brings everybody together. We are all the same religion. I am Moroccan, Tamara was from Jewish parents, one of my daughters is married to a Hungarian, the other married a Romanian. My granddaughter is probably going to marry a Czechoslovakian. We do not stop and think about borders — the circus is our nationality. When performers stand in the wings waiting to enter the arena, we reach for something deep within ourselves. One may make the sign of the cross; another may pray to Allah. Nobody condemns; we all support each other.'

With the emergence of more enlightened attitudes to animals and the ready availability of natural history films showing complex and fascinating natural behaviour, silly tricks in the circus arena began to appear particularly seedy from the 1970s onwards. In 1981 the National Union of Head Teachers recommended that children should be discouraged from attending any exhibition which involved animals in undignified displays or where they were housed in unsatisfactory quarters.

The steadily strengthening rejection of animal circuses has continued in the UK (though they remain popular in the US). Many local councils have banned them from public land and several of the larger troupes have also abandoned animal acts. Perhaps most significant of all was the announcement in 1996 by Billy Smart's Circus that in celebration of its fiftieth year it was to become animal-free. According to Gary Smart, 'animals no longer have the attraction of bygone years. Today's audiences want entertainment from talented human performers'.[2] Only seventeen years previously, his father Ronnie had told *The Daily Mail* that 'a circus without animals doesn't stand a chance. I believe animals are absolutely essential'.[3]

## 3   Animals in film: from *King Kong* to *Babe*

Stories featuring animals have proved popular and profitable for the film industry since its early days. In particular, several generations of children had their sympathies awakened by Walt Disney characters or sentimental heroes such as Lassie, Fury, Rin Tin Tin or Flipper the dolphin. In the 1950s, Hollywood even recognised the part played by trained animals in promoting its industry by introducing the Patsy awards — a sort of animal equivalent to Oscars.

Even though Patsys have long gone, the latter part of the century witnessed an increase in the number of films with an animal theme. Especially popular in the last couple of decades have been comedy scripts based upon supposedly close and zany relationships between people and eccentric animals, usually demanding an ever more sophisticated degree of training for the non-human actors. Notable examples include the dogs used in movies such as *Beethoven* and *Turner and Hootch*, the cigar-smoking orang-utan in *Every Which Way But Loose*, or the chimpanzees in *Ace Ventura*.

The use of animals in cinema has always raised controversy. From the 1930s onwards, complaints of cruelty and deliberate killing to create authenticity were persistent. War films and westerns drew particular criticism for their alleged use of trip wires on horses to add realism to battle scenes. Protests soon led the UK parliament to pass the Cinematograph Films (Animals) Act, designed to protect against cruel treatment. This was augmented by imperfect voluntary welfare protection measures, introduced by the film industry on both sides of the Atlantic. In the USA, the American Humane Association (AHA) monitored events, offering a grading system ranging from 'acceptable' to 'unacceptable'. In the UK, the RSPCA did its best to perform a similar task, though on a less formal basis.

Notwithstanding these safeguards, there remained deep suspicion that obsession to create realistic art continued on occasions to prompt unacceptable exploitation. Even in *Born Free* — a film which essentially created new standards

Keiko, the star of *Free Willy*, suffered years of isolation and neglect.

for non-exploitative film making — Virginia McKenna recalls that there was one incident which appalled Bill Travers, George Adamson and herself. 'We protested,' she says, 'but what more could we do? We were only actors.'

From the mid-1960s conditions actually deteriorated for animal actors. Objecting to what they considered a form of censorship, Hollywood producers ended their voluntary agreement. By the late 1970s and early 1980s several high profile films faced severe condemnation for alleged ill-treatment. Amongst them were *Apocalypse Now* (1979), where a buffalo was alleged to have been hacked to death; the James Bond movie *Never Say Never Again* (1983), in which a horse was dropped into water from a high platform; and the notorious *Heaven's Gate* (1981), which included horses tripped, injured and killed and also the staging of an illegal cock fight.[1]

Since the 1980s, there have been vast improvements. The big breakthrough occurred when AHA approached the US Screen Actors Guild (the union for film actors) for support. Convinced of the legitimacy of the animal welfare case, the union insisted that all future contracts between actors and producers should include a provision to provide the AHA both with full details of the use of animals and unrestricted access to filming. As a result — in the US at least — cruelty during production is mostly a thing of the past, though there is nothing to stop unscrupulous directors travelling abroad to beat the system. Nor can there be great confidence in the treatment of animals in the film industries of some less developed nations.

It is not only the abuse of animal actors on the film set that has raised concern. Animals for the cinema industry are often obtained from the same specialist sources that supply circuses, raising the question of whether the training methods employed should ever be fully trusted? Species used in relatively recent film history include dogs, orang-utans, chimpanzees, gorillas, elephants and penguins. Clearly some are easier to train than others.

Fortunately, the use of wild animals in fictional feature films is a problem with a ready solution, for advances in technology should soon dispel any justification. The possibilities of animatronic models and computer techniques — first popularised in the late 1980s by Stephen Spielberg's *Jurassic Park* — have evolved rapidly and technologists now have the ability to create amazingly realistic animal images and action without any risk of exploitation.

The true story behind the popular *Free Willy* (1992) whale movie demonstrates another potential pitfall, indicating how sympathetic stories are not necessarily matched by similar sensitivity in real life. Even though the movie promoted a worthy message in which the close relationship between boy and captive whale eventually prompted the child to set the animal free from captivity, the true story was one of abject neglect. Keiko — the killer whale used in the film — spent years after production confined alone in a tiny pool kept at a temperature far too high for his well-being. In addition to psychological deprivation and loneliness, he suffered physical symptoms of weight loss, a skin disease which evidently caused him great discomfort and a characteristic bent fin as a result of swimming in circles in a confined space.

Nor is Keiko the only animal film star to endure a nightmarish retirement. The fate of Clyde — the orang-utan featured in the films *Every Which Way But Loose* and *You Can* — exemplifies all that can go wrong even more spectacularly. Reportedly beaten during filming, he was afterwards sold several times, ending his days at a roadside zoo in Texas. His hair was burnt off and he was forced to lie in his own urine. He was covered in scars, including wire cut marks on his wrists and ankles. After his death an autopsy revealed that he had died of a brain haemorrhage.[2] Were his injuries and his death caused by his training, his treatment on set, or the neglect which he suffered latterly?

Another lucrative modern source of income for trainers of performing animals has been the advertising industry. Since the advent of commercial television, compelling images of animals have been used to sell an astonishing array of products, ranging from pet foods to toilet paper, paint, bank services and petrol.

Probably the most enduring advertisements of all have been the PG Tips tea chimpanzees — a theme taken directly from the circus tradition of the chimpanzee tea party. Its longevity suggests it is a concept that has delighted generations of children and many adults, though others have persistently questioned training methods and condemned the dressing up in human clothes as an inappropriate affront to the dignity of intelligent primates.

Another popular advertising symbol has been Tessa, also a protégé of one of the large companies which prepare animals for circuses and cinema film. She was one of the animals chosen to promote Esso petrol under the 'put a tiger in your tank' slogan. Her experience shows only too clearly that the use of wild creatures in advertising can create the same kind of difficulties as those experienced in commercial cinema. After her working life was over, Tessa, originally a circus animal, was sadly neglected. At the end of 1996 it was reported that her days were spent divided between travelling around the country in a lorry trailer as part of a mobile exhibition and confinement in a small, barren, makeshift cage. The Esso company and the tiger's circus owners were locked in dispute over her future.[3]

For all the problems it creates, the potential value of film in prompting awareness of the charm, intelligence and sophistication of animal life should never be overlooked.

Cinema has indisputably provided a powerful medium in which to convey a strong fictional message about the need for sympathetic treatment. No production has proved this more powerfully than *Babe* (1995), featuring the tale of a charming pig who earns a reprieve from slaughter after his kindness and intelligence win the love and respect of his owner. The film also provided an admirable model in its treatment of animals before and after production, the pigs apparently living out the rest of their lives on a sanctuary. So powerful and sympathetic was *Babe* that in the US, total sales of pigmeat were reported to have dropped significantly after the film's release.

*Babe* is probably the most radical of a long tradition of films which either encourage compassion and/or warn of the destructive consequences to humanity of ill-treatment of animals. Even the scary humanity-threatening monster of *King Kong* (1927) offers some element of caution about the possible results of mistreatment; a message expressed more pointedly in later decades through movies such as *Tarzan, Greyfriars Bobby, Star Trek IV —The Journey Home, Dr Dolittle, Gorillas In The Mist* and, of course, *Born Free* and *Free Willy*.

Documentaries have also played their part in altering perception. Apart from natural history films, there have been many harrowing productions which have brought fresh attention to cruel practices. Way back in the 1920s, a horrifying fly-on-the-wall style film of the slaughter of horses at a Paris abattoir strengthened public opposition in Britain to the export trade. Over the decades this has been followed by productions exposing practices as diverse as whaling, seal slaughter, *paté de foie gras* production, factory farming and vivisection. Television helped enormously, bringing abuses to a much wider audience, followed by the video age in which film footage has become an essential tool in the campaigns of pressure groups.

Perhaps the most striking documentary film of all has been American director Victor Schonfeld's *The Animals' Film* (1981), produced for cinema release. From the opening sequence in which archive footage shows a chained elephant electrocuted to prove the power of electricity, *The Animals' Film* was an endurance test for its viewers. Nearly two and a quarter hours of almost unbearably chilling images were almost impossible to watch uninterrupted. Narrated by the distinguished actress, Julie Christie, the film was 'not about them, but about us' — a relentless exposé of the depths to which humanity can sink in its exploitation of other creatures. Although it won awards and a British audience in excess of one million when broadcast in the opening week of Channel 4 television, it was inevitably too painful and controversial to gain widespread cinema exposure. But amongst those who endured it, *The Animals' Film* did change minds.

## 4   The unfortunate consequences of *Flipper*

In the 1960s — a decade elsewhere associated with the beginning of more enlightened attitudes — a new form of animal exploitation emerged. The catalyst was a film called *Flipper*, a low-budget B movie released in 1962. It was another story with a laudable animal theme: boy befriends injured dolphin and eventually abandons his plan to use the animal to perform shows for his friends in favour of releasing it back into the wild. Friendship between boy and dolphin then develops in the animal's natural environment.

The movie was a surprise box office hit, soon spawning the long-running television series of the same name. Suddenly, the world was enchanted by dolphins. They became much sought after.

Within a few years dolphinaria had sprung up in many areas of the world, each one displaying its own obligatory 'Flipper'. Dealing became a big and highly profitable global business. With no significant legal restrictions, boats were launched across the oceans in search of specimens suitable for training. For several years, a gullible public seemed to swallow wholeheartedly the created myth that captive performing dolphins were experiencing the ultimate in happiness and fulfilment.

The dolphin craze first hit Britain in 1963 at Flamingo Park (now Flamingoland) in North Yorkshire. Within a decade more than another thirty enterprises had been established. Unsuitably small pools were built in 'fun parks' and 'marinelands'; travelling shows were set up, transporting animals confined on irrigated stretchers in specially constructed wagons. Even the soft-porn industry tried to get in on the act, devising (mercifully unsuccessful) striptease shows featuring women and dolphins swimming together in underwater tanks.[1]

For nearly a decade profits flowed in. Then the bubble began to burst. Legislation to control indiscriminate dolphin catching was brought forward in the US in 1973; the UK government introduced its own temporary ban on the import of all cetaceans. Public attitudes also changed, encouraged by campaigns from animal protection groups. As understanding grew of the delightful natural behaviour of dolphins in the wild, the degradation of their existence in captivity started to seep surely into public consciousness. By the end of the 1980s only four dolphinaria remained in the UK, each of them faced with a persistent barrage of adverse publicity.

By 1991 the number had been reduced to two following the first much-publicised re-introduction of captive dolphins 'into the blue'. Two organisations, Dolphin Circle and Zoo Check obtained a protected 100-acre area of sea off Provenciales, a

small island in the Turks and Caicos Islands in the British West Indies. A temporary sanctuary was created. The first animal to benefit was Rocky, a male dolphin released after spending seventeen years at Marineland in Morecambe, much of the latter period solitarily confined. He was joined shortly afterwards by Missie and Silver from Brighton Dolphinarium. After a period of rehabilitation the three of them eventually left their protected homes, after which their fate is unknown.

Windsor Safari Park and Flamingoland attempted to continue, but the tide of public opinion was by this time so strong that it was only a matter of time before they, too, closed down their dolphin exhibits. The UK dolphin boom ended where it had begun almost exactly thirty years before, at Flamingoland in North Yorkshire.

It is a measure of the haste with which the trade took off that there are no accurate records of how many bottlenose dolphins were actually imported into the UK during that period. Estimates put the figure in excess of three hundred, with more than one hundred deaths in captivity.[2]

The eventual collapse of dolphinaria in Britain marks an inspiring conclusion to a dark chapter in our exploitation of animals. In other areas of the world, however, the Flipper craze has no happy ending. In the US and elsewhere, massive 'sea world' theme parks display not only dolphins, but also captive whales and other species. Although taking animals from the wild is not as lucrative as it was in the 1960s and 1970s, commercial hunting still continues on a significant scale. Even in this country the legacy of the dolphinarium survives in the popularity of marine theme parks which display captive sharks and other marine wildlife seized from the oceans.

In 1996 came news of a new production of *Flipper*, starring the Australian actor Paul Hogan (star of the successful Crocodile Dundee films). Leaving aside concern for the trained captive dolphins used in the film, it must be the profound hope of all those sympathetic to the cause of animal protection that the consequences of the film are rather less destructive than the original version nearly forty years before.

Opposite: Silver, one of two captive dolphins to be freed from Brighton Dolphinarium 'into the blue' in 1991.

# 6 / Down on the farm

## 1  Over the seas to slaughter

In one sense, it is a measure of how little progress has been made in the campaign to protect farm animals that the subject causing most public concern at the close of the twentieth century is strikingly similar to the major animal welfare issue at its beginning.

In Victorian England, the British obsession with beef was so great that we were unable to produce sufficient quantities to meet demand from our own lands. Faith in the link between a high red meat diet and strength and virility was largely unquestioned, with the newly affluent middle classes created by the industrial revolution adding to the already insatiable demand from the aristocracy and the military. Only the working classes were excluded from the perceived feast.[1]

To keep pace with requirements, British money was pumped into the formation of livestock companies overseas. First, it was Ireland; then prospectors searched further afield. The beef industries of the Australian outback, the grasslands of New Zealand, the Argentinian pampas and the plains of North America were all established by British companies to help to feed British appetites.[2]

In the mid-nineteenth century animals were transported live from all of these countries. Only the uneconomical high death rates stopped the trade from Australasia, while in America animals often faced appallingly long and brutal journeys across country even before the dreadful sea crossing to Britain.[3]

Although the development of refrigeration in the 1870s greatly reduced the traffic in live animals, there were still half a million imported annually from North America at the turn of the century.[4] Far greater numbers endured the shorter routes from Ireland. Cruelty was endemic. Cattle were commonly unfed, overcrowded and beaten brutally. In 1898, even *The Meat Trades Journal* complained of the Irish trade that 'our cattle, sheep and pigs are carried by sea and rail with the minimum care and the maximum cost; they are bundled and shunted about as if they were iron'.[5]

Fortunately, the already declining trade from America faded fairly rapidly in the early part of the century, leaving what limited public concern there was for the voyages from Ireland. These continued to attract criticism from the RSPCA and the vegetarian lobby, but failed to evoke the kind of concerted public hostility stirred by the transport of worn out horses to the continent. As far as human compassion was concerned, cows and sheep did not rank high on the list of worthy recipients.

It was in the 1950s that the modern trade in selling farm animals to Europe for further fattening and slaughter began, stimulated first by the demand for freshly killed British beef from American servicemen stationed in Holland.[6]

Once the precedent had been established, the trend spread quickly throughout Northern Europe and from cattle to sheep. It proved highly popular with British farmers and dealers who gained better prices for their animals abroad than they were ever likely to receive from domestic markets. Continental slaughterhouses were equally satisfied by the obvious boost from increased trade.

The RSPCA, of course, were less enthusiastic, voicing concern almost immediately and asserting the welfare advantages of a carcass trade. They created sufficient pressure to compel a government inquiry, set up under the leadership of Lord Balfour.

What became known as the Balfour Assurances followed in 1957, approving live exports in principle, but laying down strict recommendations about welfare conditions. Animals should travel no more than 100 kilometres from the overseas port; they were to be adequately fed and watered during journeys; no animal was to be re-exported to another country after arrival at its first destination; and continental slaughterhouses must always stun animals (i.e. render them insensitive to pain) before slaughter.

Whatever its reasonable intentions, the negative impact of Balfour was that it gave new legitimacy to the trade. The number of animals sold abroad increased steadily, reaching 655,000 by 1963. By laying down paper regulations, the impression was created that the welfare of animals was closely monitored, whereas in fact, as soon as the RSPCA began to investigate the trade in the mid 1960s, it became obvious that supposed safeguards were routinely ignored. On his first trip overseas Inspector Ronald Butfield witnessed 'cattle being pushed and shoved all over Ostend Docks. The crews were using bits of stick, with lengths of fire-hose tied to them'.[7]

From 1970, the society undertook regular surveillance trips and soon discovered that both re-exportation and barbaric slaughtering methods were commonplace. At one abattoir in Putte in Belgium, they found animals stunned by a blow to the head with a carpenter's claw-hammer.[8] A dossier of cruelty began to accumulate, culminating in early 1973 with the involvement of a BBC documentary film crew from the respected current affairs series *Midweek*. The report it produced was to prove highly significant.

The BBC team followed a consignment of British sheep. After the animals had already endured a journey lasting more than 36 hours, film showed them 'miserable and distressed, pawing the decks for food, sucking at pieces of chain or rope outside the vehicle for what moisture they could get'.[9] A further day passed before their final destination for slaughter was eventually reached. The programme also contained dramatic scenes of the lorry driver swerving and speeding in an attempt to lose his pursuers. At one stage he even climbed from his vehicle armed with heavy tools and chased the camera team.

Such was the strength of the film that the night before it was scheduled to be broadcast, the Minister of Agriculture, John Godber, attempted to head off the anticipated public outcry by announcing that no further export licences for live sheep to Europe would be issued. He continued, however, to sanction the trade in cattle.

By this time live exports had become headline news. Public support for a total ban was overwhelming. The RSPCA and other animal welfare groups launched fresh campaigns; the British Veterinary Association reversed its policy to favour a ban; the bestselling *News of the World* conducted its own investigation, exposing a harrowing tale of ill-treatment and horrific slaughter conditions for British cattle in Belgium. It became a major political issue, so much so that the Labour Party decided to use one of its precious 'opposition days' to put forward a motion to suspend all export licences. On 11 July 1973, twenty-three Conservative MPs voted in support of the motion, defying the government whips and helping to secure a victory by 20 votes. Left with little choice, an embarrassed Minister of Agriculture announced a ban on all export licences from the following day, pending the findings of a full inquiry set up under the chairmanship of Lord O'Brien. The RSPCA declared it a victory for 'the sense of shock and outrage felt by ordinary people throughout the country'.

Some campaigners were optimistic that a final victory had been won. But they had underestimated the power of vested interests. When the O'Brien Report was published a year later it recommended a resumption of the trade, albeit with the proviso of stricter controls. In 1975 live exports resumed, setting a predictable pattern for the next twenty years. As free trade between European states increased so did the number of animals exported, exceeding one million for the first time in 1982. At the same time, animal welfare groups consistently produced chilling evidence of how welfare regulations were routinely ignored, prompting government responses which ranged from bloody-minded denial to the introduction of yet more unenforceable 'stricter controls'.

The 1992 liberalisation of free trade determined by agreement between EC states produced added difficulties for welfare groups. The long journeys increased. More than three million animals were exported in 1993. As the trade escalated, so did the

Live export of calves.

level of public protest. Film was obtained of deplorable conditions in Spanish, Belgium and French slaughterhouses; proof of failure to observe welfare standards during transport continued to be gathered with alarming frequency. Live exports hit the headlines again.

A massive postcard campaign was launched, aimed at the three ferry companies responsible for almost all the traffic across the English Channel. All were vulnerable to public protest because their business was principally the ferrying of holidaymakers and not livestock. Pressure upon them grew. After a period of stern resistance, all three gave way during the summer and autumn of 1994, announcing that they would end their involvement with live exports. The decision was reached after they had received — in the words of one spokesperson — 'hundreds of thousands of letters and cards' from 'ordinary people'.[10] The traffic in animals was effectively curtailed.

Campaigners were delighted: government officials and farmers were thrown into panic by the apparent loss of a lucrative business. Smaller freight companies frantically scurried to set up contracts which would allow them to cash in on the new gap in the market. Within three months deals had been struck and calves were again being loaded for export, both from Coventry airport and Shoreham docks.

These developments prompted the most dramatic demonstrations against cruelty to farm animals ever seen. Hundreds of protesters from a remarkable range of backgrounds flocked to the ports. Almost overnight, the live export campaign became big news yet again. When the new trade spread to Plymouth and the small Essex port of Brightlingsea, more protests were organised. At Brightlingsea, an estimated 25% of local residents took part. Sympathetic news coverage emphasised that many of those involved had never been associated with public protest before; they were simply 'ordinary folk' outraged by what seemed a pointlessly cruel trade. Why — they asked — could animals not be killed in the UK and transported in refrigerated lorries on the hook, rather than live on the hoof?

On 1 February 1995, tragedy struck. A thirty-one-year-old protester, Jill Phipps, was fatally injured at Coventry airport after falling beneath a lorry carrying veal calves for export. Her funeral at Coventry Cathedral was attended by hundreds of sympathisers, media from all around the world and the normally reclusive former film star, Brigitte Bardot, who journeyed from France especially to pay her respects.

Bardot's presence ensured that media interest stretched from the UK to the rest of Europe and beyond. So did demonstrations. In Holland, five people tried to climb the perimeter fence of Amsterdam airport to disrupt unloading of British calves bound for Dutch veal farms. When EU agriculture ministers met to discuss developments in Brussels they were greeted by over a hundred protesters from at least five member states.

In support of the public mood, port authorities in Dover, Plymouth and Coventry all attempted to introduce their own local bans on the exporters. Aware that national law denied them the right to interfere with free trade purely for moral reasons, they based their actions on the grounds that security arrangements were proving too expensive and too disruptive. But their attempts were foiled by a High Court ruling that to prohibit live exports would be to submit to the 'mob rule' of animal rights campaigners — a decision condemned scornfully by some newspapers.

> *Dover found itself in the grip of mob rule yesterday when a group of animal rights protesters gathered to vent their frustration at the imminent resumption of live calf exports.*
>
> *There was the 66-year-old grandmother, the 19-year-old humanities student and the housewife whose husband used to be a P&O ferry captain.*
>
> *These were the sort of people described as a 'mob' on Wednesday by the High Court judges.*[11]

The protests began to acquire wider significance. Judges and politicians were characterised increasingly as divorced from the real concerns and aspirations of the general public. Commentators began to identify demonstrators as part of a 'revulsion against powerlessness' and as indicators of 'a general disenchantment with politics and the establishment'.[12]

Yet for all the indignation and almost universal public support, these remarkable months of people power were not enough to break the twin forces of vested interest and EU political policy. Determination to encourage unrestricted trade between nations continued to override the stress and suffering caused by long and unnecessary journeys to distant farms and abattoirs. More than one hundred years after refrigeration should have rendered long distant transportation of live animals indefensible, the same specious arguments used then to defend imports are now being offered to justify exports. Just as the transport in live cattle from America survived for decades because it was argued that quality beef had to be freshly 'home killed' to meet the requirements of UK consumers, so France and other European countries now churn out similar excuses for the miserable trade in British sheep. There can be no greater proof of the low ethical value still placed on the welfare of individual farm animals.

By 1997, the number of livestock facing export had soared back from the dramatic fall brought about by the headline protests of 1994/95 to exceed one million. Meanwhile, yet another set of 'stricter controls' was being denounced as unenforceable by welfare organisations.

## 2   Animal machines

In 1996, a year after the live export demonstrations had reached their peak, farm animals were once again in the media spotlight. On 20 March the UK government finally admitted what had been suspected by others for several years — a probable link between bovine spongiform encephalitis (BSE) in cattle and the degenerative disease of the brain in humans, Creuzfeld Jacob Disease (CJD). Its advisory committee revealed that ten fatal cases of a new strain of CJD in young people were almost certain to have been caused by consumption of BSE infected beef.

The news sparked a crisis of unparalleled proportion for the farming industry. 'The Roast Beef of Old England' — once feted in song as having 'ennobled our hearts and enriched our blood' — had been transformed into a potent source of disease and death. A world-wide ban followed swiftly (effectively suspending the export of calves to the continent in addition to the trade in cattle meat products) as events brought into sharp and painful focus the potentially lethal consequences of modern systems of animal farming. It was a scenario that had been predicted by critics for over three decades.

Until the 1960s, animal welfare groups and vegetarians had tended to base their campaigns against livestock farming upon transport and slaughter conditions rather than the rearing methods on farms. The children's picture book view of traditional farms where happy and secure animals lived out idyllic lives in beautiful countryside was largely accepted by the public as an accurate representation. In reality, traditional methods were rarely quite as peaceful as the romantic image presented and dubious welfare practices such as the permanent tethering of dairy cows in city dairies were commonplace, but nevertheless the majority of farm animals did at least enjoy a reasonably natural life between market and slaughter. Despite the warning signs of a relatively small number of intensive poultry farms set up in the 1930s and 1940s, most livestock were allowed fresh air, exercise and companionship for at least part of their lives.

The crucial changes began after the second world war. As we have already seen, when Clement Attlee's Labour Government was returned to power in 1945 its visionary programme of social reform included a massive commitment to increased food production. This was considered almost as crucial as the establishment of a welfare state, radical education reforms and industrial modernisation. More meat for everybody was a central element of the agricultural plan, partly as a perceived contribution towards a healthier population, partly as a potent symbol of new affluence and also as an important ingredient of a more democratic society. The harsh economic years of the 1930s followed by severe rationing during the war had ensured that meat had previously been a relative luxury for poorer people. Now the aim was to make it freely available to all.

Similar sentiments found expression throughout the Western world. Agricultural economists acquired a new importance as they set about the task of finding ways to reduce costs and maximise productivity. A cheap food policy was born. Throughout the 1950s, intensive methods were developed to meet expectations. The face of the countryside was altered dramatically.

In this quest for plentiful cheap food, farm animals were to pay a particularly high price. Economic cost/benefit analysis was applied mercilessly to their lives. The aim was to fatten the largest number for slaughter in the shortest possible time for the least possible cost. Genetic science developed to produce breeds that would put on weight quickly; indoor factory farms meant that greater numbers could be kept in a small space and food intake controlled; drugs (known as feed additives) were added

to enhance weight gain. Battery hen cages for hens, two-foot-wide wooden crates for veal calves, stalls where pigs were tethered in vast windowless buildings, broiler houses for fattening thousands of chicken — all of these systems proliferated. Under the new regimes, fresh air, sunshine, exercise, natural mating and sometimes even companionship and the room to turn around were considered superfluous.

Although a number of voices were raised in protest, the ruthlessness of this revolution in livestock rearing escaped national public scrutiny until 1964 and the publication of Ruth Harrison's *Animal Factories*. The book received widespread publicity and was serialised in *The Observer*, ensuring that for the first time the legendary British concern for animals was focused squarely upon farm animals. From that moment factory farming became a fiercely debated issue.

The government responded to the ensuing outcry by setting up a committee of investigation under the chairmanship of Lord Brambell. Published in 1965, the Brambell Report was very much a compromise, but it did recommend certain protections which, had they been enforced. would have rescued livestock from some of the suffering they continued to face. In particular, it put forward the principle of certain freedoms which should be granted to all — from hunger, thirst, discomfort, pain, injury, disease, fear and distress — plus the freedom to express normal behaviour.

Sadly, Brambell's main proposals were ignored. In spite of mounting public disquiet, conditions for farm animals deteriorated. The number reared and slaughtered continued to rise dramatically. In 1961, 19% of eggs came from hens kept in battery cages; by 1983 the figure had increased to 96%. Pig and sheep herds also grew. The broiler chicken industry multiplied at a remarkable rate. There were 52 million chicken slaughtered in 1955, 142 million in 1963, 382 million in 1981 and in excess of 760 million by 1996.[1]

From the beginning, those who condemned the emergence of factory farming had warned vehemently that ill-treatment of animals would inevitably lead to long-term dangers to the health of human consumers. In *Animal Machines*, for example, Ruth Harrison stated that 'unhealthy animals cannot make healthy food for humans' and that the 'intensification of livestock rearing' has 'made the food a definite danger'.[2] Yet the warnings went unheeded — as they continued to do in the 1970s and 1980s when scares associated with consumption of animal products became commonplace. Food poisoning incidents increased alarmingly and the bugs became more virulent as the wide use of pharmaceuticals in livestock farming was implicated in the development of drug-resistant bacteria. Slaughterhouse hygiene was condemned by a series of investigations which found 'a frightening picture of poor hygiene, slapdash organisation and blood and gore all over the floor'.[3] A black market in growth-promoting hormones with links to some human cancers was exposed.[4]

All this culminated in 1986, when the first cases of BSE in cattle were confirmed in the UK. Official reaction was to claim that the disease would soon die out. In 1988, the government-instigated Southwood Committee predicted 17,000-20,000 cases in all. By early 1998 there had been approximately 180,000 confirmed incidents. Even more disturbingly, the possible risk to humans was described as 'remote', marking the beginning of a UK government policy which seems to have been motivated primarily by a desire to protect the farming industry rather than the health of consumers. Each time new evidence emerged of a threat to human health, the Ministry of Agriculture responded with an uncompromising 'beef is safe' message. Such assurances now seem very hollow indeed.

Because of the protracted incubation period of CJD it will be impossible to predict accurately how many people will eventually develop the fatal human brain disease from eating infected beef until early in the twenty-first century. Most informed opinion seems to suggest that, at the very least, hundreds of families will suffer the anguish of watching a loved one die a particularly distressing death.

Nor have the exact causes of BSE in cattle been isolated conclusively, though it does seem almost certain that the policy of feeding animal protein to creatures herbivorous by nature in order to reduce feed costs was partly responsible. Furthermore, according to critics of intensive farming, cattle have become increasingly susceptible to infection owing to deteriorating welfare standards. Their immune systems have also been severely weakened by the constant pressure to maximise meat and milk production.

This makes the confused and disorientated 'mad cow' as much a victim of factory methods of food production as the battery chicken or veal calf — and the human suffering an inevitable consequence of our barbaric indifference. In the words of the Director of Animal Aid, Andrew Tyler, 'the BSE crisis is merely the most spectacular symptom of a sickness that goes to the heart of commercial meat production in all industrial nations. There is a simple, irreducible formula that explains it: if you exploit, stress and traumatise animals in order to extract the last penny of profit from them, then a large number will get sick. If people then eat any part of their bodies, they too risk getting ill'.[5]

## 3   Peter Roberts: from farmer to campaigner

While farmers have been condemned for their involvement in factory farming, some have been reluctant participants. The whole agricultural system has been weighted to encourage intensive methods and many have been faced with a stark choice — either go with the flow or risk unemployment. One ex-farmer crucially aware of the pressures is Peter Roberts, who — in the 1960s — struggled with the idea of introducing intensive methods on his own farm in Hampshire. He rejected the temptation and in 1967 he and his wife, Anna, formed the campaign group Compassion In World Farming.

There had been nothing in Peter Roberts' background to suggest a career in agriculture. Born in 1924, the youngest of four children, his father was a doctor near Lichfield in Staffordshire who hoped that Peter would follow in his footsteps. Yet the youngster's interest was stimulated by a job on a local farm during school holidays, after which he romantically imagined himself 'up on the Welsh hills looking after sheep on a thousand acres, roaming wild.'

Despite initial family disapproval and disappointment, Peter's determination to become a farmer never waned, though pursuit of his goal was delayed by two years conscripted military service in Egypt immediately after the war. His experiences in the army included leading a team of thirty men escorting 750 mules on a difficult journey through the Suez Canal from Burma to Greece. 'We had quite a good rapport with those mules,' Peter recalls, 'though I dread to think what future they had. They

Peter and Anna Roberts photographed in 1997.

were looked upon as very inferior animals by the Greeks and they were taken up the mountains to carry heavy loads in the campaign against the communists.' Problematic though the experience had been — at one stage they were refused permission to travel through the canal — it only increased his desire to work with animals.

At the end of his period of conscription, Peter put in for a serviceman's grant to study agriculture at Harper Adams College in Shropshire, preceded by the statutory two years employment on a farm near the family home 'to gain sufficient practical experience to base the theory upon.' Graduation was followed by employment as a farm manager on 350 acres in Shropshire; then a move down south to establish his first partnership, and finally, in 1954, by the purchase of Little Barnett Farm in Froxfield, Hampshire. It was his experiences there over the next eight years, farming a small dairy herd of forty cattle on sixty acres of land, which were to transform his life.

The first and most significant event was his marriage to Anna Hearsey, for initially it was her concern which led them both to question their occupation. Peter explains: 'The bull calves had to go to market and that used to upset my wife very badly. Also, when you separate cow and calf — which you have to do if she's going to let her milk down — the cow that had recently calved would leave the herd, come up to the buildings where the calf was being kept and bawl all night. That was very upsetting, too.'

As time passed the Roberts were confronted with an increasing dilemma: on the one hand, they greatly enjoyed the outside life working with animals; on the other, they felt growing unease at some of the practices with which they were inevitably involved. 'It wasn't only the bull calves going to market and then on to the slaughterhouse, but of course the barreners as well. A cow must have a calf every year if she is to be kept in milk and profitable production, so if she doesn't conceive after a while you have to treat her as a barren cow and send her off for beef. After she has given her faithful best to you over the years you smack her on the rump and say "off you go" and that was very hard. Also, at some stage there were French dealers buying up barren cows at market and taking them to France for ritual slaughter. We objected to that, so I used to take our cows down to Fontley abattoir and see them killed myself. I would rather do that than feel the guilt of having just abandoned them.'

Such considerations ate into income; the price paid by the slaughterhouse was less than at market. With farming trends moving towards greater size and intensification, life was already difficult enough for the smallholder and so — by now supporting a young family — the Roberts found themselves struggling financially. At one stage Peter even considered broiler chicken farming. 'I told my wife what it was all about — that it was a general throughput sort of thing, putting chicks in at one end and bringing them out as fattened chicken at the other — and she was absolutely horrified. She said, "Look, don't the chickens have any rights?" I think it was that which started me thinking about it all.'

Like many farmers at the time they also called in the government-backed National Agricultural Advisory Service, which surveyed farms and made recommendations to increase profitability. The whole thing was costed to the finest detail. It, too, suggested that broiler chicken farming might be the answer to the Roberts' problems. It was typical of the process that was to ensnare many smallholders in factory farming. 'Once on the treadmill you couldn't get off,' claims Peter. 'With official support you would apply for a hefty bank loan, build your broiler houses and stock them. Then you would try to keep ahead of the increasing competition. Fortunately, we had already decided that broiler farming was not for us on welfare grounds.'

It was a controversy in the local newspaper in 1960 which began Peter's transformation from farmer to campaigner. A broiler chicken farm was set up in an area of outstanding natural beauty and the correspondence columns were filled with letters of complaint, first because of the despoiling of the countryside and latterly because of cruelty to the birds. In response, a factory farmer residing close to Little Barnett Farm wrote a scathing letter in which he claimed that it was mostly only 'vegetarian housewives from suburbia' who were concerned. It was this that spurred Peter into action. 'I'd never written to the paper before, but that just got my goat and so I wrote and said, "I'm a neighbour of yours, I don't quite fit into the category of vegetarian housewife from suburbia and isn't it about time you had a little bit of compassion for the flock?" I remember going down to Petersfield in a great rush on the night that the paper came out and the letter was printed with such a big headline that I missed it completely at first!'

Because it had come from a farmer, the letter provoked quite a lot of support and Peter started to widen his net with regular letters to the press. 'I remember saying that these birds will not be without a voice because we will supply it and we started to get quite a list of supporters which eventually I was able to make use of when we founded Compassion In World Farming.'

By this time, Peter and Anna had both become vegetarians. 'I found my wife in tears one day as she was preparing dinner. She said, "I wonder if this joint of beef is from one of our own cows." From that time we refused to eat meat even though we were still producing it from our old dairy cows and their calves.'

This was really the beginning of the end of their time in farming. In 1961, the decision was taken to sell the farm 'because the reservations we had about the welfare of the cattle were coming uppermost. Also, this mailing list of people opposed to factory farming was growing and we thought that something should be done about it.'

Peter took a job as an agricultural representative travelling around farms. It was a position which was later to serve his campaigning purposes well. 'It was difficult for ordinary people to gain access to battery units, broiler farms and dry sow stalls for pigs, but I would go along and present my card and I was able to see things. I was astonished by the squalor in some of the battery houses. Dead birds were left in their cages decomposing and live birds would be pecking at them. Some of the nipple drinkers would be leaking water everywhere and there would be mouldy food left around. It was then that I began to equate factory farming with a deterioration in farming standards.'

Compassion In World Farming was formed soon afterwards; originally almost by default. Peter had conceived a dual programme of action called Project 70. It aimed to prevent factory farming becoming established in countries where it had not yet taken hold and to phase it out over 10 years in those where it was already common-place. 'We recognised that a run down on factory farming was necessary on an international basis because no one country could act successfully on its own. So we approached the International Society for the Protection of Animals (ISPA), which was closely associated with the RSPCA, for support. ISPA wrote to animal welfare organisations in ninety-four countries and only two — Ireland and Malta — refused to give their backing. Unfortunately, ISPA never actually took it any further.'

One day in October 1967, Peter was complaining about this lack of action to a solicitor friend. 'He said, "You'll have to do it yourself — come to my office next Tuesday and I'll draw up your Trust deeds and you can take it from there." So Anna and I turned up and out of that meeting Compassion In World Farming was set up.'

The organisation gained almost instant media attention when its first exhibition at the Ceylon Tea Centre in Lower Regent Street, London, featured the then well-known model, Celia Hammond, in a scaled-up model of a battery cage. 'The press loved it,' Peter remembers, 'and they made us carry the cage into Piccadilly Circus for photographs. We achieved a tremendous amount of publicity and from there we just went from strength to strength.'

The next stage of the campaign was to try to find a marketable alternative to meat. Textured vegetable protein (TVP) made from soya had only recently been invented in the USA and after having had samples sent over, the Roberts approached the manufacturers to ask for an exclusive agency in the UK. 'They asked us how many million we could put into the business! Eventually they took over a company in Manchester to sell it in this country themselves, but they were only marketing it to food manufacturers. It was going into meat pies, sausages and things like that as a meat *extender*, whereas we saw it as a meat *alternative*, to be sold through the health trade. So we came to an agreement by which we were able to market it as a completely vegetarian product. They thought we were very weird, but it was business.'

And so in 1969 the first vegetarian textured protein soya products found their way into UK health stores. Originally the idea was for the soya sales to finance Compassion In World Farming, 'but it didn't work out that way because we needed a lot of money to run this company and CIWF had practically none. So we were faced with having to use the remaining money from the sale of the farm to finance the soya business.' The family house — already used as a printing, duplicating and distribution centre for anti-factory farming literature — was turned over to packaging and distribution. 'The lounge was the store room for the food, the kitchen was the weighing room, the garage housed the packaging, the dining room was the despatch area and we were camping upstairs virtually! Then the planners served notice on us to cease running the business from our private home and at that stage we had to take a large bank loan and go into production on an industrial estate in Petersfield.'

It was a brave step to take and Peter recalls a time when the bank manager wrote to say that he was watching their account closely and looking for improvements. Eventually, however, the company (Direct Foods) proved so successful that the Manchester-based suppliers became 'jealous of our success'. They announced that they were going into competition for the vegetarian market and invited the Roberts to sell Direct Foods to them. 'We couldn't really compete with them so that is what we had to do.'

Meanwhile, Compassion In World Farming's message was being treated with increasing sympathy and enthusiasm. After an exhibition in Leeds, a Yorkshire television film crew suggested they make a film at vastly reduced cost on CIWF's behalf. Peter considers the ensuing documentary *Don't Look Now… Here Comes Your Dinner* as 'another turning point' in raising public awareness. The film — finally completed in 1973 — is now preserved in the National Film Archive as a significant statement of the social concerns of the period.

In the three decades of its existence, Compassion In World Farming has been at the forefront of campaigns against all areas of factory farming. Some of the main priorities when it began — battery cages, live exports, broiler chicken farming — remain as important today as they were back in the 1960s, in spite of massive public opposition. But there have also been clear victories. In particular, CIWF played a leading role in the fight against veal farming in the UK, dating back to 1969 when Peter first took pictures of calves confined in narrow crates on a farm in Kent, having introduced himself to the farmer as an 'agricultural journalist'. In 1984, he also took a test court case on behalf of CIWF against the Canons of Storrington Priory, who part-funded their religious order by rearing 650 calves in veal crates. Although defeated and forced to pay £12,000 damages, the notoriety of the case provided added impetus to the campaign, culminating in 1987 when the Ministry of Agriculture introduced the Welfare of Calves Regulations. These effectively made the veal crate illegal in this country.

Another of Peter Roberts' important initiatives has been to press for changes in the Treaty of Rome (the document governing the European Union) which would elevate animals from their low status as 'agricultural products' to a new category of

Campaigners in Amsterdam call for the recognition of animal sentience, 1997.

'sentient beings'. Under the original Treaty it is illegal for EU member states to impede either the import or export of any agricultural product. Livestock enjoys no more protection than carrots or cabbages. 'Animals are not mere agricultural products; they are not cauliflowers; yet in fact they are treated worse than cauliflowers because if a cauliflower gets damaged it loses its value, whereas you can bruise a calf without any financial loss.'

After a long struggle lasting almost a decade, the campaign finally achieved significant success in June 1997 at the Inter-Governmental Conference in Amsterdam. The EU heads of state agreed a legally binding protocol which recognises animals as 'sentient beings'. In future this must be taken into account in all Community policies on agriculture, transport, research and the internal market. The raising of status probably offers the best hope so far of an eventual ban on both the live transportation of animals and extreme factory farming methods.

Peter Roberts retired as director of CIWF in 1989. Like so many who have been involved in animal welfare over a long period, he looks back at changes with optimism tempered by a recognition of the massive amount of work which remains to be done before animals enjoy the degree of protection he seeks. His hopes are fuelled largely by 'the changing attitude of the public... Farm animal welfare now means something,' he asserts, 'whereas earlier it was simply ridiculed. The change is being led by the younger generation, many of them leading their parents into a more wholesome way of life.' On the other hand he recognises reluctantly that 'people seem to act even now as if we are the centre of creation and that everything was made specially for our benefit.'

Peter believes that factory farming will eventually cease, even if its demise is likely to be stimulated as much by health scares as an evolution in human consciousness. 'If the farmers had set out to damage their own markets they couldn't have made a better job of it. The first thing was dried poultry manure which they put in layers between silage and fed to the cows; then they recycled it into egg-laying hen food, saying that it was unused protein; then there was the salmonella scare when they put chicken waste and feather meal into foodstuffs; and lastly BSE — slaughterhouse offal including sheep brains put into cow feed. You couldn't do much more to ruin your own markets! Ultimately, I think that the level of disease and people's mistrust of meat products will go hand in hand with a growth in our innate sympathy for the animal kingdom to bring factory farming to an end.'

## 4  Assembly line animals

In the nineteenth and early part of the twentieth century, slaughterhouse reform was one of the main priorities of both the RSPCA and vegetarian campaigners. Conditions were appalling. Most animals were butchered in small, 'private' slaughterhouses, described by Henry Salt in 1906 as 'ill-constructed dens of torment'.[1] Salt described graphically how 'the clumsy butcher's pole-axe' often took several blows to render animals unconscious.

Those who sought improvements made two major recommendations: the replacement of private abattoirs by publicly owned municipal enterprises more easily open to scrutiny and the introduction of more humane methods of killing. The latter proved particularly difficult to achieve. When abattoir reform did eventually arrive it was governed primarily by economic and hygiene considerations, not welfare.

The inspiration for change arrived from Chicago, where in 1908 the first of several huge meat plants was constructed with an industrialised killing process to maximise efficiency. Rather than the 'traditional' hauling of animals manually around the slaughterhouse floor, the new methods involved a conveyor belt system. Livestock were shackled, hoisted up onto a killing line, slaughtered, and then 'processed' by a series of workers, each of whom was allotted a single task as the dead creature was systematically prepared for human consumption. Working conditions were notoriously unhealthy and hazardous and bitter disputes between workers and bosses were commonplace, but times were hard, allowing management to get away with ruthless exploitation. There were always others glad of the work.

The speedy new methods became the protocol not only for the modern meat industry throughout the world, but also for factory conveyor belts and mass production generally. For instance, Henry Ford is reported to have taken the methods initiated in Chicago's abattoirs as a model for the first assembly lines for car manufacture.[2]

Industrialised systems of slaughter took some time to establish themselves in the UK, but gradually they did gain acceptance. Although primitive private abattoirs survived, the overall trend was towards newly built and larger public enterprises and these tended to incorporate the modern American developments in their construction. With modifications, the system pioneered in Chicago remains the conventional method of killing and processing for meat to this day.

In 1907, the RSPCA first produced a 'captive bolt pistol' as a 'humane alternative' to the pole-axe. The idea was for the pistol to be fired into the forehead of the animal, thus instantaneously rendering it insensitive to pain. The throat could then be cut and the animal bled before preparation for the butcher.

For some time, the meat industry vigorously resisted implementation of the new stunning methods, but it was compelled to reform under the first Slaughter of Animals Act, passed in 1933. This made pre-stunning (i.e. ensuring an animal is insensitive to pain before the death-cut) compulsory for the killing of cattle. Pigs had to wait until 1949 to be granted similar protection and it was not until 1974 that the Slaughterhouse Act made it a pre-requisite for the slaughter of all farm animals (with the exception of those killed to meet the religious requirements of Jews and Moslems). The 1974 Act (updated in 1995) still forms the basis of welfare provision.

As the population became increasingly urbanised it became much simpler for humans to exclude from their consciousness the process by which meat reached their dinner plates Slaughter began to take place in purpose-built factory buildings away from public view: the advent of legislation to protect animals helped to sustain a sense of well-being and efficiency. It became easier to sustain the myth that animals died peacefully and painlessly in pleasant, hygienic surroundings — or in many cases, even to ignore the fact that meat on the dinner plate was actually dead animal at all.

Not everybody was appeased, of course. A slowly increasing minority of vegetarians continued to question and contest.

Since its formation in 1847, the UK Vegetarian Society had always attracted respectable levels of support. By the beginning of the twentieth century its members represented a diversity of interests — amongst them humanitarians, campaigners against cruelty to animals and those convinced that avoiding meat was beneficial to health. The Society still suffered, however, from a reputation for austerity linked to its radical religious origins. Both the British and the American Vegetarian Societies (the latter established in 1861) had been founded by members of the Biblical Christian Church, a group as dedicated to abstinence from intoxicating liquor as it was to avoiding meat.

At the time of the first world war, links between vegetarianism and pacifism had also become well established. Some of those who opposed conflict most vociferously were notable food reformers — Henry Salt and his humanitarian circle offering an obvious example. Nonetheless, vegetarians did serve in the armed forces, facing the horror of life in the trenches with the added indignity of being denied special rations. It was a choice either to eat meat or to go exceedingly hungry.[3]

Things improved. In 1920 came the first official government recognition that there might actually be health benefits in reducing meat consumption. The President of the Board of Trade declared that 'as a result of war rationing the people have learned to eat less meat and are probably more healthy as a result'.[4] Vegetarianism had begun to gain respectability.

When war returned in 1939, a Committee of Vegetarian Interest was formed to lobby successfully for official recognition of a non-meat diet. Special vegetarian ration books were provided, allowing extra rations of cheese and nuts to those who registered. Apparently, the non-meat alternative was considered sufficiently attractive to draw an increase in converts![5] Soon after war ended, *Vegetarian News* — the magazine of the London Vegetarian Society (the national society having divided into two separate organisations, north and south) — claimed a membership of 3500 to 4000.[6]

By modern standards, however, the choice of foods for non-meat eaters remained very limited, particularly during the years of rationing. British vegetarians looked on enviously at the literature of their American counterparts, packed as it was with advertisements for tinned Californian fruits and nuts. A correspondent to the *Vegetarian Messenger* in 1946 lamented that 'tinned fruits are such a luxury… I have not tasted any since before the war'.[7]

Yet it was during this austere period that a minority of vegetarians set out on a new path, establishing an organisation to legitimise a diet free from *all* animal products.

## 5   Kathleen Jannaway: visionary or crank?

In many respects Kathleen Jannaway is an untypical vegetarian, for it is not everybody whose decision to give up meat is followed by half a lifetime dedicated to radical pioneering work on behalf of the cause. Yet in other ways she is wholly representative of a significant number of her generation whose involvement in animal welfare was prompted originally by support for the peace movement and the campaign against human hunger.

Kathleen was born in 1915 into a working class family. Her mother died when she was still a baby; her father when she was only three years old. An only child, she was brought up by her paternal grandparents. Times were hard and money short, particularly after her grandfather also died when she was hardly into her teens.

She recounts the financial circumstances with fascinating detail.

'When my grandfather died we had a total income of 17s 6d, plus the 15s granny's sons gave her. Out of this we had to pay 14s weekly rent. But my grandmother was a good manager and I never went hungry — though I can remember that sometimes on Thursday nights we had to go to bed early in the evening because we hadn't a penny left for the gas meter. There was no electricity in those days.'

At school Kathleen progressed well, winning a scholarship to grammar school and obtaining examination results which — had funds allowed — could have won her a place at university. Instead, the need to bring in a wage to help her grandmother dictated a career in teaching. She took a position as a biology teacher at a secondary school, 'hating the discipline of it all'.

From such a background is it possible to discern the seeds of radicalism which later created an indefatigable and visionary campaigner? Kathleen herself believes that it is. Her father was a member of the Socialist Party of Britain (before it became the Labour Party) and regularly preached a message of peace and the dignity of working people from a soapbox in the local park: her grandmother was sufficiently unconventional to be deeply disturbed when young Kathleen wanted to join the local girl guides, considering the organisation unhealthily representative of the status quo! Kathleen also cites her good fortune in attending progressive schools where she was always encouraged to question and to think for herself.

Before the second world war she married Jack Jannaway, creating a life-long partnership in which they have both constantly re-evaluated their beliefs and confronted fresh challenges. The first of these came at the outbreak of war. They were both pacifists and registered as conscientious objectors. Unlike many others in a similar position they encountered little hostility. 'We were lucky,' she says. 'People have always been able to respect Jack's honesty and integrity and they realised that it was simply impossible for him to kill or to be part of the killing of another human being.'

It was during the war that the couple turned vegetarian. At precisely the same moment as Kathleen was slicing up their meagre ration of roast lamb there was 'a bit of a commotion in the corner of the field outside our window and all the lambs hastily raced for their mothers. I realised that it would be no good crying for mum when the slaughterhouse lorry arrived,' she recalls. Both she and Jack decided never to eat meat again.

The war years also saw Kathleen Jannaway undertake her first public speaking engagement, though it was not for the animal cause. She helped to organise a meeting in Tunbridge Wells of the newly formed Oxford Movement for Famine Relief (later to become Oxfam) to protest against a war cabinet policy not to send dried milk to help the starving children of our allies. The decision had been taken on the grounds that there was considered a danger of supplies falling into the hands of the enemy. 'People often think that my main motivation is animals,' says Kathleen, 'but actually my principal concerns have always been peace and world hunger. My involvement in the animal movement developed out of these, particularly when I began to make connections between the different issues.'

By this time, the first of three children had been born. Raising a family (as vegetarians) dominated most of the next two decades of their mother's life. It was not until 1964 that she took the step which led to the most important of her working achievements. The catalyst was a two-page review of Ruth Harrison's book *Animal*

Kathleen Jannaway as a young woman (left), and (right) more recently with friends.

*Machines* in *The Observer*. It revealed how veal calves were separated from their mothers, solitarily confined in two-foot wide crates where they were unable to lie down comfortably and denied solid food. Kathleen: 'It was at this point that I realised that these calves were the surplus of the dairy industry and that the milk which nature intended for them was being fed to us. I decided to give up milk and to try to live without any animal products there and then. At the time I didn't know that an organisation to support vegans existed or even how I would survive.'

In fact, the Vegan Society had already been campaigning since 1944, formed by a small group of pioneers who did not wish to consume any animal products because of what they perceived as the inherent cruelty of all livestock farming. 'We believe that the spiritual destiny of man is such that in time he will view with abhorrence the idea that men once fed on the products of animal bodies', wrote co-founder Donald Watson in the first edition of *Vegan Views*. At the time, theirs was an extremely courageous decision to take, not only because of the limited choice of foods, but more particularly because most contemporary medical experts were convinced that a diet without meat or dairy products was a sure recipe for malnutrition, disease and probably premature death.

Eva Batt was not one of the original members, but her own account of how — in the 1950s — she converted overnight from a conventional meat to an animal-free diet illustrates both the overwhelming sense of purpose and the bravery of the early vegans. It also offers another telling example of the kind of chance incident which so often prompts individuals to change their lives.

*There was this railway station platform, and there were cows herded at one end making very pathetic noises and at the other end were baby calves, very, very young, crying for their mothers. Of course I asked an official why they could not be put together, and he explained that the cows were going to market and the calves were going to the butcher.*

*'To the butcher,' I said, 'Why?'*

*'Well,' he said, 'you can't have milk unless cows keep having calves, and you can only rear a few of the calves. Most of those poor little things will be in veal and ham pies before too long.'*

*This shook me, I hadn't realised that milk production was responsible for suffering and slaughter. I had pictured gentle, placid cows grazing in green pastures and thought how kind the farmer was to relieve them of their milk. I turned again to the cows, one was now nudging my shoulder, trying to attract my attention, and as I turned she gazed straight into my eyes and there was a real message. I knew I could never drink milk again and I never have, but believe me I had a terrible time over that weekend wondering how I was going to manage. I knew people could live without meat, but without milk! I really thought that I was going to die.*[1]

Eva went on to become one of the leading figures in the Vegan Society, researching and writing *What's Cooking* (1973), one of the first vegan cookbooks and nutrition guides to become widely available.[2]

It was thanks to individuals such as Eva Batt and her predecessors that by the time that Kathleen Jannaway became General Secretary of the Society in 1972, some of the health worries associated with veganism had been dispelled — if only because there were original members who had proved the point by living for nearly three decades. Nonetheless, there was still a great deal to be done before medical and nutritional practitioners would begin to be convinced. It was not really until the late 1970s and early 1980s that studies began to acknowledge that 'the consumption of a properly balanced vegan and vegetarian diet does not endanger health'.[3]

Kathleen Jannaway's role in promoting the healthiness of veganism over the last thirty years should not be undervalued, yet her particular strength has been in another area, linking the compassionate desire to avoid animal products with rational use of world food resources. Her own half-acre of garden in the heart of suburban Leatherhead was soon turned over to a horticultural experiment where she and Jack successfully developed green manure techniques (i.e. manure from plant sources only), food-bearing trees, vegetable and fruit beds. The aim was simple: to provide living proof that more people could be sustained on less land in a more self-sufficient way on a vegan diet.

This work has continued since Kathleen left the Vegan Society in 1984 to form — with Jack — her own Movement For Compassionate Living. At the end of 1996, she insisted that the garden was 'not what it once was', but at the age of eighty-one and with Jack no longer mobile enough to help, she was still harvesting bumper crops of which any gardener would be proud, grown from her own vegan compost. She was particularly proud of her perfectly formed carrots, averaging 6oz each and carrot fly free! Stores of vegetables, fruit and protein crops such as haricot beans lay neatly packed away in sufficient quantities to provide most of the food needed to see the Jannaways through the winter.

'I think it is important to show people how much of our food is home produced,' says Kathleen. 'I don't grow the wheat for bread, though I do have enough land and could do so. And, of course, the soya we use is imported. Haricot beans are an alternative I use in many dishes, but I would like to see a lot more work put into developing different plant protein crops which would grow successfully in this country.'

In addition to the time she still spends in the garden, Kathleen remains remarkably active, researching and writing for the Movement for Compassionate Living.

She is at her desk by 7.00 most mornings. All the literature is produced and distributed from home, written by her and — until a recent illness — typeset, illustrated and photocopied by Jack. 'I am not very good at working with people,' she admits, 'I haven't got the patience. But Jack and I made a good team.'

Old age has not slowed down the pursuit of new ways of carrying forward her message of compassion. One of her leaflets carries the provocatively tongue-in-cheek message that 'veganism is not enough', exhorting readers to grow as much of their own food as possible, to buy local produce, or — as a last resort — to purchase imported crops only from fair trade sources such as Oxfam. She urges people not to depend upon Third World cash crops which cause environmental degradation and human hunger.

Elsewhere she champions the potential of 'a tree-based culture' where forests would be planted to replace animal farming, claiming that these would not only provide ample food, but also improve soil fertility, prevent soil erosion and reverse the effects of global warming. Most revolutionary of all, she envisages 'a world-wide network of self-reliant, tree based, autonomous, vegan village communities' based loosely on the ideas of Mahatma Gandhi, to replace 'the huge conurbations of the industrial era… Taking a broad view, Gandhi's beliefs are closer to my own than those of any other person,' asserts Kathleen. She was an early member of the Gandhi Foundation and served on its executive committee for many years.

Visionary or crank? Like all those who offer a utopian vision of the world, some of Kathleen's ideas are so radical that they are sometimes ridiculed. Yet even those who do not share her views could not fail to be impressed by her energy, presence and the inspiration she has provided for so many over the years.

'Disinterested compassion is the most important motivation for doing anything,' she concludes, 'but the practical side of our work in promoting an alternative future is also important. If I've done anything in my life I am really proud about, it is the number of people who've gone over to veganic growing following our example. They write to me saying that they've only got a small garden or patio, but now they are producing at least some of their own food.'

Despite her obvious disenchantment with many features of modern civilisation, Kathleen Jannaway maintains a warm and compelling optimism about her fellow humans. As a Quaker (albeit an agnostic Quaker!) she believes in 'a capability of compassion in every human being' and that 'if life is going to go on we must develop that capacity. Otherwise we're finished. Eventually I think we will come through.'

In the last thirty years she has seen thousands adopt a vegan diet and believes that the trend will continue. With a smile she adds that her only regret is that she will

• • • • • • • • • • • • • • • • • • • • • • • • • • • • • • • • • • • • •

not be around to find out how far her vision will be fulfilled. 'My saddest comment on my age is the Browning one,' she says:

> 'O what the world will do
> And I not here to see it.'

## 6 The vegetarian revolution

Compared to the horrific conditions described in private Victorian abattoirs or the early meat plants of Chicago, modern abattoirs do appear comparatively efficient and ordered. Yet all is relative. The focus upon live exports may have tended to encourage the view that appalling slaughterhouses are now mostly only a foreign problem, but a 1984 report from the UK government's own advisory committee demonstrated clearly that conditions remain barbaric — even in nations which enjoy the highest reputation for animal protection. Poor design, concern for speed and throughput at the expense of welfare, insensitive handling and inefficient slaughter methods were all heavily criticised.[2] Alongside disquiet about standards of care have come consistent reports of poor hygiene leading to carcasses cross-contaminated with dangerous bacteria.

One of the achievements of the modern animal protection movement has been to bring the previously secret world of the abattoir into sharp public focus. Combined with numerous health scares, the effect has been to turn vegetarianism into a mass popular movement for the first time. Numbers have increased dramatically, both for health and compassionate reasons. Vegetarian foods have become accepted in shops, restaurants and supermarkets.

According to a 1997 Gallop opinion poll, 5.4% of the UK population (over 3 million) have now adopted a vegetarian diet, a massive increase from 2.1% when regular surveys were first conducted in 1984. The earlier figure was itself almost certainly a significant advance on previous decades. The move towards a non-meat diet is particularly prevalent amongst young women, where it rises to more than 22%.[2]

In the US, 5% of the population now consider themselves to be vegetarian, though the true figure is thought to be somewhat lower.[3]

Even amongst the remaining large majority who still eat meat, there are some dramatic signs of food reform. The 1997 Gallop poll shows that nearly half of the population (46%) is eating *less* meat. The number of people who avoid red meat stands at 14.3% (over 8 million) of the total population, compared to only 4% in 1984.[4]

For those who can afford to pay, there has also been a significant rise in sales of organic meats, guaranteeing minimum welfare standards in addition to freedom from potentially harmful additives.

Conversely, it is probably amongst those who need it most that dietary reform has had the least impact. Cheaper meats — sausages, burgers, pies — continue to be the staple diet of many of the poorer members of society — almost certainly contributing towards a widening gap between the health of the haves and have nots. The high fat, low fibre diet associated with high meat consumption is increasingly implemented in the epidemics of heart disease and cancers affecting Western civilisation.

Although people in many parts of the developed world are now eating less meat than for several decades, the number of animals killed for the table is still rising at a considerable rate. This is largely because of the trend towards consumption of cheap (and comparatively small) poultry, rather than larger red meat animals. By 1996, in the UK alone approximately 850 million animals were killed for food.

In the US, the annual figure is around 7 billion.[5]

# 7 / Animal experiments: 'Everything changes and everything remains the same'

## 1  Shambles of science and the Brown Dog

Two separate events from either end of the twentieth century offer a revealing insight into progress in both official and public attitudes to animal experiments. Both involve campaigns instigated by courageous women in their early twenties, so dedicated to the anti-vivisection cause that they were prepared to infiltrate laboratories in order to expose practices which they could hardly bear to witness.

In 1900, two young Swedish women, Emilie Louise Augusta Lind-af-Hageby and Liesa Katria Schartau, arrived in Paris with a letter of introduction to the famous Pasteur Institute. Both came from privileged backgrounds and, even though she was only twenty-one, Miss Lind-af-Hageby in particular had already made an impact in Swedish humanitarian circles. She had lectured extensively on issues as diverse as prison reform and women's rights and had also contributed regularly to the Swedish press.

With Miss Schartau she shared a keen interest in science: hence their visit to the 'famous centre of medical research' in Paris 'to learn and admire'. What they found, however, incited their contempt rather than respect. Rabbits, cats, dogs and monkeys were found amongst what Louise later described as 'vast rooms filled with hundreds of animals that had been inoculated with diseases'. In particular, 'the suffering and intense appeal' of one dog 'with strangely expressive eyes' affected her profoundly when 'it stood up and tried to reach me with his front paws'.[1]

On their return to Sweden, both women determined to expose what they considered to be the evil of animal research. They became active in the anti-vivisection movement and Louise publicised their findings in articles.

Convinced that they needed first hand experience to enhance their credibility as campaigners, Louise and Lisa next planned an anti-vivisection initiative which, arguably, created more impact in the United Kingdom than any other that has followed. In 1902, they enrolled as students at the Women's School of Medicine in London, thus gaining the right to attend courses and demonstrations in physiology and other subjects. As students they fared well — regarded by their physiology tutor as 'very advanced and intelligent' — but their real purpose was subversive; to record details of the treatment of animals, both in kennels and during experiments. From autumn 1902 to the spring of 1903 they kept a diary, later to be published in book form under the title *The Shambles of Science*.[2]

In the book, descriptions of the suffering of individual animals are described under chapter headings such as 'The Quiet Cat', 'The Dog That Escaped' and 'The Struggling Cat'. Another chapter, entitled 'Fun', exposes the callous and cavalier attitude which often accompanied animal demonstrations. It cited the appalling treatment of a particular small brown dog which — apparently inadequately anaesthetised — was still alive and in pain when taken from the lecture room after having an incision made in its neck. Its struggles were ignored. Failure to ensure proper anaesthesia throughout a lecture or demonstration was itself an infringement of the law. But more significantly, Lisa and Louise noticed that the dog also had a recent abdominal wound, thus breaking the legal clause which stipulated that an animal should not be used in more than one experiment.

Enter Stephen Coleridge, then Honorary Secretary of the National Anti-Vivisection Society (NAVS), who read the book and understood the legal implications. Realising that a criminal prosecution was impossible because the statutory six months had passed since the incident had occurred, he decided instead to force a court case by publicly accusing the lecturer in question. (Names and addresses had deliberately been omitted from *The Shambles of Science*.) At a public meeting at St James Hall he read a statement in which he named Professor William Bayliss, leaving the researcher little choice other than to take action for libel against Coleridge and NAVS.[3]

The subsequent court case revealed fuller details of the dog's ordeal. It was admitted that it had been used twice. An experiment on its abdomen by a Professor Starling had deprived it of proper use of its pancreas in December 1902; it was then kept in a cage for two months before a second abdominal cut had been performed. Half an hour later, Professor Starling clamped the wound and presented the dog to Bayliss, who made an incision in the neck before taking it to the lecture room for the demonstration which had been witnessed by the Swedish anti-vivisectionists.

The original Brown Dog memorial in Battersea.

Another half an hour passed before the dog — in great pain — was killed.

Despite the emergence of these facts, the case against Dr Bayliss was lost on the grounds that the anaesthetic condition of the dog could not be proven. Considerable costs of £2000 were awarded against Coleridge and the National Anti-Vivisection Society. But far from being the end of the matter, the court's decision simply served to stir public outrage. *The Daily News* — a popular national newspaper of the time — took up the cause in no uncertain manner:

> *We can only say that the whole admitted details of the operation — the laughter of the students, the throwing down of the unhappy animal after the operation, the careless indifference of all concerned — throw no favourable light on the state of mind and morals produced by scientific study under modern conditions…*
>
> *Is it not worth considering whether the human race may not pay too heavy a penalty for knowledge acquired in this manner? Are we to leave out of count altogether the hardening of heart and searing of sensitive feeling that must be produced by the constant spectacle of such unmerited suffering?… This is not a matter which can be allowed to rest here. We are all responsible for the hideous defiance of the laws of humanity.*[4]

The newspaper opened a subscription fund for the defendants which — alongside other contributions — raised £5735 in four months. This was a large sum for those days.

More was to follow. Anger at the verdict remained so strong that another fund was opened, this time to erect a memorial to the unfortunate dog. In September 1906, a drinking fountain and monument was unveiled in Battersea Park by the local authority. Battersea had been chosen partly in recognition of its radical council, but also because it had become the home of an Anti-Vivisection Hospital, opened in 1902. This was the main source of medical treatment for the local community, dispensing mostly homeopathic remedies. The hospital had a

> In Memory of the Brown Terrier Dog
> done to death in the Laboratories
> of University College in February
> 1903, after having endured Vivisection
> extending over more than Two Months
> and having been handed from
> one Vivisector to another
> till Death came to his Release.
>
> *(Inscription on the statue)*

policy which prohibited not only animal experiments, but also the employment of any doctor who had been involved in them. This remained in place until its closure in 1971.

The story then moves on to November of the following year when a group of medical students from University College — outraged by the specific condemnation of their college on the memorial — attempted to smash it up. Although they failed and ten were arrested and fined, the incident marked the beginning of three extraordinary years of agitation which became known as the Brown Dog Riots. At regular intervals medical students descended upon Battersea to try to destroy the monument, only to be opposed by its defenders — the Metropolitan Police and the youth of the borough. At times these encounters reached considerable ferocity. On one occasion about a hundred students arrived at the park at five o'clock in the evening and were involved in seven hours of violent confrontation, described as follows in the next day's *Standard* newspaper:

> *At Battersea, the demonstrators met with a warm reception. Hostile crowds sided with the police, and attacked anybody whom they imagined to be students. None of the demonstrators was able to approach the statue, but at times it looked as if the disturbances might assume a dangerous character.*[5]

Local feelings ran high. Residents in this working class area seemed to see the dog as a symbol of their own oppression by the more privileged members of society. They distrusted science and modern medicine, believing correctly that poor people were themselves sometimes victims of medical experimentation by ambitious and unscrupulous doctors. The distrust was also fuelled by the arrogance and contempt displayed towards them by some members of the medical world. This was best illustrated by a comment in a 1903 edition of the *British Medical Journal*, condemning those 'who doubtless find the blood and thunder of the anti-vivisection drama a stimulating addition to the drink, betting and other wanton indulgences, which … are their natural amusements'.[6]

One witness to events in Battersea was Edward Ford, who recorded his observations in *The Brown Dog and Its Memorial*, published in 1908. On arriving by bus in South London to begin his investigation, he asked a young boy if he knew where the monument was located. 'Our dorg, sir?' came the reply. 'I should think I know! I helped to fight the stoodents. And if they're coming again, we'll give 'em what for!' According to Ford, the boy went on to condemn 'them stuck-up chaps who yell and shriek 'cause they want more haminals to cut up' and to claim that his dad had told

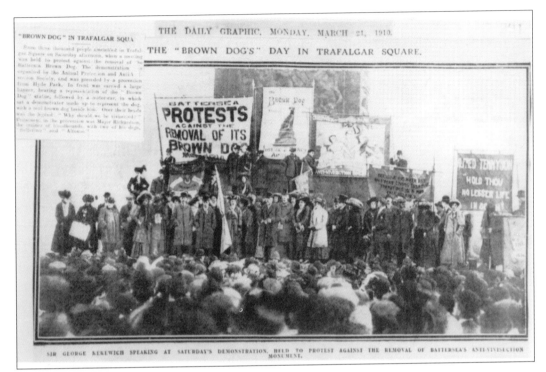

Protest against the removal of the Brown Dog memorial, Trafalgar Square, 1910.

him that he would 'rather die in peace than have them doctorin' 'im… We don't trust them 'ere in Battersea,' the boy concluded. 'We've got an 'orspital of our own, where the doctors don't believe in cutting haminals up alive.'[7]

The ramifications of the controversy were extensive. University College students took to attending anti-vivisection gatherings, heckling speakers and breaking up meetings. All that this achieved was to ensure far greater publicity than would otherwise have been afforded. According to *The Star* newspaper the students achieved 'more for the anti-vivisection movement than all the anti-vivisectionists have ever done'.[8] The costs of protecting the monument soared; questions were asked in the House of Commons; the Home Secretary was requested to intervene (he refused) and pressure was put upon Battersea Borough Council to have the reference to University College removed from the statue in order to avoid the mounting police bill. It responded defiantly in January 1908, voting to retain the inscription.

Although the next two years saw a gradual quietening down in the conflict, sporadic incidents continued until 1910, when the Brown Dog affair ended suddenly and anti-climactically. Under the instruction of a newly elected borough council the statue was removed secretly in the middle of the night. A protest march and rally was organised to call for the memorial to be returned, attended by between 1000 and 3000 people. But the monument was never to be seen again. Fairly rapidly, events faded from public spotlight.

Nevertheless, the affair was not forgotten by anti-vivisectionists. In 1985, a second brown dog memorial was erected in Battersea Park, jointly funded by the British Union for the Abolition of Vivisection and the National Anti-Vivisection Society. It remains there to this day, tucked away in a quiet area of the grounds.

The level of public debate stimulated by *The Shambles of Science* was so great that the government was roused into a response, setting up a second Royal Commission in 1906 to investigate whether changes in the law were necessary. How far this was a genuinely disinterested attempt to establish the validity of vivisection or an elaborate attempt to allay public disquiet is open to question, particularly as there was a heavy bias of pro-vivisection interests serving on the eight man committee. Either way, it was certainly scrupulous in its attention to detail, taking six years to produce a final report which ran to six volumes and included the full evidence of all witnesses. As ever, defenders of experiments reasoned that pain inflicted on animals was always kept to an absolute minimum and that this could be justified because of the great medical discoveries that had been and would continue to be achieved. Against this, it was argued that experimentation on animals was morally indefensible and scientifically crude. None stated the anti-vivisectionist position more powerfully than Louise Lind-af-Hageby herself:

*I wish to plead the priority and the ultimate persistence of the moral objection and revolt against experiments upon living animals… Moral evolution has forced us to include the sub-human races in the circle of our compassion and our sympathy. Kindness to animals, gradually passing into a conscious acknowledgement of their rights and our duties towards them, is the last and the finest product of our developing altruism. In the light of progressive morals, anti-vivisection is not an isolated fad, or the expression of uncurbed sentiment — it is part of a great whole, of a humanitarianism which includes every sentient creature in its protective embrace, and which condemns every form of cruelty to man or beast…*

*I am prepared to say that nothing which I would call useful has been obtained by experiments on the lower animals… I believe that the abolition of vivisection when these methods are discarded will be followed by new scientific methods and new scientific light, and that science need not suffer. Science has immense possibilities.[9]*

With her natural eloquence, it was little wonder that Louise was establishing herself as an unofficial figurehead of a powerful and popular anti-vivisection movement. Public meetings were well attended and an audience of 'several thousands' attended 'the great demonstration' in Trafalgar Square in 1908 at which she spoke. A year later she organised one of two international congresses held in London. Two hundred and fifty societies attended, representing thirty countries.[10]

A further measure of the seriousness with which the anti-vivisection message was embraced is that active support was forthcoming from several leading politicians and intellectual figures. George Bernard Shaw gave two public lectures in 1900 and four members of what was later to become the first Labour government were among the vice-presidents at one of the anti-vivisection congresses of 1909. These included Ramsay MacDonald, Labour's first ever Prime Minister, and R. J. Clynes, who became Home Secretary.

Faced with such impressive opposition, pro-vivisection interests also became better organised. Mr Stephen Paget — whose father had been a leading proponent of animal experiments in Victorian times — was particularly outspoken. In 1908 he formed the Research Defence Society (RDS) with a specific mandate to defend animal experiments and to promote what it claimed as 'the immense importance of such experiments to the welfare of mankind'. The RDS continues to fulfil this role to this day.

The breadth of the vivisection debate during the first years of the century reaffirms what the earlier portrait of Henry Salt indicated — namely, that in this period people were probably more responsive to enlightened humanitarian ideas than at any other time until the last decades of the century. Not all those who passionately abhorred vivisection would have shared Louise Lind-af-Hageby, Liesa Schatau or Salt's coherent vision of a world in which cruelty to animals was seen as inseparable from exploitation of humans, but widespread gut-feeling opposition to experiments was sufficiently strong to create an anti-vivisection movement of considerable influence.

In the end though its achievements were less than they might have been. At the same time as public disquiet was at its most vehement, experimental medicine was also becoming more firmly established. In percentage terms, the period 1880-1910 represents the most rapid period of growth ever in the number of vivisections conducted annually (from 311 to 95,731). Perhaps the last chance to curb its further escalation ended when the Royal Commission published its Final Report in 1912 and rejected the moral case for total abolition as 'inconsistent if not preposterous' given 'the present state of society and of public opinion'.[11] Nor did it recommend any more than minor modifications to the 1876 Cruelty to Animals Act, which remained the governing legislation up until 1986. This huge disappointment to the anti-vivisectionist movement was soon to be followed by the outbreak of war and a diminishment of influence from which it did not really begin to recover for a further sixty years.

While Liesa Schatau faded from public life, Louise Lind-af-Hageby went on to champion humanitarian causes for many decades. Some of her life-long achievements on behalf of animals have been mentioned earlier, notably her rescue of Ferne Animal Sanctuary after the death of the Duchess of Hamilton in 1951. She also formed her own organisation, the Animal Defence Society, for which she worked tirelessly for decades. It was established 'on the principle that the cause of humanity to animals is not a side-issue but a vital part of civilisation and social development'. Its scope extended to many areas of animal welfare, from setting up veterinary hospitals to campaigning against hunting, slaughterhouse conditions, fur-trapping and the use of pit ponies in coal mines.[12]

Louise was equally involved in charitable work for people. In the 1920s, she wrote a book calling passionately for women of the twentieth century to lead a campaign to prevent future war and another on the right of women to work. In Europe, she helped to house children from distressed families, funding much of the work from her personal fortune.

She died in 1963, aged eighty-three.[13]

## 2   Silent suffering: Sarah Kite and Huntingdon Laboratories

Eighty-five years after the two young Swedish women had exposed the use of animals at University College, a twenty-five-year-old social worker embarked on her own initiative against vivisection. In the autumn of 1988, Sarah Kite — employed as an undercover investigator by the British Union for the Abolition of Vivisection (BUAV) — answered an advertisement for a weekend worker at Huntingdon Research Centre in Cambridgeshire, as part of a plan to infiltrate the secret world of the largest commercial animal research centre in Europe.

Her task was in some ways very different from that of her predecessors. When Liesa Schartau and Louise Lind-af-Hageby took up their position as 'students' in London, the Home Office put the total number of experiments conducted in the UK at 19,084: when Sarah actually began her employment in 1989, the figure had risen to more than 3.3 million. Animal experiments had become sophisticated big business, spawning several 'contract laboratories' such as Huntingdon which exist solely to carry out research on behalf of any company anywhere in the world which chooses to employ it. In 1988 alone, Huntingdon used more than 128,000 animals, employed more than 1000 staff and ran offices overseas in Paris, Tokyo and Washington D. C.[1]

Another development was the very great secrecy associated with animal research by the latter part of the century. Large and isolated industrial complexes, fans and furnaces, security guards, high wire fencing topped with barbed wire, video cameras and blacked out windows had become characteristic features of the environment. Although this was in part a reaction to the threat of attack by the Animal Liberation Front, it was also governed by the acknowledged need to hide the nature of the business from public scrutiny. Back in 1974 — before the active days of militant animal rights campaigners — the Research Defence Society had produced guidance notes 'compiled with the collaboration of the Home Office Cruelty to Animals Act Inspectorate'. It advised:

> *Premises selected and prepared for experimental animal usage should ideally be in a quiet place undisturbed by traffic and out of sight of the general public and afforded minimal publicity.*[2]

Given the degree of security, it is something of a surprise that Sarah Kite found employment at all. She was not the first person to infiltrate laboratories by taking a job and the animal research industry was known to operate a screening service based upon a large databank of animal rights sympathisers held by the Research Defence Society. Yet despite her involvement in campaigns over several years, Sarah's past activity was not spotted. On Saturday 21 January 1989 she was able to join the Huntingdon staff, employed to feed and water animals and clean out cages.

Her account of the next eight months at Huntingdon does not make pleasant reading. Although she failed to gain access to the large primate complex, she did spend five months in the Rodent Toxicology Unit, followed by a further three working in Dog Toxicology. She criticises the housing conditions. 'Most rats', Sarah writes, are 'squashed five to a cage with no bedding, living on metal grid floors, so that urine and faeces could fall through onto the trays below'. In the dog unit she found 'beagles that lived out their lives in small, bare cages isolated from each other'. She either witnessed personally or else found documentary evidence of animals dosed with an astonishing array of substances. These ranged from drugs for psoriasis, arthritis, fungal infections and psychosis, to food colourants, ingredients for cling film and insecticides. Products were administered by a variety of methods, including capsule, implant by tube into the stomach, being mixed with food, applied to skin, or force fed through a tube pushed down the throat.

According to Huntingdon's own day record book, symptoms of suffering in the rodent house included 'red discharge from anus', 'wet ulceration', 'swollen abdomen', 'hyperactive', 'gasping', 'limbs splayed out', 'unsteady gait', 'emaciated' and 'lethargic'. Sarah herself describes dogs with 'weeping sores', 'grazed raw skin, covered in blood' and 'vomiting and retching'. She also recounts beagles 'rigid with fear' and 'petrified and cowered in their cages'.

Pain and suffering apart, another of Sarah's observations which recalls *The Shambles of Science* is what she considered the 'callous, uncaring attitude' of many of the staff at Huntingdon. She tells how 'the rats and mice became the object of ridicule and their suffering an amusing topic for conversation during coffee breaks' and criticises the method by which technicians grabbed dogs 'roughly', often by the scruff of the neck.

Sarah finally left Huntingdon for the last time on 16 September 1989, 'overwhelmed by the grief and anger that had built up inside me for the last eight months'. On that day, she witnessed beagle dogs desperately trying to avoid unsympathetic handling while a long tube was 'forced down their throats and directly into their stomachs'. She decided that she 'could take no more'.

Her investigation came to the nation's attention on 20 November 1989 in the now defunct daily newspaper, *Today*. The paper ran a four page special report and an editorial demanding that the Home Secretary give 'top priority' to the findings. There were demonstrations held outside the gates of Huntingdon and a local protest group was formed. Local television and national radio covered events extensively. Both *Today* and the BUAV were inundated with calls and letters from shocked and outraged members of the public.

Despite the considerable level of public support and sympathy, however, the reaction of officialdom merely served to affirm how deeply entrenched the system of animal experimentation had become. Peter Lloyd — Home Office minister of the day — chose a knee-jerk reaction, praising the 'standards of care and the conduct of scientific procedures' at Huntingdon and stating that 'in many ways, it would serve as an excellent example to others'.[3] His only positive move was to suggest that his advisory committee should examine whether it would be possible to relax the level of secrecy in laboratories — a question which remains unanswered nearly ten years on.

Like Louise Lind-af-Hageby and Lisa Schartau before her, Sarah Kite's life was changed for ever by the experience of witnessing animal experiments. For one thing it left a determination to continue campaigning. In addition to working full-time for the BUAV for most of the last decade, she has also given a home to a number of beagles rescued from breeding establishments that have closed down. 'Their happiness and zest for life is a joy to watch as they hurtle around on the heath, totally oblivious to the fate that could so easily have been theirs,' she comments.

But she also bears emotional scars. 'I will never be able to forget those months I spent working undercover. The sickening smell, the noise, the attitude of the staff, but most of all the suffering of the thousands of animals imprisoned there will remain permanently etched in my memory. In particular, I remember the plight of the beagles. Dogs rigid with fear, cowering in the corner of their cages as staff reached to grab them for their daily dosing. Others offered little resistance as they sat forlornly, their spirits broken and a look of utter dejection in their eyes.'

Nonetheless, she has no regrets. 'I would like to think that I was able to be the voice of the thousands of animals imprisoned there, to bear witness to their pain and despair and to present to the outside world the reality of life behind the locked door of the research laboratory,' she affirms. This she certainly achieved. Her investigation changed other lives besides her own — ordinary people who were drawn to the anti-vivisection cause by the force of her evidence.

Regrettably, however, we now know that it brought little change inside Huntingdon. In 1996, Sarah was involved as a consultant on a Channel 4 television documentary which succeeded in gaining employment inside the laboratory for Zoe Broughton, another investigator. What was filmed with a secret camera proved conclusively both the validity of Sarah's original claims and the failure of authority to respond to them. When broadcast in March 1997, the appropriately titled *It's a Dog's Life* revealed how beagle dogs were punched, violently shaken and roughly handled by laughing technicians. It showed animals yelping as repeated attempts to draw blood from their veins were bungled. Callous treatment, incompetence, scientifically banal procedures and humiliating treatment were all disclosed.

Some action did follow the documentary. Two technicians (both of whom had been employed when Sarah had undertaken her investigation) were suspended and later prosecuted. Huntingdon Life Sciences — as it is now known — was rebuked and given only a few months to persuade the Home Secretary that 'measures have been put in place to prevent any recurrence of events shown in the television programme'. Predictably, the laboratory was deemed to have succeeded in this and its licence was renewed in October 1997. In a statement to the House of Commons, the government had previously stated its concern about the potential loss of 1400 jobs if the laboratory were permanently closed down.

In 1997, Huntingdon experienced further condemnation when People for the Ethical Treatment of Animals published the findings of its own eight month under-cover investigation at one of the company's subsidiary US laboratories. In early 1998, this led to a decision by the US Department of Agriculture to invoke charges for multiple violations of the US Animal Welfare Act.

## 3 Fifty years in the wilderness

The hopes and optimism of early twentieth-century anti-vivisectionists proved unfounded as science and technology were increasingly embraced as the potential saviours of humanity.

Between the two world wars the number of experiments rose dramatically, spurred by the availability of public funds through the establishment of the Medical Research Council in 1920. More than this, however, it was simply advancing faith in the powers of science which provided impetus. In the field of experimental medi-cine, research was hastened in new areas such as chemical drug development, hormone therapy and vitamin supplements — as well as the longer established disci-plines of immunology, pharmacology and physiology. By 1943, the official number of animal experiments exceeded one million for the first time.[1]

Against this tide of confidence in science, the anti-vivisection movement proved helpless. From time to time it enjoyed brief moments of influence, but with medical practitioners regularly producing effective new treatments and the constant promise of a stream of 'wonder drugs', defenders of animal experiments became ever more untouchable. The status quo view was exemplified succinctly in an article written for the *Sunday Express* in 1927 by the novelist, H. G. Wells. Entitled 'The Way the World is Going', it defended vivisection, arguing that the pain inflicted was insignificant when compared to the knowledge to be gained in the quest of science to create a better world.

George Bernard Shaw was invited to respond on behalf of anti-vivisectionists, maintaining that knowledge should never be produced by what he labelled 'criminal methods':

*The Anti-Vivisector does not deny that physiologists must make experiment and even take chances with new methods. He says that they must not seek knowledge by criminal methods, just as they may not make money by criminal methods. He does not object to Galileo dropping cannon balls from the top of the leaning tower of Pisa; but he would object to shoving off two dogs, or two American tourists.[2]*

No doubt Shaw's view did have many sympathisers and the fact that he was asked to state his opinion at all is evidence that the beliefs propounded by Wells were not universally popular. Nonetheless, it is certainly true that by this time many of the doubts and suspicions about the legitimate boundaries of science, debated so fiercely during and immediately after the Victorian Age, had largely been dispelled.

With the scientific community enjoying unprecedented popular prestige and all but a tiny minority of its spokesmen championing vivisection as vital to medical progress, researchers were also able to develop a persuasive political voice. In 1929, when the Labour government came to power for the second time, the Prime Minister, Home Secretary and two other senior members of the cabinet were personally committed anti-vivisectionists (readers may recall that they had been vice-presidents at a Congress organised in 1909), but not only did they withdraw support for an outright ban from the Labour agenda, they also refused to uphold less radical proposals to exempt dogs from experimentation. The Home Secretary, J. R. Clynes, stated that 'he had to harmonise his public duties with his private opinion' and that 'the best possible advice' opposed any change.[3] Such 'advice' was, of course, the evidence of the Medical Research Council and others from the research lobby.

The period after the second world war witnessed further escalation in the use of animals. Medical experiments were one source of the increase, stimulated particularly by the rapid development of the pharmaceutical industry following the discovery of antibiotic and antibacterial therapies. The vaccination industry was another major factor, provoking a near holocaust in the capture and exploitation of primates for their tissue in polio and other viruses.

But medicine was only one factor. Commercial interests recognised the potential of science to develop an astonishing range of hitherto unknown products. Household cleaners, cosmetics and over-the-counter medicines all began to proliferate on the market, symbolising an easing of post-war austerity. For younger readers, it is difficult to comprehend that not even washing-up liquid was widely available in shops until well after 1945, let alone any of the other specialised cleaning products which are now taken for granted as part of everyday life.

Animals paid a high price for these changes in human living standards. The proliferation of new products stimulated crude testing procedures to assess potential dangers to consumers. For example, the LD50 test had been invented in 1927 to assess the strength of drugs: now it also became the standard means of predicting the potential toxicity of all commercial goods, ranging from weedkillers to lipsticks and toothpastes.[4] (LD50 is shorthand for the lethal dose at which 50% of a batch of animals are poisoned to death. Despite consistent criticism of its efficacy, with some modifications it has remained the most common method of measuring toxicity.)

First used in 1944, the Draize test also became an integral part of routine research procedures.[5] It involved dripping the test substance into the eyes over a period of days to observe the damage caused. Rabbits were soon established as the favourite 'animal model'. As the years passed by thousands were blinded annually in an attempt to assess a bewildering array of powerful chemicals.

In the decades following the second world war, it seems that almost every human hope, fear, aspiration and folly was a signal for largely unquestioned experimentation. Humanity was swept away in its enthusiasm for the possibility of a technological 'brave new world', compared to which the moral question of our exploitation of animals seems to have been mostly ignored. There were also fresh demands from newly popular academic disciplines such as psychology, while the rapid expansion of ingredients for agricultural and industrial chemicals created further excuse for expansion.

The Cold War proved to be yet another cause of suffering. It provided impetus for an escalation in poison gas and other weapons experiments conducted at the top secret Chemical Defence Establishment at Porton Down and by all major powers. Massive budgets were allocated to military research. At its most obscene, this led in 1946 to the US government dropping an atomic bomb in the Pacific Ocean on a target of 75 ships loaded with 4500 live animals in order to assess injuries and the effects of radioactivity. Ignoring any ethical implications, President Truman stated that 'these tests are in the nature of a laboratory experiment' which 'should give information … essential to intelligent planning'.[6]

Probably the most potent symbol of how twentieth-century worship of technological progress has been accompanied by a correspondingly primitive abuse of non-humans is offered by our ultimate scientific quest: the space race. From its conception, animal sacrifice was crucial to the vision. In 1957, the Soviets fired the first dog, Laika, into space. She was lost in orbit after a week. A year later the Americans responded by launching a squirrel monkey named Gordo. He was blasted 300 miles up in the nose cone of a missile and travelled 1700 miles before he died over the South Atlantic. In January 1961, the first chimpanzee astronaut, Ham, was

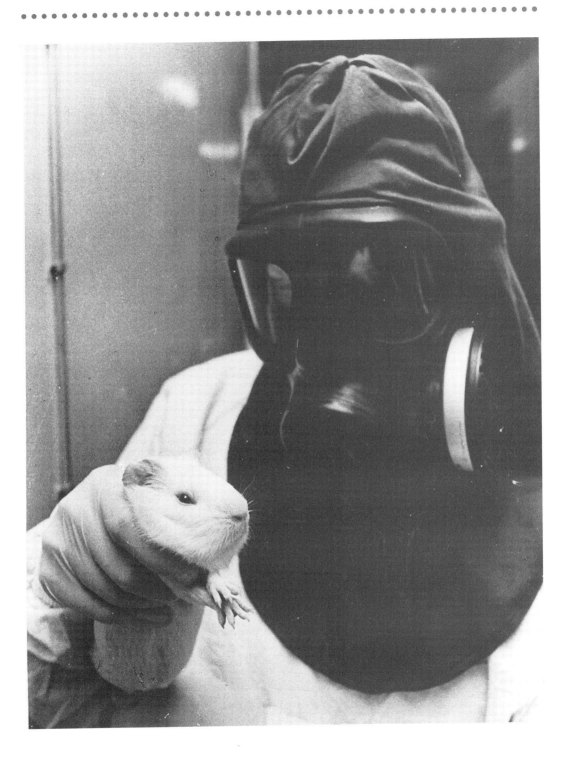

This guinea pig was one of hundreds of thousands of twentieth-century victims of warfare research.

propelled into space. Not only did he survive the ordeal, he was even feted as a national hero on his return. He is now buried in the International Space Hall of Fame in New Mexico.[7]

When President John F. Kennedy made his famous speech in 1961, prioritising the programme to put a man on the moon by the end of the decade, he let loose an even more insane commitment of resources. Animal suffering increased. Many thousands of unnamed victims died in the quest, some in orbit, but most during almost equally barbaric routine space simulation experiments back on earth. The famous 'one giant leap for mankind' achieved by the moon landing in 1969 had been accompanied by a giant leap backwards for animal welfare.

In spite of an end to uncritical support for space programmes, research on animals has continued into the 1990s. It became the centre of protests in 1997, following revelations about the Bion 11 Project carried out at NASA. A joint mission by the USA, France and Russia forced monkeys through an agonising series of experiments on earth before they were blasted into space for a period of fourteen days. The experiments were designed to help study the effect of weightlessness on human astronauts. It was at least a sign of some enlightenment that on this occasion NASA was pressurised into giving way to public protest, suspending the experiments in April 1997. Other less publicised animal research continues.

While the priorities of the decades after the second world war left little room for a vibrant anti-vivisection movement, it ploughed on as best it could. Probably its most influential spokesperson of the period was a British war hero who had been knighted for services in defence of his country. Air Chief Marshal Lord Dowding had been supreme commander of the Royal Air Force during the Battle of Britain and his brilliance as a military campaigner won him recognition for having played a crucial role in the defeat of Nazi Germany. After he was honoured he spoke only infrequently in the House of Lords, but cruelty to animals — particularly vivisection — was a favourite theme whenever he did. His speeches often linked opposition to animal research with the pursuit of permanent peace that preoccupied many of those who had experienced the horror of war:

> *Failure to recognise our responsibilities to the animal kingdom is the cause of many calamities which now beset the nations of the world… Nearly all of us have a deep rooted wish for peace, peace on earth; but we shall never attain to true peace — the peace of love, and not the uneasy equilibrium of fear — until we recognise the place of animals in the scheme of things and treat them accordingly.*[8]

Despite his eminence, Lord Dowding's pleas were not taken seriously by authority. He found virtually no support in the House of Lords and was told in a private meeting with the Home Secretary, Lord Butler, that the government was prepared to take no measures against animal research unless requested to do so by its advisors.[9]

His family did succeed, however, in launching one far-reaching initiative. In 1959 his wife, Lady Muriel, founded Beauty Without Cruelty and produced the first range of cosmetics and toiletries to be marketed as cruelty-free.

In spite of government inflexibility, protests grew against the inadequacy of the 1876 Cruelty to Animals Act to control a practice which — by 1960 — was responsible for the death of 3.7 million animals a year in the UK. Eventually, the Conservative administration gave way and agreed to set up a new inquiry. Chaired by Sir Sydney Littlewood, its final Report carried little comfort for anti-vivisectionists when it was published in 1965. It had no significant impact.

Throughout the 1960s, the number of experiments continued to increase rapidly, soaring to 5.58 million in 1970 (the year of Lord Dowding's death). By 1980, however a slow change had begun, prompted by the beginnings of a renaissance in the anti-vivisection movement which saw it start to rock the complacency of both the scientific community and politicians.

## 4  Biting back

More attention will be given to the reasons for the re-emergence of the anti-vivisection movement in a later chapter, but one crucial element was again the influence of the hippy generation and with it, the popularisation of 'green' values. As we have seen in the emergence of the Hunt Saboteurs Association, many young people viewed opposition to cruelty to animals as inseparable from a general concern to protect and nurture the threatened environment. Alongside these feelings grew a deepening disenchantment with some aspects of science and technology. Rather than the road to any future utopia of equal rights and good health for all, to a steadily increasing minority 'progress' became associated increasingly with weapons of mass destruction, pollution and the means of ruthless suppression of the poor by the rich and powerful.

This period also saw the publication of several critical books which brought the issue of animal experimentation back into sharp focus. *Victims of Science* (1975), written by Richard Ryder — a clinical psychologist who spoke from experience, having worked with laboratory animals while he was a research student — and the hard-hitting *Slaughter of the Innocent* (1978) by Hans Ruesch, both attracted converts. Even more significant was Peter Singer's *Animal Liberation* (1975).

One person upon whom Singer's book was to have a profound impact was Jean Pink, then a junior schoolteacher near Tonbridge in Kent. She was so moved and shocked by what she read about vivisection that within a few months she had quit her teaching post to form Animal Aid and launch her own campaign. Armed with bagfuls of literature produced on a secondhand duplicator set up in her kitchen, she and a handful of colleagues regularly took the train to London to distribute leaflets at main-line railway stations during the rush hour. The results were staggering. Within months of its formation in 1977, two thousand people had joined Animal Aid and offers of active help flooded in. Offices were found; local groups were set up all over the country. Driven by boundless energy and optimism, Jean Pink asserted that a mass popular movement would be created to achieve abolition world-wide within ten years.

As unrealistic as this was to prove, her enthusiasm and unerring determination acted as a catalyst to refresh and revitalise the British anti-vivisection movement and to stimulate thousands of fresh recruits. Within a couple of years local groups were holding stalls and handing out leaflets and petitions most weekends in hundreds of British towns; regular demonstrations or vigils were held outside research laboratories; national marches were organised in several cities and attended by thousands. The immediate success of Animal Aid had a dynamic effect on the older and better established anti-vivisection societies, too. Younger and more radical staff were brought in and they also began to organise regular marches and demonstrations.

Another boost to the campaign around this time was provided by several high profile exposés of life in the vivisection laboratory. Particularly important was the rescue by a young hunt saboteur, Mike Huskisson, of two beagle dogs used in smoking experiments by the giant multinational company, ICI. He also stole documents from the company. When published in the *Sunday People* newspaper, it was revealed that dogs had been held in head clamps and forced to breathe tobacco smoke for long periods. An outcry ensued. Burglary charges brought against Huskisson were swiftly dropped, almost certainly because ICI feared even more adverse publicity.

Membership of national societies soared. By the early 1980s, animal experiments were rarely out of the news. Pressure on government to bring in new legislation to update the 1876 Cruelty to Animals Act grew. In 1983 its plans to do so were outlined in a White Paper.

Most anti-vivisection societies perceived the proposals as woefully inadequate and joined together to launch a campaign to amend them. Their aim was to ensure that certain specific tests (including cosmetics, warfare, psychology, tobacco and alcohol research) would be banned outright when plans were finally put before parliament.[1]

Powerful images such as this added new impetus to the anti-vivisection movement in the late 1970s and early 1980s.

But despite considerable investment and extensive support the initiative did not succeed, doomed from the moment that the opposition Labour Party decided it would give its backing to the government. The Animals (Scientific Procedures) Act eventually passed onto the statute book in 1986, hailed by its proponents as the best legislation in the world and as a whitewash or 'vivisectors' charter' by those opposed to animal research.

After the disappointment of its failure to influence the new legislation, the anti-vivisection movement never quite recaptured the impetus of the previous few years.

It lacked unity of purpose and direction. Different factions and organisations quarrelled over tactics. The failure to influence the legislative process gave the militant approach added credibility, particularly for young supporters.

Nevertheless, campaigns did become increasingly sophisticated. Carefully planned infiltration of laboratories to demonstrate the inadequacies of the law became one priority and several establishments found themselves embarrassed by damaging revelations. Apart from Sarah Kite's work at Huntingdon, an exposé of the world-wide trade in primates for vivisection by the British Union for the Abolition of

Vivisection proved particularly damning. The fearless Mike Huskisson also re-emerged (not for the first time since the smoking beagles) to create further controversy. He and a colleague, Melody MacDonald, first won the confidence of 89-year-old Professor Wilhelm Feldberg and later gained permission to film him at work at the Medical Research Council headquarters near London.[2] Feldberg had been an eminent scientist in his day, but as the investigation was to prove, his day had long passed. Huskisson's video camera revealed an incompetent and confused old man performing pointless and painful experiments upon rabbits and cats. It showed blatant infringements of the new legislation and cast further doubts over the level of protection granted to animals in laboratories. How, anti-vivisectionists demanded, could somebody so clearly incapable be granted a licence to perform animal work?

Official response was to treat Feldberg's case as an aberration. His licence was suspended, but predictably no prosecution followed. Although a private case was contemplated by the organisation, Advocates for Animals, it was concluded that Feldberg was probably not even mentally capable of standing trial. In over 120 years since legislation on animal research was introduced there has never been a prosecution for cruelty brought by the state against a scientist.

After a century of more or less unhindered growth, the number of animals used in the UK finally began to decline significantly. From a peak in 1974, figures have been more than halved to less than three million animals per year (2.72 million in 1996). This is a sure testament to the significant impact made by the anti-vivisection movement in the last quarter of a century.

There is also now massive public support for an end to the use of animals in the cosmetics industry and for products such as tobacco and alcohol. Protesters have succeeded, too, in raising public awareness and creating a growing market for companies which manufacture 'cruelty-free' products. Compulsory dissection for students taking GCSE examinations has been abandoned. Many powerful commercial companies have adopted a non-animal testing policy on their toiletries and household goods. More money is now invested in scientific methods which do not rely upon animals (though commitment remains pitifully small). Organisations such as the Dr Hadwen Trust pioneer new science which does not involve animals. And, perhaps most positively of all, the vitality of British campaigners has been instrumental in encouraging new initiatives all around the world.

Admirable as such achievements are, however, the right of researchers to exploit animals in pursuit of medical progress remains firmly established throughout the world.

# 8 / Animal rights revisited

## 1 Peter Singer and *Animal Liberation*

After the first world war, the concept of rights for animals more or less disappeared from public debate for sixty years. Even though by their actions many individuals showed their fellow-feeling for the kind of ideas expressed by Henry Salt, there was no focal point for concern until publication of Peter Singer's book *Animal Liberation* in 1975.

Peter Singer was born in Melbourne, Australia in 1946, the son of Jewish refugees who had fled from Vienna after the Nazis invaded Austria. Three of his grandparents failed to escape and later died in concentration camps. He describes his father as 'a businessman, quite conservative both politically and personally'. His mother — a doctor — 'came from a much more intellectual family, but that side of her was somewhat suppressed by being with my father'.

It may not have been an obvious background for a radical social reformer, but nevertheless Peter Singer describes himself as 'very much a product of the sixties'. As a young university student, he took up many of the popular social causes of the period, particularly campaigns against conscription for the Vietnam war and the movement to liberalise abortion laws. Feminism and free speech were other initiatives he 'strongly supported'.

After graduating in philosophy from Melbourne University, Peter moved to England to take a post-graduate degree at Oxford University. It was there that a chance encounter with a fellow philosophy graduate sparked his participation in the animal rights movement.

'For the first twenty-three years of my life I had no particular involvement with animals and no connection with the animal movement,' he recalls. 'Nor did I consider myself an animal lover. Then, in the autumn of 1970, during some discussion after a philosophy lecture, I started talking to a fellow student — a Canadian named Richard Keshen. The debate continued over lunch and I discovered that he was a vegetarian on ethical grounds concerned with animals. To meet a vegetarian was a much rarer thing in those days and indeed, I couldn't remember having met anybody who didn't eat meat for ethical reasons before that.'

Over lunch, Singer quizzed Keshen about his attitude to animals and the Canadian responded by posing the question: 'What do you think entitles us to treat animals in the way that we do?' Peter took this as a challenge. Surely, he thought, conventional attitudes to animals cannot be wrong? He went away — as any good philosophy student would do — and looked up what others had written.

'This was a time in the early seventies when one of the burning philosophical questions was, "What is the basis of equality for all human beings?" So I decided to approach the subject by asking why the principle of equality — which all decent people agreed should be granted to humans irrespective of their particular qualities or capacities — should apply *only* to us?'

Peter's research showed that most philosophers had either ignored or neglected the question. The minority who *had* discussed the ethical position of animals he found unconvincing. 'They maintained that only humans possess an intrinsic moral worth, but nobody satisfactorily explained why. What was this intrinsic "moral worth" that just happens to belong to all members of one species and is denied to all members of every other? When you think of the great variety of humans that exist and the great variety of animals, by whatever standard you compare them you are going to find an overlap. Some non-human animals are more rational, more intelligent and more aware than some human beings — for instance, a very young human being or a person with severe mental disabilities.'

The more that Peter Singer read, the more he became convinced that there were no good reasons why the basic principle of equality that most philosophers advocated for all human beings should not be extended to non-human animals. 'Gradually it dawned on me that rather than finding a key that would solve the riddle of why we treat animals the way we conventionally do, I had found a systematic prejudice which people could not see past. It was the same kind of thing that had previously allowed otherwise perfectly decent people to assume that they were entitled to treat Africans as slaves because they had a prejudice against extending the basic moral principles that applied to Europeans and some other races to people outside that priv-ileged group. Once I had seen this my attitude changed.'

Peter then began to discuss the issue of animal rights with fellow Oxford philos-ophy students. He soon discovered that others had been thinking along the same lines. There was not only Richard Keshen and his wife Mary, but also Englishman John Harris and another Canadian couple, Stanley and Roslind Godlovitch. In fact, the latter trio were already in the process of editing a collection of essays on the subject for a book entitled *Animals, Men and Morals*. Some of the contributions were by well-known writers such as Brigid Brophy and Margaret Duffy.

Hopes that *Animals, Men and Morals* would have great influence after its publication in 1973 were soon dashed. 'It was effectively ignored, overlooked or neglected by the entire British media. I think it merited one paragraph in the 'in brief' column of either the *Sunday Times* or the *Observer*. It was a great disappointment.'

There remained some hope, however, in that the book was later to be published in the US, which was then considered a less conservative and more open society than Britain. 'The US had been in a state of considerable ferment due to the activities of the black liberation movement, the women's movement and the anti-Vietnam war movement. Perhaps they might take the arguments a little more seriously? In particular, it seemed to me that the *New York Review of Books* — which at that time was read by every self-respecting radical intellectual — might be responsive. So I wrote

to the editor and suggested why I believed that *Animals, Men and Morals* was in a sense a manifesto for a new kind of movement and why I thought it important that it should be reviewed. I got a letter back inviting me to submit a review for consideration and that is what I did.'

It was the response to Peter Singer's review, published in the *New York Review of Books* in the spring of 1973, which created the impetus for *Animal Liberation*. In addition to correspondence praising the sentiments, the author also received a letter from a publisher suggesting the possibility of a book. And so Peter soon had a new project on his hands, writing on the basis that there was scope for an approach

that would differ from *Animals, Men and Morals* by presenting a single coherent perspective rather than a series of essays reflecting different views.

*Animal Liberation* was completed in 1974, at which time Peter Singer held the position of visiting assistant professor at the New York University Department of Philosophy. It was published in the following year. Probably for the first time in print since the writings of Henry Salt, it offered a logical vision of animals as 'independent social beings' and not 'a means to human ends'. The author's conclusion was that 'there is no reason — except the selfish desire to preserve the privilege of the exploiting group — for refusing to extend the basic principle of equality of consideration to members of other species.'

While Peter Singer was not the first to articulate such ideas, his book is considered by many to be the 'bible of the animal rights movement', providing the intellectual basis for what was to become one of the fastest growing popular causes of the 1980s. The author, however, is much more modest about his achievement. 'It is very flattering, but I think it takes more than a book to start a movement of the size of animal liberation. I think that it was going to happen anyway. There were people in different groups getting more radical about animals, thinking their way through the same questions and issues that I'd been thinking through. In fact, nothing happened immediately after the publication of the book. It was some years afterwards before you could say that there was actually an animal liberation movement.'

In more than twenty years since publication, Peter Singer has combined a successful academic career and a keen interest in other important ethical issues with consistent involvement in animal rights. He has toured the world giving talks, edited books, written articles and campaigned with the Australian organisation, *Animal Liberation*. Almost uniquely qualified to assess progress, he believes that campaigners can take 'justifiable pride' in some improvements in animal welfare and also in managing to open up a debate about the idea of equal consideration for non-human animals in many countries. Less optimistically, he concludes that 'there is a long way to go before it is truly an international movement,' citing in particular a visit to Japan in 1993 where his lectures on animal rights were greeted with 'bafflement and incomprehension.'

In 1993, Peter launched The Great Ape Project, 'a book, an idea and an organisation' with the specific aim of achieving for the first time at United Nations level a declaration which applies to non-human animals. It seeks to gain recognition for the rights of chimpanzees, gorillas and orang-utans 'to life, liberty and freedom from torture'. Great apes were selected for special treatment partly because of the high degree of public sympathy they enjoy and also because those who profit from their exploitation — smugglers, entertainers and some animal experimenters — are less powerful than some other interest groups which abuse animals. 'Above all great apes illustrate the prejudice of our attitudes more easily than any other species. To some degree they clearly possess the same capacities as humans. Intellectually, they are more sophisticated than any child under two years old or any human suffering from a severe mental disability, so where is the justification for saying that they are so different from us that rights apply to us and not to them?'

In spite of its focus upon a relatively small group of non-humans, Peter is adamant that the Great Ape Project does not represent a compromise of his beliefs. 'It is an attempt to find another route to the goals of animal liberation by breaking down the gulf between humans and animals. Hopefully, apes will become a bridge to allow wider consideration of the rights of other animals.'

Four years after its launch, Peter admits that progress has 'not been as fast as I would have wished,' though the existence of the project has helped to gain the release of some chimpanzees from laboratories into sanctuaries. He is now working on the possibility of taking a legal case in the USA in a bid to establish a precedent for the protection of apes.

Although it was never a bestseller, the steady presence of *Animal Liberation* did have considerable impact. It was read, talked about and gave significant intellectual credibility to a viewpoint which had previously tended to be dismissed as the territory only of sentimentalists. Suddenly, the rights of animals became a subject worthy of serious debate. Other philosophers responded, arguing about its legitimacy. Writers from different disciplines became involved. In the next two decades, sociologists and political historians also produced books and undergraduate students now regularly study courses in which the rights of animals are discussed. Peter Singer's own standing is such that even the *British Medical Journal* — bastion of the medical establishment — has invited him to write an editorial expressing his anti-vivisection views.

But perhaps the greatest quality of the book was that whilst its argument was sufficiently rigorous to stimulate widespread academic interest, it was written with a refreshing simplicity which made its philosophical case easily accessible to non-specialists. It also contained a new and disturbing exposé of recent developments in factory farming and animal experiments, ensuring that it maintained the power to stir readers at an emotional as well as an intellectual level.

For a multitude of reasons, many new supporters were attracted to the cause of animal protection as a result of reading it. It inspired the formation of new societies around the world. In the UK, Animal Aid was set up. In the US, it was a strong influence upon one of the co-founders of People for the Ethical Treatment of Animals. And in Peter's native Australia, the Animal Liberation organisation was formed. All are now established as powerful voices against cruelty.

The deep impulse to protect animals has always come naturally to many individuals who have not needed any establishment approval to be stirred into action. But even to dedicated 'everyday' campaigners who had been struggling on behalf of animals for decades, *Animal Liberation* gave fresh focus and new heart. One example is Irene Williams, already almost fifty years old when Singer's book was published.

## 2   Irene Williams: the original Spice Girl

Irene was born in 1927 in a small mining village near Barnsley in South Yorkshire. Her father was himself a miner and she was brought up in the harsh poverty of the place and time, alleviated partly by the clever management skills of her mother.

Her family had no pets and animals played no direct part in her early life. Yet the sentiments that later prompted her to become a committed campaigner for animal welfare were clearly evident from when she was still 'very small'. She recalls screaming with horror at the sight of a struggling fish pulled out of a pond; at the age of six her older brother told her about the annual Waterloo Cup hare coursing event, prompting similar dismay.

Although as a child she 'desperately wanted a rabbit', Irene was fifteen before she

first looked after her own pet. By this time she had left school and was working in a local commercial library. It was wartime. A colleague needed homes for kittens and Irene took one. It was to be an important event in her life. 'I really did love that kitten,' she recalls, 'but more than that I saw her vulnerability and it made me want to help other animals.' So she joined the

Irene in 1943 ...

RSPCA and became what was known as an 'auxiliary secretary' for the local branch, mostly organising flag days and running garden parties.

Between 1945 and 1949, she and her friend who was later to become her husband, Eric Williams, ran a small group of young RSPCA Animal Defenders. It met at her house regularly to discuss such issues as hunting, circuses and zoos. Irene would send off for literature and carry out research, but Eric would have to do most of the talking because she was so shy. (Eric came from a similar mining family in the neighbouring village. They met when she was eleven and he was twelve.) Irene's mother played her part too, encouraging the youngsters to attend by supplying home-made toffee!

From there, Irene and Eric progressed to the giddy heights of the committee of the local RSPCA in Barnsley. Although in some ways the two young people from the outlying industrial villages stood out from the better-off folk who dominated both this and other RSPCA committees, it is a testament to the affection they inspired that when they married in 1952 they were presented with a Shelly tea set — a gift treasured to this day. Irene's other abiding memories of the time are of her own enduring shyness; of Eric cycling for many miles around the area to collect the money from RSPCA collection boxes; and of helping out at the Society's town clinic and finding it very upsetting to witness sick animals, particularly those that had to be put down. 'I used to dread going,' she remembers.

In 1960, the Williams moved to Havant in Hampshire with their two-year-old son, Chris. Irene became more involved in anti-hunt campaigns, joining the League Against

... and campaigning against factory farming in the 1990s.

Cruel Sports and becoming one of the early members of the Hunt Saboteurs Association. 'I thought they were wonderful. I admired people that were doing that and wanted to do something myself, but I didn't know what. I always hoped that I would find others as desperate to help as I was.'

She began writing to newspapers and in 1965 the *Daily Mail* printed a letter of hers attacking stag hunting. Amongst dozens of sympathetic replies, one correspondent enclosed a leaflet about the treatment of farm animals. It was an issue Irene had not really considered before. She soon became a vegetarian.

During the next few years, Irene quietly involved herself in the embryonic stages of the modern animal rights movement. She joined Compassion In World Farming shortly after its formation and attended the launch of its film *Don't Look Now* at the Café Royal; she wrote letters and attended numerous marches, demonstrations and lobbies of parliament.

It was during this period that *Animal Liberation* was published. Irene explains its impact: 'I read it soon after it was published and it made me feel that something was really happening. It was inspiring. The fact that an academic like Peter Singer had written a book about animals at all — I felt that there was really some hope at last. Before it had all been so frustrating. It was a new focus for us all.'

By the time that Irene and Eric returned to the Barnsley area in 1977, local animal protection groups were being formed all over the country. She attended a meeting to discuss the organisation of an animal welfare show in her small local town of Penistone. Realising that factory farming might be considered too radical a subject for rural Yorkshire, she proposed instead a stall on the work of Beauty Without Cruelty. But this, too, was considered inappropriate by the organisers.

Nevertheless, the idea interested one member of the committee sufficiently for her to introduce herself to Irene at the end of the evening. The new acquaintance was a member of the Townswomen's Guild and suggested that if Irene was to join the local branch, other members could be persuaded to invite a speaker from BWC. 'I didn't really want to join, but I did so just to get the speaker,' Irene recalls. It was to prove a far-reaching decision.

At a Guild tea party the following year Irene was approached by the local social secretary, who had noticed that she was not eating any of the meaty refreshments that had been laid on! Irene explained her reasons for not consuming animal products and, much to her amazement, soon found herself invited to speak about factory farming to the local group. Torn between her natural shyness and a passionate desire to 'spread the word' she decided that, while she could not possibly give a speech, she would be willing to try to answer questions.

'The meeting was held in the Council Chambers and there I was sitting in the big chair. I introduced myself and fortunately the questions came thick and fast.' In her own words she 'did all right', so much so that at the end of the meeting it was proposed that a motion against factory farming should be taken to the National Union of Townswomen's Guild and that Mrs Williams should present it!

So it was that in May 1980 the naturally reticent miner's daughter found herself faced with the prospect of speaking to 6000 women at a packed Royal Albert Hall. She had to speak for five minutes and later to answer questions.

'I remember sitting there on that platform, steeling myself by thinking about those pigs and chickens,' she says. She also recalls watching Princess Anne leave the auditorium just before the factory farming motion was raised, presumably because the subject was considered too controversial for royalty to be associated.

Irene's motion against factory farming was passed with a large majority and was later described in the Guild newsletter as the issue which drew the largest response on the day. Her reaction was a typical mixture of joy and relief: 'I was elated, though if I hadn't got it through I would never have forgiven myself!'

In the subsequent years, Irene Williams has proved a dedicated and determined campaigner, mostly on behalf of farm animals. She helped to form a group in Sheffield and continued to organise regular stalls in town centres all across the north of England. Now a skilled speaker and broadcaster, she is one of those rare people who enjoys the challenge of campaigning for her beliefs, talking and arguing with supporters and opponents alike. She also helps to run the office of the respected Farm Animal Welfare Network and is a trustee of Compassion In World Farming — a position she holds with considerable pride.

Irene looks upon the progress that has been made in the fight for animals with some satisfaction. 'Just to see products marked as "not tested on animals" shows me how far we've come. Also, it is so easy to be a vegetarian now,' she adds. 'When I first stopped eating meat I didn't know one other person who felt the same and advice on diet was not easy to find. I thought you had to buy lots of spices to survive. I must have spent a fortune on spices!'

## 3   Militancy

Another sign of the dramatic impact of Peter Singer's book is that in the year after publication its name was being adopted by the emerging militant contingent of the animal protection movement. The Animal Liberation Front came into existence in 1976, changing its name from the Band of Mercy, which had itself been formed four

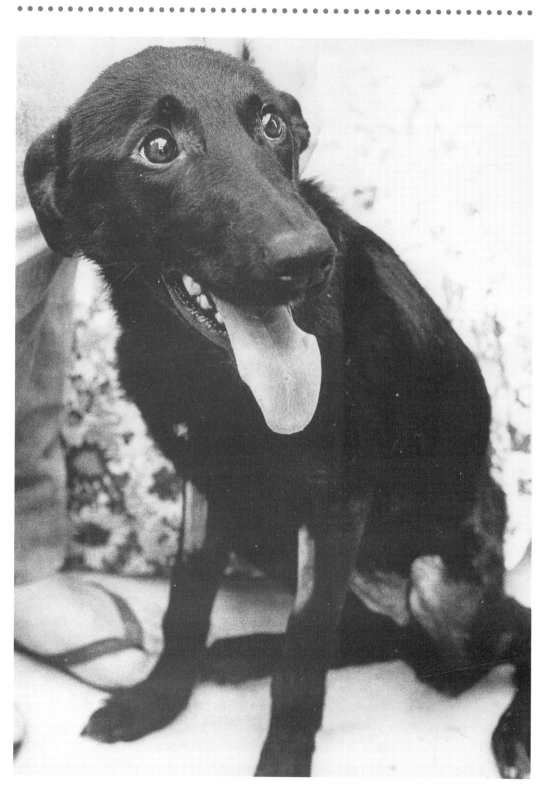

years earlier by a breakaway group from the Hunt Saboteurs.

The original purpose of the Band of Mercy had been to damage vehicles and property belonging to hunts, but it soon extended its activities. Early initiatives included setting fire to a new building belonging to a drug company involved in vivisection and the destruction of a sealhunter's vessel harboured on the Wash.

These activities evoked a surprisingly high degree of support from media and public alike, as did the early efforts of the Animal Liberation Front and associated direct action groups. Sympathy was kindled in particular by Mike Huskisson's rescue of the two beagle dogs from the laboratories of ICI in 1975 and the subsequent exposure of the company's smoking experiments. Support for the 'criminal' was almost universal, with ICI characterised as the heartless villain rather than the victim of crime.

In the wake of Huskisson's coup, media coverage of ALF activities tended to focus upon animals 'liberated' from farms and laboratories and to play down the considerable damage caused to property around the country. Indeed, the atmosphere was such that often the victims of ALF activity did not even bother to report the crime, preferring to meet the financial costs quietly rather than to risk public exposure of their activities. The police, too, often seemed reluctant to expend much effort on pursuing the activists. The prevailing image was of brave young freedom fighters saving animals from a fate worse than death at the hands of uncaring big business.

The influence of the ALF soon began to spread abroad. By the early 1980s similar groups existed in France, Canada, the USA, Germany and Australia, while in Britain increasing numbers of young people were swept with enthusiasm for what they perceived as an effective and exciting form of campaigning. Local 'liberation groups' were established. One of these, the Northern Animal Liberation League, pulled off another huge propaganda successes in 1981 when it broke into the animal holding centre of Sheffield University and rescued a black Labrador dog named Blackie. When he was later reunited with his previous owner, it provided the first concrete evidence of the existence of organised pet stealing for sale to laboratories.

In the same year, however, there were signs of a wane in public sympathy. More militant activities began to receive widespread media attention. The houses and cars of forty animal experimenters were vandalised (mostly with paint) in a co-ordinated night-time attack; then in 1982 a group calling itself the Animal Rights Militia sent letter bombs to several people viewed as 'animal abusers', none of which exploded; and in 1984, David Mellor — then Home Office minister responsible for animal experiments — had his home daubed with paint.

Left: Blackie, a stolen pet dog, after being rescued from Sheffield University in 1981

Next a campaign of 'contamination' began. Cosmetic products produced by companies involved in animal testing were 'spiked', forcing their withdrawal from shops and supermarkets. Most famously, a hoax warning was issued, claiming that Mars chocolate bars had been poisoned because of company sponsorship of dental research on primates. This strategy propelled the ALF into national headlines in November 1984, but unlike earlier times, the publicity was almost all negative. The organisation was presented as a terrorist threat to freedom and democracy, comparable to the IRA.

The Mars Bar incident provoked a much more serious response from authority, too. Scotland Yard announced the formation of a special police squad to 'hunt down animal rights fanatics'.[1] Those who were arrested on charges connected with any illegal activities on behalf of animals found themselves facing stiff prison sentences.

Some within the ALF seemed to thrive upon the terrorist label, almost deliberately inciting hostility. ALF literature began to carry provocative headlines, encouraging readers to 'devastate to liberate'. Arson was advocated; carefully illustrated descriptions of how to make incendiary devices were distributed. The police crackdown was met with hopelessly naive and immature defiance: 'the special squads and the vicious sentences represent the last desperate cries of a dying monster', stated the ALF Supporters Group in February 1985. Campaigns, too, became more outrageous. The Animal Rights Militia reappeared, threatening to injure and kill. In 1986 it claimed responsibility for placing small bombs under the cars of four animal experimenters. All were safely defused.

At the same time as a vociferous minority were beginning to advocate anarchism and violence, others embarked upon a different style of venture. Laboratories were broken into during daylight hours; documents were taken, video film was obtained and animals were rescued. Particularly effective was a group calling itself the South Eastern Liberation League, which, over August Bank Holiday in 1984, entered the laboratories of the Royal College of Surgeons (RCS) in Kent and gathered film and photographs. One of the monkeys they discovered was so dehydrated that its condition was to form the basis of an initially successful prosecution of the RCS (later overturned on a legal technicality) by the BUAV. Perhaps even more disturbing than the case that went to court were the pictures obtained of another monkey, upon whose forehead researchers had tattooed the word CRAP. It was a powerful image which prompted understandable outrage.

For a short period the efforts of SEALL and other similar groups received enormous publicity and significant support, but success was shortlived. Daylight attacks on laboratories involved large numbers of people and identification and surveillance of participants was relatively easy. Mass arrests and harsh sentences resulted in the tactic soon being abandoned.

Meanwhile, the more militant wing of the ALF had embarked on a campaign of arson against fur shops. Small incendiary devices were timed to ignite at night, thereby setting off sprinkler systems and ruining coats. After £200,000 worth of damage was caused at one shop in Sheffield, the authorities stepped in. More than twenty people were arrested, including Ronnie Lee, long-term public spokesman for the ALF. One of the original founders of the Band of Mercy, Lee had already served two prison sentences when, ten years later, he found himself in court again.

## 4   Ronnie Lee: 'Dangerous criminal'?

The man described by the judge at his 1987 trial as a 'fanatic' and a 'dangerous criminal' was brought up in Stevenage in Hertfordshire. As a child he was 'no more fond of animals than the average kid,' caring for the family pets but not thinking far beyond them. He did reasonably well at school, 'scraping a couple of A levels,' and when he was eighteen became an articled clerk for a firm of solicitors in nearby Luton. It was during his four years of employment in the legal profession that the cause of animal rights began to assume increasing significance for him.

It began when his sister started going out with a vegetarian. 'He was a very fit guy, a good athlete who threw the javelin for the county,' recalls Ronnie. 'I hadn't thought much about it before, but after a while I tossed and turned for a few nights and decided I couldn't find any excuse not to be a vegetarian! Fortunately, my sister came to the same decision at roughly the same time, so we were able to support each other against our parents, who were not very sympathetic.'

A couple of years passed by fairly uneventfully until Ronnie sent off for information to a number of animal protection societies who had advertised in the back of a Vegetarian Society magazine. When the literature came back he was 'shocked and overwhelmed' and immediately 'spent a fortune' joining an array of organisations. He became a vegan and soon afterwards joined the Hunt Saboteurs.

It was frustration at the impotency of saboteurs to prevent cub hunting during the summer months that led to the creation of the Band of Mercy. ('Cubbing' involves hunters surrounding the woods in which the cubs are present in order to prevent their escape. This tactic makes it almost impossible for protesters to penetrate and to prevent a kill.) Ronnie and a handful of colleagues decided that the only effective course of action was to prevent the hunt vehicles from leaving the kennels at all. So they embarked upon a night time campaign, slashing tyres, placing tacks in locks and leaving the Band of Mercy calling card underneath windscreens. (The name of the organisation was chosen by Lee, recalling nineteenth-century animal activists who had sabotaged guns in order to damage the activities of 'sportsmen'.)

The decision to expand the group's activities came about when the protesters read about plans by the Hoechst drug company to build a new research laboratory at Milton Keynes. Radiation experiments on animals were proposed. Twice Ronnie was involved in setting fire to the building during construction, on each occasion causing more than £20,000 of damage. Despite the delay caused, the new facility did eventually open.

The Band of Mercy reign of sabotage lasted roughly eighteen months until Ronnie and his colleague Cliff Goodman were caught red-handed in the grounds of a company supplying animals for vivisection in Oxfordshire. Naively, they had left evidence linking them with several other offences. In 1975, they became the first people to be imprisoned for animal rights activities when they were each sentenced to three years.

Ronnie found prison 'a shock to the system at first. The prisoners were not too bad, but the prison conditions were appalling.' Yet he adjusted, helped by a move from the bleak conditions of Oxford jail to a semi-open prison in Dorset. He was treated with a degree of sympathy by prison guards and prisoners alike, though the general response was one of disbelief that anybody could have risked their freedom for the cause of animals when they could have stolen 'a hundred grand' and still faced the same sentence!

With parole, Ronnie was released in March 1976, after serving twelve months. By this time the ranks of those ready to take part in direct action for animals had swelled considerably from the half dozen involved in the Band of Mercy, partly inspired by the publicity surrounding his case. The decision was taken to change the name to the Animal Liberation Front and the new group began to increase its activities.

Within a year, Ronnie Lee was in jail again after the police raided his house and found 150 mice stolen from a company which bred animals for vivisection. He was sentenced to a year's imprisonment, most of which was served in a semi-open prison on the Isle of Sheppey. Better prepared for jail though he was second time around, he came to the firm decision that he had had enough and would not risk any further loss of freedom after his release.

By this time, however, the number of young people attracted to the activities of the ALF was rising rapidly and for many of them Ronnie had acquired cult hero status. Admiration also extended beyond his ALF colleagues to many of the mainstream organisations and their supporters, attracted by what they saw as his dedication and courage. The media, too, was becoming fascinated by the expansion of the ALF. Ronnie became much sought after for comments and interviews. Almost by default he acquired the position of spokesman for nearly all Animal Liberation Front campaigns, appearing regularly on television and in newspaper features.

The ALF soon became a little more sophisticated. A supporters group was set up for those who wished to give financial help; newsletters were published; an official press office was established. Ronnie was the linchpin, publishing the literature, organising most of the finances and running the press campaign.

When the ALF began to acquire a harder, more militant edge in the early eighties, Ronnie's views seemed to alter with the times. Previously, he had been a convinced pacifist, but now he was prepared to sanction the principle of 'justifiable violence' against individual 'animal abusers'. It became policy never to condemn any act committed in the name of animal liberation. The ALF *Newsletter* itself reflected this new outlook, openly entertaining the possibility of violence towards those involved in vivisection, the meat trade and hunting.

In 1986, the authorities decided that it was time to try to crush the ALF. Ronnie Lee became their number one target. He was arrested and charged with conspiracy to commit arson and conspiring to incite criminal damage to fur stores, butchers' shops and laboratories. The all-encompassing conspiracy charges meant that he could face imprisonment even though he had not actively participated in any illegal acts.

At first he was shocked by his arrest, believing that in merely writing and publishing he had not committed any crime. But soon the gravity of his position became clear. He was to be made an example to discourage others. The prosecution stigmatised him as 'the general' of a highly organised military regime. Even though this was far from the reality of the chaotic structure of the ALF, his legal advisors told him to expect a long spell in jail. After being held for over a year on remand, he was sentenced to ten years imprisonment in February 1987. By the time the trial was over he had begun to expect even worse.

For the first few months of his

sentence, Ronnie Lee was classed as a high security risk Category A prisoner in the notoriously grim Armley Prison in Leeds. He was accompanied everywhere by three prisoner officers and endured permanent lighting in his solitary cell. It was fortunate that he maintained the ability to be philosophical about his situation, looking forward to each improvement in his conditions and using his time as constructively as he possibly could. He stopped smoking, ate healthily and took up a strict fitness schedule as his way of 'fighting back' against his fate. 'I figured that if they were going to take years of my life, the best answer was to compensate by trying to live longer!' He learnt four languages and thought long on the events and campaigns that had landed him in jail. Slowly, life improved. In the latter years of his sentence he was re-classified as Category D in a semi-open prison, which allowed him home leave every couple of months. Denied parole, he was finally freed in November 1992 after serving six years and eight months in jail.

Since his release, Ronnie has lived a quiet life, though he is still as dedicated as

ever to the animal cause. He assists his partner in an initiative to protect grey-hounds and 'helps different campaigns, doing things where I am not on show'. He maintains a passionate disdain for all 'animal abusers', which seems all the more intense in the context of his otherwise cheerful and gentle character. 'If any of them came to any harm, I cannot say I would be sorry,' he freely admits. He is also completely unrepentant about the controversial role he has played in the modern animal rights movement. 'With hindsight, there are a

Dog rescued from Oxford University, 1984.

lot of things I would do differently,' he says, 'but I have no regrets about helping to form either the Band of Mercy or the ALF. We gave a real kick start to the animal rights movement when it most needed it.'

Ronnie Lee maintains a firm belief in the principle of direct action, though he now thinks 'it should be targeted much more selectively than I did in the past.' On the whole, he feels that illegal campaigning is best focused upon practices where public opinion is already strongly on the side of protesters. 'With things like the fur trade, we were able to push them over the edge,' Ronnie asserts. 'It is in such situations that direct action can be really effective.'

In the short term, the draconian sentences handed out to Lee and others did little to curb ALF activities. In fact, violence increased. The incendiary devices became bigger, culminating in the complete destruction of Dingles department store in Plymouth (the store had a fur department) and a high explosive attack at Bristol University (though the latter was never proved to be an ALF initiative). The bravado also became more pronounced within the organisation's literature. There were calls to 'learn from the IRA',[1] to 'sympathise with the use of lethal violence against animal abusers'[2] and to avenge 'every day our comrades and fellow animals who stay behind bars'.[3]

Such was the level of concern amongst established animal protectionists that when the second edition of *Animal Liberation* was published in 1990, Peter Singer felt it necessary to confront the issue of direct action in a newly written preface. While he praised the 'courageous, caring and thoughtful people' who had planned the kind of activities that had led to video tapes of the most appalling head injury experiments being stolen from the University of Pennsylvania in 1984 (and eventually led to the experiments being stopped), Singer also condemned bombs and 'the spectrum of threats and harassment of experimenters, furriers, and other animal exploiters' as 'a tragic mistake'. He pleaded for the movement to stick to a 'principle of non-violence', whatever the provocation it encountered.[4]

The Animal Liberation Front has continued to make the headlines spasmodically in the 1990s, though there has been less activity than in the previous decade. Undoubtedly, the severe crackdown by the police and courts played its part in this, but probably the main reason is simply that the new young generation had different priorities. For a period in the 1980s, animal liberation was *the* cause through which rebellious youth most readily expressed dissatisfaction with the status quo and natural indignation at injustice. By the mid-1990s much of that youthful energy had been transferred to the campaign against road building and car culture. Inspired at first by the US-based organisation Earth First!, 'eco-warriors' have been propelled into the headlines at the expense of 'animal liberationists'.

This does not mean that animal protection is no longer an important issue amongst the caring young. On the contrary, one of the reasons that concern for animals is no longer the centre of radical campaigning effort is that for many it has become taken for granted as part of 'alternative' life. Some of the camps set up to oppose new road schemes were actually formed by Hunt Saboteur groups and large numbers of those who take part are committed vegetarians or vegans. Typical is Swampy (real name Daniel Hooper), the protester who achieved folk-hero status when in January 1997 he stayed in a home-built tunnel for a week, defying the efforts of bailiffs to clear the way for a new road improvement scheme in Devon. On his emergence from the tunnels, Swampy told reporters that his objections to the building scheme were motivated primarily by a belief that 'animals have equal rights to humans and should not be evicted from their homes.' 'All animals deserve their life,' he declared, 'not just endangered species.'[5]

Swampy is probably the most notorious of a generation for whom vegetarianism and a general acceptance of the arguments for animal liberation are no longer contentious. This applies not only to those who campaign actively for environmental causes, but also to the more conventional. The concept of rights for animals may still invoke strong hostility from some quarters, but opinion polls suggest that the majority of young people now feel some sympathy with some aspects of the campaign. For example, a 1993 poll on youth attitudes conducted by the *Daily Telegraph* showed that 88% of young people worry about animal cruelty.[6]

The message of Peter Singer's book now influences the everyday thinking of large numbers of people unaware even of the existence of the Australian philosopher and his work. No doubt it would come as a surprise to many of them that only twenty years ago the advocacy of vegetarianism or other aspects of cruelty-free living could have been considered so new and controversial. In part, this is a testament to the impact of *Animal Liberation* and the campaigns it helped to trigger, though more than this, there does also seem to have been a degree of inevitability in it all. Animal rights had simply become a concept whose time for more popular acceptance had arrived.

# 9 / Animal world

## 1   A nation of animal lovers?

In many ways, the reputation of the United Kingdom for leading the world in animal welfare is well deserved. Campaigners in other countries look on with envy and admiration at Britain's vibrant and well-supported organisations and the perceived advancement of its legislation. The danger is that this does sometimes stimulate a sort of patronising xenophobic complacency — a tendency to dismiss animal cruelty as a problem caused almost wholly by less enlightened foreigners.

In truth, some nations — particularly in northern Europe — have tougher laws than Britain on a variety of issues. Finland banned the use of most species of wild animals in circuses in 1986 (only dogs, domestic cats, sea lions, ponies, donkeys and tame horses can be used). Swedish animal welfare laws are probably the most sophisticated anywhere in the world, prohibiting the close confinement of sows and phasing out the battery cage for hens over a ten-year period; the same laws have effectively led to a ban on the use of animals for testing cosmetics, tobacco and alcohol. Battery cages are illegal in Switzerland, too; Austria does not permit the use of dogs in experiments; Germany reduced its dependence upon animal research at a greater rate than the UK and has banned the testing of weapons, tobacco and cosmetics; the Netherlands has announced a ten-year run-down programme leading to a permanent ban on fur farming. Even in the overall less sympathetic areas of southern Europe, Italy — a country not considered to be at the forefront of animal protection — has enacted progressive legislation to recognise the right of students and researchers to refuse involvement in animal research without fear of penalty.

On the other hand, mainland Europe has many cruel traditions which still hit the headlines with depressing regularity. Force feeding of geese in *pâté de foie gras* production, particularly in France and Belgium; the annual ritual slaughter of thousands of sheep in the open air near Paris to mark the Muslim festival Eid-el-Kabir; animal sacrifice in bullfights and fiestas in Spain and Portugal; the popularity of hunting and shooting in Italy which results in the deaths of an estimated 200 million creatures every year; the widespread neglect of domestic cats in Greece; dancing bears in Russia

Signs of hope: rescued dancing bears in a WSPA sanctuary in Turkey.

and Turkey; the export of horses from Poland and other parts of Eastern Europe; the growth of the fur trade in the same areas, much of it to fuel the fashion centres of Paris and Milan; the appalling conditions in many zoos and slaughterhouses around the continent. These are only a few of the most blatant manifestations of barbarity.

Eastern Europe poses a particular problem, labouring as it does under the effects of the old communist ideology in which animal welfare campaigning was considered 'insurgent activity'. Consequently, most former members of the Soviet block are only now introducing (or in some cases re-introducing) animal protection legislation. Although some have made rapid progress in the last decade, notably Slovenia and the Czech Republic, lack of tradition and lack of resources combine to ensure that progress is difficult in many nations.[1] At least, however, there are some indications that the combined developments of an animal welfare movement and a free press may eventually help to curb the excesses of mindless animal cruelty which could not be questioned under the old regime. For instance, in 1997, a Russian hunting party — which included the then Prime Minister — killed two bear cubs and their mother after first sending dogs into the den to rouse them from hibernation. The magazine *Ogonyok* responded with strong words of condemnation: 'One is overcome by a feeling of bitter irritation that the leaders of a country with great humanitarian ideals should find time for a hunt which is more like common murder', it commented.[2]

With many Eastern nations seeking to join the European Union, perhaps the most promising advance will prove to be the legally binding agreement granting animals the status of 'sentient beings', signed by the Community's fifteen heads of government at the June 1997 Amsterdam Inter-Governmental Conference. While it is in some ways a measure of how much remains to be done that it has taken so long to achieve an agreed distinction between cows and cabbages (France and Spain leading the opposition), the decision does at least create a more sympathetic philosophical basis from which to campaign for practical reform. At the same time, however, the reforming impulse has been tempered by a restatement of the policy that any practices which 'arise from religious rites, cultural traditions and religious heritage' will be exempt from any EU legislation. This would appear to present a formidable barrier to the possibility of prohibiting 'entertainments' such as bullfighting and fiestas.

While the extension of European political union offers some hope, the globalisation of world trade under the General Agreement on Tariffs and Trade (GATT) presents new obstacles to animal welfare, not just in Europe, but throughout the world. Currently, GATT rules make it practically illegal to ban imports or exports to or from another country on ethical grounds. In the words of leading critic, Dr Vandana Shiva, GATT has 'established a rule of cruelty… Until you can find the most cruel, violent method you are GATT illegal'.[3] Already, one of the EU's most progressive actions — the proposed outright ban on the import of furs from nations in which leghold traps are legal — has been shelved on the grounds that it would be against GATT regulations.[4] Resistance to powerful global free trade agreements which ignore moral considerations (GATT was ratified by 138 nations in 1994) is crucial to the future of animal welfare — as it is to other initiatives for social justice.

## The movement in the US

Like its counterpart in the UK, the US animal welfare movement dates back to the nineteenth century and enjoyed growing popularity in the period up until the first world war. After that its influence faded until the last quarter of the twentieth century.

By 1890, many major US cities had local organisations of the Society for the Prevention of Cruelty to Animals and the American Humane Association (AHA) had been formed to oppose horrific long-distance transport conditions for livestock. There was also a small intellectual humanitarian movement, similar to that pioneered by Henry Salt on the other side of the Atlantic. Particularly impressive was John Howard Moore, who considered Salt to be 'truly an intellectual brother'. The admiration was mutual. Salt called Moore's major work, *The Universal Kinship*, 'the best book ever written in the humanitarian cause'.[5]

As we saw in Chapter 6, the American Vegetarian Society was set up in 1861 by members of the same Bible Christian movement responsible for the formation of the UK Vegetarian Society. By the beginning of the twentieth century a non-meat diet enjoyed sufficient respectability for several major US cities to have established their own local vegetarian organisations. By 1906 even Chicago, the slaughterhouse centre of the US, had 'four vegetarian restaurants' serving 'many hundreds of people daily'.[6] Anti-vivisection views enjoyed reasonable support, too. The novelist Mark Twain (1835-1910) was amongst those vociferous in his condemnation on ethical grounds and until his death in 1916, the physiologist Dr Albert Leffingwell gave credibility to scientific arguments against the practice.

Where the US failed (and has continued to fail) to emulate Britain is in its enforcement of legislation. While some states have been more progressive than others, national (federal) legislation has proved difficult to achieve. Compulsory stunning of farm animals was not introduced nationwide until 1958 and there were no laws to regulate vivisection until 1966. To this day the legislation governing more than 20 million animals used in research every year (more than in any other country) is considerably less comprehensive than in many European countries.

On the other hand, US wildlife did at least benefit from the establishment of national parks many decades before the UK. By 1930, 600 state parks already covered 2.75 million acres.[7] Even though North America's native fauna and flora have been subject to the same pressures and exploitation as every other nation, they have continued to enjoy levels of protection in some states which compare favourably to almost anywhere else in the world. This was exemplified by the government's decision in 1994 to designate a sanctuary of over 6 million acres in desert areas of California, Nevada, Arizona and Utah, principally to conserve some 2 million native tortoises. Plans by developers to mine natural resources and to build a nuclear dump were resisted in favour of the conservation measure.

The renaissance of interest in animal protection in the US came later than in Britain, inspired largely by the twin factors of the publication of *Animal Liberation* and admiration for the vitality of the British movement. Characteristically though, when animal rights did stir the American consciousness it did so with considerable fervour. Philosophers (notably Tom Regan) added to the academic debate stimulated by Singer. Henry Spira — whose interest was aroused by participation in a course on animal liberation taught by Peter Singer in New York — led boycott campaigns against American cosmetic companies that tested their products on animals. In particular, his initiative against the multinational Revlon organisation was soon

"I'd rather go naked than wear fur."

Nadja
Auermann

Every fur coat means animals died a painful death by strangulation, electrocution, drowning, or being gassed.

PETA
PEOPLE FOR THE ETHICAL TREATMENT OF ANIMALS
P.O. Box 42516, Washington, DC 20015; 301-770-PETA

PETA have attracted unprecedented support for their campaigns from actresses, models and other celebrities.

taken up by groups in many areas of the world (including Britain) and proved influential in developing a concerted international movement against cosmetic testing. Spira's boycott tactics were critical in creating the conditions which eventually allowed 'cruelty-free' companies to thrive.

Another significant event was the formation of People for the Ethical Treatment of Animals (PETA) in 1980. With imaginative campaigning and skilful marketing it soon established itself as one of the largest and most innovative animal organisations in the world — its success proving instrumental in revitalising some of the longer established US groups.

PETA's original impact was due to co-founder Alex Pacheco's undercover investigation at the Institute of Behavioural Studies in Silver Spring, Maryland in 1985. His evidence led to the first and only arrest and criminal conviction of an animal experimenter in the US on charges of cruelty. Indeed, it was the first US Supreme Court victory for animals in any case involving vivisection. This success has been followed by a series of similarly high profile (and damning) investigations of American laboratory practice.

PETA's approach to campaigning has attracted unprecedented support from celebrities in the world of film, rock music and sport. Using methods that would have been impossible to implement in the UK, the organisation has combined undisguised support for the illegal activities of the Animal Liberation Front with glitzy galas and award ceremonies where stars and senators sit down to enjoy elaborately prepared vegan food served at plush venues. Its impact bears witness to the readiness of liberal areas of American society to embrace radical new ideas.

Conversely, the ultra-conservative elements of the farming and scientific communities have responded with almost frightening intensity to campaigners they dismiss disdainfully as 'bunnyhuggers'.

While massive levels of financial support, charity rock concerts, albums, galas, academic studies and fervent philosophical debate all demonstrate how some areas of the US have embraced the cause of animal rights with an earnestness unparalleled anywhere else in the world, the overall impact of campaigners upon legislators has so far been limited. According to Peter Singer, progress is in some ways slower in America than in his native Australia, even though the US movement enjoys far greater levels of support. He believes that massive vested interests are the principal obstacle. 'Compared with the US, we are probably a little better off in Australia, because big business is not quite so dominant over the political process here as it is there,' Singer speculates. 'It seems to me that farm animals in the US are no better off and their lab animals are clearly worse off.'[8]

## Progress in Australia

Although its RSPCA was formed in the 1890s and has achieved some legislative protection, Australia had no deep-seated tradition of animal welfare before the last quarter of the twentieth century. Since then, many groups have sprung up at both state and national level, Animal Liberation being the most prominent.

Despite its only recent development, the Australian animal welfare movement has made its impression. Peter Singer believes that the country's recent code of practice on animal experiments 'is one of the strictest anywhere, and we have advocates for animals on all the ethics committees that are required to approve experiments.'[9] Another considerable achievement has been the banning of duck shooting in Western Australia (1990) and New South Wales (1995).

Where campaigners have proved less successful is in their initiatives on behalf of farm animals. Inevitably, in a nation so heavily dominated by farming interests it has proved desperately difficult to make progress. Attempts to emulate Switzerland's ban on the battery cage or the UK's phasing out of sow stalls have, thus far, been in vain, though not for want of trying. Especially worthy of attention have been the efforts of the tireless activist Pam Clarke, imprisoned several times for her protests against the battery system. In 1993, she inspired a landmark prosecution of a farm in Tasmania, leading eventually to guilty verdicts on seven counts of causing cruelty to battery hens. In his summing up, the magistrate concluded that 'in my strong view all these birds have been treated with unjustifiable and unnecessary cruelty, constituted by great indifference to their suffering and pain'.

As this was considered a test case, it effectively placed all battery farmers in Tasmania in danger of prosecution. It was a threat which prompted the state government to take a decision which highlights only too clearly the frustration often experienced by animal welfare campaigners around the world when faced with powerful vested interests. Rather than the introduction of a ban, an amendment to the state Cruelty Act was implemented to exclude battery hens from the protection afforded to other species.

The overwhelming influence of the Australian farming lobby is demonstrated even more decisively in the survival of the much condemned export of live sheep on horrifying long journeys to the Middle East. Approximately 5 million animals are exported every year. Those that survive the horrific three-week journey are ritually slaughtered for the Islamic meat trade.

*In the developing world...*

It is far from a complete truth, but there is a tendency for economically poorer nations to be less advanced in their concern for animal welfare than their wealthier counterparts. The reasons are obvious: extreme poverty is rarely a condition for enlightened social reform. Where there is struggle for human survival, compassion for animals (or indeed other humans) is often considered a luxury. It is, therefore, unsurprising that progress in the majority of developing nations has either been slow or non-existent — or that British expatriates have often been at the centre of what limited change has been achieved. From Greece to Egypt, India, Algeria, Japan and Tunisia, animal welfare initiatives can be traced back to the pioneering efforts of British men and women living and working abroad.

In addition to traditional indifference to animals, a further problem is that the institutionalised cruelties of the western world — factory farming in particular — are now being exported to developing nations at an alarming rate. In Africa, for example, the poultry industry is evident in all areas of the continent, from Nigeria to Ethiopia. It is a similar story in Asia. As affirmed by the World Cancer Research Fund in its recent comprehensive report on the links between diet and cancer, this trend is likely to increase rather than decrease ill-health:

> *... The trend in Asian countries in rapid economic transition, is towards mass animal breeding and/or the import of meat, meat products, and dairy products. Thereby, the meat, animal fat, and protein content of the diet is approaching that of Western economic countries. The consequences include less productive use of land, and increased incidence of many diseases such as those cancers now most common in the West.*
>
> *Policy-makers in all parts of the world should be informed that increasing consumption of meat and fatty foods will lead to a massive increase in incidence of a large number of diseases that are expensive to treat.*[10]

A further difficulty linked to the expansion of meat eating in developing areas is that it necessitates an inefficient and ecologically-damaging use of land, likely in the long-term to contribute towards rather than to alleviate world hunger. Claims that such expansion is a useful way of providing food for the local population are grossly simplistic, for the reality is that factory farming provides a luxury product of no value to poorer people struggling to produce even enough grain for survival. To quote the World Cancer Research Fund again:

*Intensive agricultural methods originating in Europe and the USA, and now also used in other parts of the world, have led to irreversible degradation of much agricultural land. Much of this intensive land use has been to rear animals and to grow crops for animal feed. More appropriate ecological and nutritional use of the land would involve their use for plant-based food production for direct human consumption.*[11]

There are a few more encouraging signs for wildlife protection. In large parts of Africa and the Indian sub-continent, at least there is now widespread acceptance that native wild animals should be protected and viewed as a vital resource — if only because of the economic advantages of doing so. By providing reserves to support endangered species, Kenya, Tanzania, India and others have not only helped to conserve animals threatened by habitat destruction, but also reaped the benefits of important income from tourism.

Nonetheless, poaching is still an acute problem all across the world. Valuable larger animals such as elephants and great apes are hunted by ruthless and highly organised gangs. Elsewhere, destruction is often the result of local people trying to

Another admirable initiative from WSPA: rescued orang-utans in an Indonesian sancturay.

eke out a living from the small price which foreign dealers pay for (say) wild birds. Senegal, Tanzania, Guyana and Indonesia are amongst the main exporters in the world.[12]

Parts of Asia hold the dubious distinction of possessing probably the worst reputation in the world on animal welfare issues. Typically, animals are viewed with a total absence of care and compassion, highlighted by well-publicised practices such as the strangling of dogs for human food in Korea; the destruction of Taiwan's estimated two million stray dogs; and China's live animal markets, where starving creatures are stuffed into cages, some seeming more dead than alive.

In the technologically advanced areas of Japan and China the cultural limitations are exacerbated by the existence of a large and mostly unregulated animal experimentation industry. Japan alone is responsible for approximately 8 million painful experiments every year, many of such severity that they would not be permitted in Western Europe.

Japan also earns persistent condemnation for its enduring enthusiasm for the import of products outlawed by the vast majority of the international community. Demand for whalemeat and elephant ivory stimulates killing by poachers and pirates, thus increasing pressure on Western governments to sanction controlled quotas of slaughter.

China is another nation guilty of encouraging the slaughter of wildlife from other parts of the world, partly to provide ingredients for its traditional medicines or — as in the case of its recent trade in the import of seal penises — to meet the consumer boom in supposed aphrodisiacs.

It is a bleak picture with a discouraging outlook, but even in the less enlightened nations there are dedicated minorities campaigning valiantly for improvement. The Japan Anti-Vivisection Association (JAVA) was formed in 1986 and built up a membership of over 2,000 in its first decade; during a 1996 visit to China to inspect zoo conditions, Virginia McKenna was struck not only by the 'intolerable' level of cruelty, but also by the dedicated efforts of a few to combat it. She also praised the 'hundreds of wonderful students, eager to give their energy to help the tragic animals about which I told them.'[13]

Attitudes and practices are similarly largely unenlightened in South and Central America. Neglect is allied to the worst aspects of macho Latin behaviour, producing particularly barbaric festivals such as Brazil's *Farra do Boi* (Oxen Fun Days). Ironically timed for Holy Week, each year these events result in the torture and killing of dozens of animals, first starved in preparation, then set free in town centres and chased by villagers armed with sticks, stones, knives and bamboo canes. The celebration ends in slaughter. Brazilian critics label it 'blind torture for the pleasure of torture';[14] like so many other abuses of animals around the globe, supporters defend it as 'cultural heritage'.

Cockfighting and bullfighting are also common in South America, the latter particularly in Peru, Honduras, Costa Rica and in Mexico. Mexico City now houses the biggest bullring in the world, capable of accommodating 50,000 visitors.[15]

Nor is wildlife exempt from cruelty. In Brazil, illegal trafficking of wild fauna is second only to the trade in drugs;[16] Argentina is one of the largest exporters of wild birds in the world.

Once again, however, tiny signs of progress — such as the surprising ban on dissection in schools introduced by Argentina in the last decade — should not be ignored.

## 2 Maneka's ark

India offers a more interesting and favourable scenario for animals, influenced as it is by the more sympathetic Hindu culture. The Indian nation also has a stronger recent political emphasis on the importance of respect for animals than any other nation. For Mahatma Gandhi, the founding father of the modern state, animal welfare was a priority. He asserted that 'the more helpless a creature, the more enti-

Maneka at a conference organised by Compassion in World Farming in 1998.

tled it is to protection by man from the cruelty of man'.[17] Gandhi was also a vegetarian and stigmatised vivisection as 'the blackest of all the black crimes that man is at present committing against God and His fair creation'.[18]

The Indian constitution, introduced after independence in 1947, is one of the few to incorporate animal welfare provisions. Article 51 includes a pledge that the country should safeguard its wildlife and take steps to eliminate cow slaughter.

Despite the fine sentiments, however, animal protection did not prove to be an issue of major political concern in the early decades of the independent nation.

India epitomises the irrationality of human attitudes to animals probably more acutely than any other nation. At one extreme, the Jain sect take their opposition to killing so far that they cover their mouths with masks lest their breath should cause harm to living organisms. Yet in the same country where the cow is considered sacred and in many parts is left free to roam (a fact that itself causes enormous welfare problems for many diseased and starving animals), 300,000 cattle are killed daily in abattoirs.[19] While few Hindus do the killing themselves, increasing numbers eat the produce, rationalising that as long as a Moslem performs the act of slaughter then the consumer is somehow excluded from implication. A Jain was even responsible for the establishment of the largest slaughterhouse in the country.[20]

On the other hand, the positive power of cultural beliefs still ensures that interest in animal protection is generally greater amongst the native Hindu population of India than in any other developing nation. It still has the largest number of vegetarians in the world, estimated at between 25% and 30% of the total population.[21]

India is also probably the only developing country to have had its own weekly television programmes dedicated solely to animal welfare issues. The series, *Heads or Tails* and *Maneka's Ark*, are written and presented by Maneka Gandhi, one of the most admired campaigners in the world who is at the centre of India's protection movement.

Although proud of the compassionate culture into which she was born, Maneka is, nonetheless, openly critical of 'a romantic world view of Hinduism and the protection it affords to animals.' She believes that her fellow Hindus long ago sacrificed their right to be viewed as 'gentle people coexisting and caring for all plants and animals and setting an example to the rest of the world… India has become the largest exporter of meat in Asia. Factory farming is becoming the norm,' she laments.[22]

Mahatma Gandhi once wrote that 'the greatness of a nation and its moral progress can be judged by the way its animals are treated'.[23] For all its positive history, there remains much to be done before the nation he helped to create can come near to measuring up to his ideals. Nevertheless, in the inspiring work of Maneka, the Gandhi legacy does live on.

Maneka Gandhi was born into a high-ranking Indian army family which lost most of its land during the partition of Pakistan from India after independence in 1947. As a child, life was relatively nomadic, her father's occupation leading to posts in various parts of the country. It was not a background in which animals played a significant role, though from an early age both she and her sister did show signs of the innate sympathy with suffering creatures which was later to produce one of the most remarkable campaigners of her generation. Several stray dogs were rescued from the streets and given food and shelter.

At the age of seventeen, Maneka became part of India's most famous family. She married Sanjay Gandhi, youngest son of the then Prime Minister, Indira, and brother of Rajiv, later also to become head of state until his assassination in 1991. It was the kind of fairy tale romance beloved universally, but particularly in India — Sanjay having proposed within half an hour of meeting his future bride at a wedding in Delhi.

Membership of the Gandhi dynasty granted Maneka new privilege and security and she began to devote increasing amounts of time to animal welfare work. At the time, however, this now-outspoken proponent of vegetarianism was still eating meat. All this changed suddenly one evening when Sanjay, finding his wife tucking into a bowl of meaty soup, teasingly pointed out the inconsistency of her spending her days trying to protect animals and her leisure time eating them. She turned vegetarian immediately.

In 1980, Maneka began to plan India's first animal hospital in her home town of Delhi. It was funded by a surprise legacy from Ruth Cowell, an Australian woman unknown to both her and her husband. It was the first of several occasions on which financial support for animal welfare initiatives has appeared almost miraculously.

Tragically, before the project could be completed, Sanjay was killed in a plane crash. Maneka's life was shattered. Aged only twenty-three, she was left with a baby son only one hundred days old, little money and no security. Although she opened and continued to run the animal hospital, naming it after her late husband and dedicating it to his memory, it was a difficult time, personal unhappiness contributing to uncertainty about the direction her life should take.

It was several years later that the prospect of a campaigning and political future materialised. In 1984 — at the age of twenty-eight — Maneka Gandhi stood for election to the Indian parliament. Defeated, she decided to learn from the experience, spending the next few years studying and travelling around her country in order both to define her own beliefs and to gain a sense of what India most needed. This brought her to environmentalism — at the time a concept unheard of in India. 'Most of all I thought about leaving something of value to my son and how useless all the material possessions I was putting away for him would be if I couldn't leave him a glass of water, or if he never saw a park to play in,' she recalls.

After winning a seat in parliament at the next election, Maneka was invited to become Minister of Environment in 1989. She was thirty-three years old. It was not, she claims, quite as powerful an appointment as it may seem. 'You can tell how important it was considered by the fact that the word "environment" was spelt incorrectly on the official headed note paper!'

Over the next two years, Maneka embarked on a radical clean-up campaign, ensuring almost single-handedly that environmental concerns became firmly established on the Indian political map. She declared war on polluting big business, shutting down her huge local distillery because of its destructive impact upon river water. Even more important in the long term was the setting up of many NGOs (non-governmental organisations) and her personal support for the establishment of centres such as the Research Foundation for Science, Technology and Ecology in New Delhi, now an internationally respected environmental protection organisation under the directorship of Dr Vandana Shiva.

Within a year, influential members of India's business community had seen more than enough of Maneka Gandhi and her radical reforms, as had the Janata Party government of which she was a member. She began to be viewed as a liability. In the 1991 elections, the government was defeated (an event for which she claims some credit!) and Maneka lost her seat with her own administration actually 'rigging the election against me' — an action for which she was later to receive an apology.

The loss of political office resulted in a shift of emphasis. By now the environmental movement was fully flourishing. 'In only a year and a half it had become mature and there were many good people to guide it,' says Maneka, 'so I took the opportunity to come out of the closet and head into what I really wanted to do all along, which was the animal protection and vegetarian movement.'

With the 'moral background' of her animal hospital and her veganism, she was soon given her own television programme and also began to write a column on animal issues for twenty newspapers. Her family and her friends were persuaded to turn vegetarian and to support her campaign, forming 'a charmed circle'. They succeeded in making animal welfare fashionable, 'with lots of film stars, artists, writers and politicians standing up for vegetarianism.' Her television programme became so successful that it led to a second prime time show, entitled *Maneka's Ark*.

Both programmes now draw audiences of around 200 million. She also has her own weekly radio show. In a country in which she believes pessimistically that the overall trend is 'to measure progress in the move from vegetarianism to non-vegetarianism,' she has, nevertheless, built an influential movement for change. 'Although the environment movement has done very well in India, we have succeeded in making the animal movement even larger,' she states proudly.

The focus for Maneka's animal welfare work is People for Animals, an organisation which friends from India's artist and media world helped her to set up in 1994. 'Having lived with my concern for animals for so long, but recognised my impatience with modalities and formalities, they took upon themselves the task of dealing with all the paperwork and legal requirements and then gave the organisation to me. It has become an umbrella organisation for most of the animal work in India… I now have 72 units across the country — my aim is to have one in all 600 constituencies. We set up shelters ourselves and fund similar efforts from others. I plough on from morning to night trying to raise money to give one an ambulance, another a shelter and to train staff how to operate them. Nobody who asks for money ever goes away empty handed.'

People for Animals now has 150,000 members. While its celebrity origins might suggest an organisation better suited to public relations than animal rescue work, it is first and foremost dedicated to practical improvement. 'Amongst our biggest achievements has been to change the concept and focus of animal welfare from holding debates and painting competitions to real on-ground work for animals — rescuing them, feeding them, learning about the laws to protect them and first aid to treat them, propagating vegetarianism strongly and so on. I remain impatient with achievements on paper and that feeling has communicated itself to the whole movement, who now know it is more important to have picked up one animal or punished one birdtrapper than to have attended a seminar on the subject of cruelty. One example is worth more than a thousand words.'

Behind her extraordinary achievements are forces which Maneka describes as 'God-given… Sometimes I sit in the morning and say, "Listen to me. I need 10,000 rupees because I have somebody coming who needs money for a shelter." In the day, somebody will come to the house and say, "You know I had a dream that I must give Maneka Gandhi something," and they' ll hand me 10,000 rupees. It is amazing.'

Equally mysterious is her own personal magnetism, about which she is delightfully honest. 'Nobody knows how to say no to me. There is a certain magic which God has given. It's a combination of being a Gandhi, being determinedly aggressive and permanently pretending to be happy. Nobody sees the amount of struggle and pain.'

Alongside her cheerfulness, Maneka Gandhi has deliberately developed a public persona that is 'overly-arrogant… It has to be done. I get a huge amount of bad press about how bad tempered I am, but that's very good for me. If I was always courteous and gentle, the vegetarian movement would be dead, but because I am perceived as rude and argumentative, everybody who opposes my views has become apologetic to me. I throw my weight around.'

Despite her critics, she remains hugely popular with the Indian public. She attributes this to several factors: the Gandhi name which helps to ensure that she is constantly in the public eye, the existence of a culture where kindness to animals has always mattered, and also because 'Indians like eccentrics and they see that I have so much fun.'

Maneka was re-elected to parliament as an independent candidate in 1994. Her majority was the largest anywhere in India. In the 1998 General Election, she once again triumphed by an enormous margin. 'I never attempt to be different — I talk about what concerns me. On my way to one election meeting I found a wounded donkey, so I cancelled and took the donkey home and treated him. We named him after the biggest rock star in India and he became a celebrity. Everybody loves him. In my election speeches I talked about how one night he sang to the stars. I said, "Look this is life; think of the fun I have gained from a donkey." It changed so many people.'

Alongside Maneka's personal charisma exists enormous dedication and courage. She runs the biggest cow shelter in India. She is Governor of the SPCA in Delhi and personally stands on roads and stops overloaded trucks. She writes books. She visits zoos and insists that animals kept in particularly appalling conditions are removed. She is Chairperson of the Committee for the Study and the Control of Animal Experiments, a once unconsidered government quango she has used to end compulsory dissection and cosmetic testing. 'When I was out of office, a government minister came to me and said, "Look, Mrs Gandhi, just to get you off our backs, what would you like?" I said, "Give me this rubbish committee that does nothing and has no power." He gave it to me and I have turned it into a monster!'

She has also stopped animal sacrifice in certain temples and cruelty in the Indian film industry; she has implemented a Pound Act to forbid the use of stray dogs in experimentation and introduced a sterilisation and vaccine programme for strays. 'Hardly a week goes by without some progress,' she remarks.

Nor is her energy confined to animals. She runs India's largest group for kidnapped children, helping to organise three schools for them. She is Chairperson of Rugmark, an international trademark scheme introduced to identify Indian carpets which have been produced without exploitative child labour.

At the end of March 1998, Maneka Gandhi enjoyed further success. She became a government minister again. Within days of accepting an offer to join the Ministry of Welfare, she had ensured that her remit included animal protection.

Meanwhile, a multinational drug company became the latest powerful institution to wilt under her remarkable personal power. Late one evening, airport authorities telephoned to tell her that fifty beagle dogs had arrived in the quarantine centre, bound for animal experimentation. They were the first animals imported into India for this purpose. Maneka telephoned the owner and told him that the licences he had received were useless since 'I am the law on animals.' ('My eighteen-year-old son, listening into the conversation, told me that I sounded exactly like Judge Dread,' she jokes.) The editor of India's largest newspaper was persuaded to write a front page article condemning the development; the story soon spread to television news. Pressure grew on the company to change its policy. After less than a fortnight it actually asked Maneka to take away the beagles.

She followed this victory by passing a proposal through her 'rubbish committee' for a law to ban completely the import of animals for experimentation. It will now go before parliament. 'I am like the Wizard of Oz,' she concludes, 'in that nobody knows how far my power goes. I make sure it goes a lot further than it has any right to go.'

The commitment Maneka Gandhi has made to help India's animals is well rewarded. 'Just to hold those rescued animals in my arms or to see that wounded elephant look back after it has been saved makes it all worthwhile,' she believes. 'I am so lucky. I get a telephone call from Madras to say an injured elephant has been found on the road. I ring up the local MP, the police — anybody I can think of. Everybody answers my calls and nobody refuses to help. Two days later somebody rings to tell me that the elephant has been picked up by the army, taken to a sanctuary and treated. You can't imagine how my heart leaps.'

## 3   Antony Thomas and *To Love or Kill*

Someone better qualified than most to comment on cultural differences in attitudes to animals is the world-renowned film maker Antony Thomas. Since establishing his reputation in 1977 with the award-winning anti-apartheid documentary trilogy, *The South African Experience*, he has produced a number of highly regarded films — all inspired by a hatred of injustice. Amongst these, the drama *Death of a Princess* is probably the best known.

In 1996, Thomas turned his professional attention to the relationship between people and animals, writing and producing the documentary film, *Man and Animal* (US title — *To Love or Kill; Man vs Animal*). It was a project undertaken with some reluctance, partly because he considered it 'such a complex subject', but mainly because 'I knew I was going to experience dreadful things I didn't want to experience.' It was — he adds — 'a coward's resistance.'

*Man and Animal* took Thomas to the far ends of the planet, not only exposing barbaric practices which are 'manifestly wrong and should be stopped,' but also including scenes 'to induce in people a real respect for animals — a real understanding of their sensibilities, feelings and intuitions.' He aimed to 'fire bullets' at the idea there is a 'hard and fast dividing line between humans — who supposedly possess an immortal soul — and other "things".'

Probably the most harrowing of many painful sequences in the documentary were obtained in China. At a restaurant the film crew recorded dogs and cats being prepared for human food. Antony takes up the story:

'They had an outside pen where animals were kept and customers could choose which they would like to eat. To begin preparation for the table, cats were gripped around the neck by a sort of instrument like a pair of tongs. Then they were stunned — but not killed — by being clubbed on the head. Next, they were dropped into very hot water. This produced some kind of shock which enabled them to strip the fur more easily. The naked little animal was then thrown under a cold water tap and finally slaughtered.' Thomas considers it amongst the most difficult things he has ever had to record. 'If we had reacted as we felt, they would have realised that we didn't view this as a normal day's happening. It was very difficult to maintain the neutral persona that I believe film makers should always try to adopt.'

The crew had arrived in China equipped with sophisticated secret filming equipment, only to find that the Chinese were so indifferent to animal suffering that a tourist video camera was all that was required. Cruelty was blatant and unquestioned. 'It does occur to me that sometimes there is a correlation between the way that people treat their animals and the way that they treat their people,' he concludes. 'The Chinese have a culture where there simply isn't the same respect for life.'

One of the principal themes of the film is the detrimental effect of both conventional religion and superstition upon animal welfare. In India, a Jain temple was filmed where rats — thousands of them scurrying around the building — were fed and worshipped. While Antony admires the Jain and Hindu principle of 'respect for all life' which helps to makes the Indian response to animals so unique, he believes that this, too, can ultimately cause suffering. 'The Jains believe that an animal's life is so sacred that even if it were going through an extreme form of suffering you should

Antony Thomas with Ellie, a dog rescued after a sadistic attack on the Greek island of Skopelos.

do nothing. I respect the spirit of that, but I find the reality painful.'

In southern Europe, Thomas focused upon a Spanish fiesta where there was an absence of even the remotest form of respect. Animals were chased through the streets, taunted, tortured and eventually killed in a frenzy of ritual hysteria. He believes that traditional religious teachings are at least partly responsible. 'If you think that only humans have an immortal soul, that causes a fundamentally different attitude to animals. I have some personal experience of this having lived for some years in Greece. Cruelty is simply flung in your face over there. I once stopped a little boy who had a cat cornered in a little alleyway and was throwing stones at it from each hand. When I stopped him he yelled at me that it doesn't matter because the cat has no soul.'

In spite of his harrowing experiences, the film maker remains optimistic that progress against religious superstition can be made. 'A lot of evil in the world is not conscious. The way that progress is made possible is by opening people's eyes to things they have not considered before. The influence of one or two people can dramatically change attitudes. I think that the main problem is that the message simply hasn't got through to a country like Greece yet.'

Condemnation of abuse in other areas of the world has not led Antony Thomas to embrace wholeheartedly the theory that the English speaking world is superior in its treatment of animals. On the contrary, he is adamant that neither Britain nor the USA has any cause for complacency. 'We may treat our pets relatively well, but our farming methods are refined to new levels of cruelty. If you judge a nation by its treatment of animals I don't think that we fare particularly well.' He believes that the British attitude exemplifies a schizophrenic national characteristic evident throughout our history. 'Take our colonial history. The passion of the anti-slavery movement and the idealism of many figures in politics goes side by side with our cruel, crass, antediluvian, imperialist politics. We're a class-conscious society as well as being a nation with great democratic ideals and we are polarised about our animals as well. On the one hand, we lead the world with support for our protection movement; on the other, we are still capable of supporting obscene practices like factory farming.'

In *Man And Animal* we see that the USA is equally extreme and irrational in its contradictory attitudes. On the negative side, animals are shown as the object of emotions ranging from ghastly 'slightly psychotic over-sentimentality' to 'naked lust for killing'. Sentimentality is represented by scenes of the dressing up of pets in fashion coats and swimming costumes; lust for killing by the practice of canned hunting in Texas. 'You go to a ranch and you have a menu of animals which you can kill,' explains Thomas. 'Species can range from rhinoceros at 50,000 dollars to Hawaiian rams at 275 dollars. You choose your animal, go out with a guide and position yourself close to a trail. On the other side there is a fence so the animal can't get away. The guide goes off and rounds up some animals and herds them towards you. When they are about five yards away you shoot. In the case we filmed the weapon used was a crossbow. All the arrows were aimed at the body because if you shoot at the head you ruin your "trophy". The animal dies a slow and painful death. The guide then takes it away and skins it whilst all these guys stand around and discuss "the drama of the hunt". The reality is that it is nothing other than point blank slaughter and an ugly fascination in killing.'

To show how others in the USA display more admirable understanding and respect for the positive potential power of animals, Thomas took his cameras to record a remarkable and controversial reform programme at a prison for the criminally insane. Inmates are allowed the companionship of a number of species, including cats and birds. 'These are people to whom no-one has ever related, mixing with animals who don't care whether or not they are axe murderers: they just give them love. It is a sentimental message, but I think it is a true one. When the programme started people thought that the inmates would murder the birds and cats, yet no animal has ever been harmed.'

Anthony Thomas' film has now been shown in more than forty countries and has won several prestigious television awards. These include the 1996 Grierson Award for the best British Television Documentary and the Basle Prize, awarded by the European Broadcasting Union for the best educational programme. In addition to the profound impact it has made upon many of the individuals who have watched it, perhaps its greatest practical achievement has been to persuade the Chinese author-ities to allow the World Society for the Protection of Animals to be represented in its country for the first time. That the nation with arguably *the* most deplorable repu-tation for its attitude to animals has taken its first tentative steps towards recognising welfare offers a distant sign of hope in a world still far too often dominated by thoughtless brutality.

# 10 / Past, present and future

To *draw any sweeping conclusions* about the ways in which attitudes to animals have progressed in the last hundred years is a dangerous enterprise. As the great English poet and visionary William Blake succinctly put it, 'to generalise is to be an idiot'! Nonetheless, there are certain trends so distinct that it is feasible to reach some tentative judgements.

For example, it is evident that the period from the later years of the nineteenth century to the outbreak of the Great War saw important advances in philosophical thought about animals, in the level of campaigning, and in enforcement of legislation. Momentum for change was then stifled and took nearly half a century to begin to recover. Despite the indefatigable efforts of a dedicated minority, progress was slow in the period 1915-1960, brightened mainly by an emerging interest in conservation from which some species of wild animals began to benefit. Significant improvements in the welfare of horses were also achieved.

As with many twentieth-century social reforms, the pivotal decade was the sixties. It was then that the mass media started to focus concertedly upon issues such as seal slaughter, factory farming and the threat to survival faced by wildlife. This was also the period in which several new animal welfare initiatives were launched. These ranged from the ultra-respectable World Wildlife Fund to the anti-establishment Hunt Saboteurs Association; from the innovative International Fund for Animal Welfare to the influential Compassion In World Farming. Above all, the sixties was a time in which young people questioned conventional attitudes and confronted the status quo with unprecedented vigour, assuming a degree of power and independence that previous generations would not have thought possible. Borrowing from the esoteric ideologies of the East, the youth movement also offered a relatively new (if still rather vague) spiritual respect for the natural world.

Yet the sixties was only a beginning. As Celia Hammond points out, 'I don't remember it as a particularly sympathetic time for animals. People still thought you were crazy if you spent much of your time trying to care for them.' It was more a case of the foundations being put in place that would allow interest to flourish from the mid-nineteen seventies onwards.

From approximately 1977 to 1990, animal protection in the UK enjoyed its heyday as far as active campaigning is concerned, prompting changes which are now so much taken for granted that it sometimes difficult to remember how recently they were achieved. Vegetarian options on most restaurant menus, health food stores in almost every town, vegetarian food sections in supermarkets, cruelty-free cosmetics and household goods available widely, non-animal circuses, hunts banned from assembling in many town centres for their traditional Boxing Day activities, free-range eggs easily attainable, progress in international efforts to protect whales, elephants and other threatened wild species, the decline of the fur trade in the UK (and certain parts of the US), the abandonment of compulsory dissection of animals for school biology students, the formation of investment policies by a high street bank which avoids support for factory farming, the fur industry and companies which test cosmetics on animals,[1] a reduction of more than 50% in the number of animals used in experiments in the UK in the period 1970-95, the banning of veal crates and the phasing out of confinement stalls for sows — all these are advances that are, to a large extent, the achievement of the post-*Animal Liberation* generation of campaigners. Of course, they have to be measured against a less promising overall picture which includes increases in cruelty to some domestic pets, an obscene escalation of the intensive poultry industry, more wild species than ever before threatened with extinction and the emergence of genetically engineered animals in medical and agricultural research. Nonetheless, they do represent enormous progress.

Analysing current trends is even more risky than summarising the past, but in the 1990s animal protection remains an issue that incites great passion and commitment. This has been demonstrated especially by the scale of protests against the live export trade. Overall numbers involved in organised campaigning may have declined from the 1980s, but there are almost certainly more people than ever before making personal statements of concern, be it purchasing free-range eggs, writing letters to politicians, supporting welfare organisations financially, turning vegetarian, or purchasing cruelty-free products. And with animal issues discussed freely in most schools, support would seem to be particularly strong amongst the young.

There is a sense, too, that some of the arguments about the need to respect and be kind have been accepted. There is a groundswell of public sympathy, distinguished by the immense popularity of pet welfare programmes on television. These often carry an underlying message that cruelty to animals is about as low as humanity can sink.

Equally emphatic is the demand for heartwarming stories about pets, wildlife or even farm animals. A recent illustration is the remarkable tale of Butch and Sundance, two pigs who, in January 1998, escaped from Malmesbury Abattoir in Wiltshire, swam across an ice-cold river and avoided re-capture for over a week. It is only a slight exaggeration to say that their fate gripped the nation. The saga ended when a daily newspaper — purporting to be responding to the wishes of its readers — paid to save the two animals from slaughter and provided a home for life in a local sanctuary.[2]

In one sense the Butch and Sundance incident can be dismissed as an example of acute sentimentality when thousands of other pigs are dispatched routinely for the dinner table each week. But more positively, does it not provide evidence of a profound recognition of animal sensibility and intelligence lurking ever-nearer the surface of everyday human consciousness? Despite the often yawning gap between our deepest feelings and our actions, there is growing acceptance of the complexity and sensitivity of *all* animals. Eventually this must surely find expression in greater protection?

This book has represented most of those who have fought for animals as courageous, liberal-minded individuals whose care and compassion is an extension rather than an alternative to their concern for humans. It would be foolish, however, to argue that this has been the only motivation. As the historian Keith Thomas expressed it when describing the nineteenth-century origins of the animal welfare movement, 'not all animal-lovers were either social reformers or lovers of humanity'.[3] That this is still the case is best demonstrated by the wholehearted commitment of Brigid Bardot, probably the most famous celebrity in modern times devoted to the animal cause. If persistent media allegations are to be believed, Bardot's unquestionable dedication is combined with support for the French National Front and a belief in compulsory repatriation of immigrants. It is not untypical for right-wing groups promoting a 'new world order' for human society to advocate a sympathetic new *ordering* of its relationship to animals.

The all-too-common caricature of animal welfare campaigners as sentimentalists who bestow affection on the four-footed to substitute for an inability to relate to their own kind is not completely without foundation, either. Examples could readily be found to support such allegations. But the point that needs to be emphasised constantly in the face of such derogation is that neither lack of respect for fellow humans nor personal isolation have ever been the prevailing ethos within the animal protection movement. Compassion for all life has always been at its centre.

### *The role of religion and the churches*

I have made a conspicuous lack of reference to the efforts of orthodox religion to speak out against animal exploitation. Is this an unfortunate oversight? Or is it rather a justified reflection of absence of care?

Since most elements of western civilisation are based very broadly upon Christian teaching it is inevitable that the best of Christianity has had some beneficial impact upon animal welfare, as it has on every other area of our lives. Mercy and compassion are, after all, as much the core values of animal protection as they are central to the teachings of Jesus Christ. More specifically, there have been numerous Christian apostles — as well as Isaiah in the Old Testament[4] — who have emphasised the importance of kindness to animals. Many centuries later, St Francis of Assisi became probably the most remarkable of all.

In more recent times, the establishment of an organised movement for animal welfare in the early nineteenth century was linked specifically to elements of the Christian church. As mentioned before, the first vegetarian societies on both sides of the Atlantic were formed by members of the Bible Christian Church. Earlier, the Revd Arthur Broome, previously the Rector of Marylebone, had become the first Secretary of the (R)SPCA. Indeed, the Christian roots of the (R)SPCA were so strong that they sometimes manifested themselves in deplorable religious intolerance and prejudice towards non-Christians. Its second Secretary, Lewis Gompertz, was a Jew who had little choice other than to resign in 1832 when the Society announced that it was open to 'Christians only'.[5]

In this century, a minority of Christian teachers have been outspoken in their condemnation of cruelty to animals. Societies for animal welfare have been formed to represent both Anglican and Catholic faiths.[6] Theological treatises have been written advocating vegetarianism and an end to animal exploitation on religious grounds.[7] Some of the less orthodox Christian churches have also strongly advocated the right of animals to live free from persecution, particularly Quakers and Seventh Day Adventists. Kindness to animals featured in the preaching of John Wesley and has continued to play a part in Methodist thinking, too.

Similar positive comments could be made about other major world religions. Hinduism is based upon attitudes which are particularly sympathetic, many of its ancient teachers stressing the virtues of both abstinence from animal flesh and compassion towards other creatures.[8] Even the Jewish and Moslem faiths can boast members who have spoken out passionately in favour of animal protection,[9] though both have a poor overall reputation. Insistence upon ritual slaughter (i. e. killing for meat without pre-stunning) has proved particularly contentious.

Yet while the great religions have inspired many individuals to care for non-humans, with the exception of Hinduism the official stance of the hierarchies has been reactionary in the extreme. At best the church has been lukewarm in its support for animal protection, perpetuating the view that there are fundamental differences between people and other animals which bestow an intrinsically greater value upon human life. In particular the insistence of the Catholic church that only humans possess a soul remains a fundamental stumbling block. Admittedly, Pope Paul II displayed considerable enlightenment when, in 1990, he declared that 'animals possess a soul and men must love and feel solidarity with our smaller brethren',[10] but seven years later an alleged leak from the Vatican suggested that guidelines in the new catechism on the relationship between people and animals will continue to preserve the ancient view that 'one should not give affection to animals that only people deserve. It is unworthy to spend money for the animals'.[11] There is clearly a long way to go before historical prejudices are overcome.

So it is that on animal protection — as traditionally on many other areas of social reform — religious leaders tend to side with a pro-establishment view, lagging some distance behind progress in public opinion.

## Politics: on the side of business interests

Comments comparably disparaging could be made about politicians. Ever since Dick Martin succeeded in introducing the first law against animal cruelty in 1822, individual parliamentarians have fought doggedly to enhance legal protection. In the UK this century, the majority of these have tended to hold left of centre beliefs, though this has by no means been exclusively so. For example — as discussed earlier in this book — the most important political advances in the welfare of horses were due mostly to the efforts of a Conservative MP, Sir George Cockerill.

While the achievements of many politicians have been praiseworthy, the commitment of the parties they represent has usually been less admirable. Although a great many new laws from which animals have benefited have found their way on to the statute book, the major political parties have consistently fought shy of radical reform.

In opposition, Labour has often raised the hopes of animal welfare campaigners, only to frustrate them when in power. This dates back to that period of its first administrations in the 1920s, when committed anti-vivisectionists from the Prime Minister downwards failed to support any new efforts to legislate. More than fifty years later, Labour performed a comparable U-turn on vivisection, this time while in opposition. In 1985 it reached private agreement with the Conservative government to support the latter's Bill on animal research, having indicated previously that it would join with the majority of anti-vivisectionists who had condemned the proposals as hopelessly inadequate. The most feasible explanation for the change of heart was that Labour saw itself as likely to form the next government (wrongly as it happens) and wished to avoid responsibility for introducing its own legislation on a subject so controversial.

In October 1997, there were indications of another weakening of policy, this time by Tony Blair's Labour government. Speculation increased that a pre-election promise of a new Royal Commission on vivisection was no longer on the agenda.

In summary, the official Labour Party has consistently concluded that animal welfare is insufficiently important to warrant a challenge to powerful vested interests. A further example of this is offered by the way in which it now (1998) seems likely that Tony Blair's government will follow the example set by Clement Attlee's post-second-world-war administration by subjugating pressure from grassroots Labour campaigners for a ban on hunting. The indications are that rather than support the wishes of both parliament and the public, it will shy away from confrontation with the influential minority of hunt followers.

As for the Conservative Party, anti-cruelty sentiments have traditionally been constrained by active support for many of those interests who benefit most readily from animal exploitation. This applies not only to land-owning farmers and aristocratic supporters of hunting, but also to the forceful business concerns who profit from factory farming and animal experiments. The following extract from a 1983 White Paper in which Margaret Thatcher's government spelled out plans to update the law on vivisection, encapsulates tellingly the obstacles to progress:

> *The UK has a large pharmaceutical industry which makes a big contribution to our balance of payment and employs 67,500 people. In devising new controls it is very important not to put industry at risk unnecessarily.*[12]

As Labour, too, has allied itself progressively with powerful business interests, so the desire 'not to put industry at risk' becomes an ever more formidable barrier to reform.

Ultimately, the main obstacle to radical parliamentary reform during the twentieth century will endure through to the next. Animals cannot buy support, they cannot vote for themselves and — unsurprisingly — they have too few supporters willing to make their welfare a political priority.

Marching against vivsection in Britain in the early 1980s, at the height of popular opposition to animal-experimentation.

### The struggle continues

In the nineteenth century, some men roamed the country with bears in chains and others entertained themselves by watching spurred cocks fighting each other in a pit. Nowadays, in Britain at least, almost all public exhibitions which involve overt animal suffering have either been banned or — like hunting and hare coursing — face some possibility of abolition in the not too distant future.

On the other hand, many forms of institutionalised exploitation — principally factory farming and the routine testing of commercial products — are sharp reminders that our growing empathy with non-human animals is not always accompanied by more enlightened practices.

What of the next century? Impossible though it is to predict, a few comments are pertinent. Firstly, none of the progress that has so far been achieved is so secure that it can be taken for granted. Unlike advances in (say) attitudes to child welfare which ensure that legal protections will almost certainly never be rescinded, animals remain vulnerable for some time after legislation is passed. If fox hunting is eventually abolished, the ban will remain vulnerable for a considerable period. It is still conceivable that the fur trade might regain its former popularity.

On an international scale the possibility of retrogression has already been proved by the lifting of the international moratorium on the elephant ivory trade. Banned in the 1980s to save elephants from the threat of extinction, numbers have increased to the point where the 1997 CITES conference voted in support of a motion from Zimbabwe, Namibia and Botswana to re-open trade with Japan. Critics claim that the decision opens the door not only to elephant slaughter in the southern African states, but also to poachers in India and other nations who will exploit the Japanese market.[13] The possibility also remains that some commercial exploitation of whales will be legalised again.[14]

Another major new challenge to those who wish to reduce animal suffering is presented by genetic technology (and whatever become the scientific obsessions of the twenty-first century). While much of the criticism thus far has centred upon the potential risk to humanity from genetically modified material entering the environment, the impact of genetic science upon animal welfare has already proved disastrous. Practices developed in recent years include mice designed to grow a human ear on their backs; animals programmed to develop painful diseases ranging from cancers to cystic fibrosis; sheep engineered to produce drugs in their milk; monkeys, rabbits and genetically-modified pigs reared solely for the xenotransplantation industry; and cloned sheep. The 1996 UK annual Home Office statistics show that the number of animals bred with harmful genetic defects has doubled to 233,000 since 1990. In the same period the number of transgenics (i. e. genetically manipulated creatures) multiplied sixfold to more than 300,000 per year. The high price already paid in pain and suffering seems certain to rise incalculably in the coming years.

Against these disturbing developments must always be measured the unwearying efforts of thousands of individual campaigners who have contributed to remarkable advances. Never before has human dependence upon animal exploitation been questioned with such vigour and by so many.

Who can say how far this re-evaluation will eventually take civilisation towards the vision of Henry Salt and others? At best, animals are always likely to encourage our deepest sympathy, care and compassion; conversely, they will probably continue to prompt our most arrogant insensitivity. The irrationality of our responses remains extreme.

Probably the only safe conclusion to be drawn is that campaigners in the twenty-first century are certain to find much to hearten and inspire them in the courage and dedication of their predecessors and the reforms they have helped to create. Perhaps the greatest cause for optimism is the probability that there will be many others ready to carry forward the struggle with similar spirit and resolution.

# References

## Chapter 1 — In the beginning

**1  The climate at the turn of the century**

1  Figure quoted in Francisco Martin, *150 Years in the Forefront of Vegetarian Campaigning*, International Vegetarian Union, 1998.

2  Quotation taken from the chapter entitled 'Evidence Before First Royal Commission' in *A Century of Vivisection and Anti-Vivisection*, E. Westacott, C. W. Daniel Company Ltd, 1949.

3  Ibid.

4  Ibid.

5  Ibid.

6  Ibid.

7  *Who Cares For Animals — 150 Years of the RSPCA*, Antony Brown, Heinemann, 1974.

8  From the *Complete Works of Abraham Lincoln*, quoted from *The Extended Circle, An Anthology of Humane Thought*, ed. Jon Wynne Tyson, Centaur Press, 1986.

9  Ibid.

10  *The Creed of Kinship*, Henry S. Salt, Constable and Co., 1935.

**2  Salt of the Earth**

1  *Manifesto of the Humanitarian League*, quoted from *The Savour of Salt, A Henry Salt Anthology*, ed. George Hendrick and Willene Hendrick, Centaur Press, 1989.

2  From *Seventy Years Among Savages* by Henry Salt (1921), quoted from *The Savour of Salt*.

3  Ibid.

4  Ibid.

5  Ibid.

6  Ibid.

7  Ibid.

8  Preface to *Animals' Rights, Considered in Relation to Social Progress*, Henry S. Salt, Centaur Press, 1980.

9  *Animals' Rights, Considered in Relation to Social Progress*, Henry S. Salt, Centaur Press, 1980.

10  Ibid.

11  *The Humanities of Diet*, Henry Salt, The Humanitarian League, 1897.

12  Ibid.

13  *The Logic of Vegetarianism*, Henry S. Salt, George Bell and Sons, 1906.

14  From *Seventy Years Among Savages*, quoted from *The Savour of Salt, A Henry Salt Anthology*, ed. George Hendrick and Willene Hendrick, Centaur Press, 1989.

15  Ibid.

16  Ibid.

17  Ibid.

18  Ibid.

19  Ibid.

20  *The Logic of Vegetarianism*, Henry S. Salt, George Bell and Sons, 1906.

21  See 14.

22  From *On Cambrian and Cumbrian Hills*, A. C. Fifield, 1908, quoted in *A Savour of Salt*.

23  See 14.

24  See 22.

25  *Collected Works*, Vol 3, K. Marx and F. Engels, London, 1975.

26  Letter to Bertram Lloyd quoted in *Salt and His Circle*, Stephen Winston (with preface by George Bernard Shaw), Hutchinson and Co, 1951.

27  Ibid.

28  Quoted in Introduction to *The Savour of Salt*, ed. George Hendrick and Willene

Hendrick.

29 Preface to *The Creed of Kinship*, Henry S. Salt, Constable, 1935.

30 George Bernard Shaw, Preface to *Salt and His Circle*, Stephen Winston, Hutchinson, 1951.

31 See 1.

32 *The Creed of Kinship*, Henry S. Salt, Constable and Co, 1935.

## Chapter 2 — Domestic bliss

**1 Man's best friend**

1 *A Dog Is For Life — Celebrating the first hundred years of the National Canine Defence League*, Peter Ballard, NCDL, 1990.

2 Ibid.

3 Ibid.

**2 Shelter from the storm**

1 *The Chronicles of Ferne*, Animal Defence Society, 1951.

2 Ibid.

3 Ibid.

4 Ibid.

5 Ibid.

6 Ibid.

**3 From catwalk to cattery: the work of Celia Hammond**

Based on an interview with Celia Hammond conducted in March 1997.

**4 The century advances**

1 *Daily Telegraph*, 6 October 1996.

2 Ibid.

3 Ibid.

4 *The Problem With Rabbits*, compiled by Pat Rees, Green Fork, 1997.

5 'Little life forms to call your own', Caroline Daniel, *New Statesman*, 15 November 1996.

**5 Horses and humans: imperfect companions**

1 *Debt of Honour: The Story of The International League For The Protection Of Horses*, Jeremy James, Macmillan, 1994.

2 *Animal Revolution*, Richard D. Ryder, Basil Blackwell, 1989.

3 *Animals In War*, Jilly Cooper, Heinemann, 1983.

4 *The Chronicles of Ferne*, Animal Defence Society, 1951.

5 *Who Cares For Animals, 150 Years of the RSPCA*, Antony Brown, Heinemann, 1974.

6 *Debt of Honour: International League for the Protection of Horses*, Jeremy James, Macmillan, 1994.

7 See 4.

8 See 1.

9 'Flogging a live horse: the hidden trade in neglect', Greg Wood, *The Independent*, 14 February 1995.

10 *Betrayal of Trust*, Animal Aid, 1996.

11 See 1.

## Chapter 3 — Born to be wild

**1 Cruelty or conservation**

1 From *Inversnaid* by Gerard Manley Hopkins (in *Poems 1876-89*).

2 From *To What Purpose This Waste*, Christina Rossetti (1872).

3 *W. H. Hudson: A Biography*, Ruth Tomalin, Oxford University Press, 1984.

4 *Nature In Trust*, John Shaeil, Blackie, 1976.

5 Ibid.

6 Ibid.

7 Ibid.

8 'They Think it is All Over — The Fur Trade', Mark Glover, from *The Living Without Cruelty Diary 1998*, ed Mark Gold, Jon Carpenter, 1997.

**2 Birds fly ahead**

1 *W. H. Hudson: A Biography*, Ruth Tomalin, Oxford University Press, 1984.

2 *Birds*, the magazine of the RSPB, Winter 1997/98.

3 *Flight to Extinction, The Wild-Caught Bird Trade*, A report by the Animal Welfare Institute and the Environmental Investigation Agency, 1992.
4 *Costing the Earth*, BBC Radio 4, 25 October 1996.
5 'Ex-thieving Magpie cleared of slaughtering our songbirds', David Derbyshire, *Daily Mail*, 16 December 1997.

**3 Capturing the wild**
1 *Zoo Quest to Guiana*, David Attenborough, Lutterworth Press, 1956.
2 Ibid.

**4 Virginia McKenna and the legacy of *Born Free***
Based on an interview conducted in January 1997.
1 Personal correspondence from Sir David Attenborough, 31 October 1997.
2 Ibid.
3 *Joy Adamson: Beyond The Mask*, Caroline Cass, Weidenfeld and Nicholson, 1992.

**5 Jane Goodall's African dream**
Most of the material is from an interview conducted in January 1998.
1 *My Life with the Chimpanzees*, Jane Goodall, Minstrel Books (US), 1988
2 Ibid.
3 'Crusading for Chimps and Humans', Peter Miller, *National Geographic*, December 1995.
4 See 1.
5 See 3.

**6 Life on Earth**
1 Interview with Jane Goodall, January 1998.
2 *The Dark Romance of Dian Fossey*, Harold Hayes, Chatto and Windus, 1991.
3 Personal Correspondence from Sir David Attenborough, 31st October 1997.
4 Ibid.
5 'Forty years of animal magnetism', Gareth Huw Jones, *Radio Times*, 11-17 October 1997.
6 Personal correspondence, 31 October 1997.
7 *Introduction to Life On Earth*, Enlarged version, David Attenborough, Reader's Digest/Collins, 1980.

**7 Beyond conservation: Saving the whales**
1 *The Hull Whale Fishery*, Jennifer C. Rowley, Lockington Publishing Company, 1982.
2 *Whale Nation*, Heathcote Williams, Jonathan Cape, 1988.
3 Ibid.
4 Ibid.
5 *Moby Dick*, Herman Melville, Penguin Classics, 1986.
6 *The Greenpeace Story*, Michael Brown and John May, Dorling Kindersley, 1988.
7 Ibid.
8 Ibid.
9 Ibid.

**8 Conservation, cruelty and conservation**
1 *Animal Language*, Michael Bright, BBC Books, 1984.
2 Ibid.
3 Interview with Jane Goodall, January 1998.
4 'A Dog's Life', Claudio Silliero-Zubiri, *Wildlife Times*, Autumn/Winter 1996.
5 *The Zoo Enquiry*, World Society for the Protection of Animals, July 1994.

# Chapter 4 — The hunt is up

**1 A changing country**
1 *The Hunt and the Anti-Hunt*, Phil Windeatt, Pluto Press, 1982.
2 Ibid.
3 Ibid.
4 *All Heaven in a Rage*, E. S. Turner, The Kinship Library, Centaur Press, 1992.
5 'Grasping at a forty-five year old straw', John Bryant, *Wildlife Guardian*, No 34, Summer 1996.
6 Ibid.

7 *Report of the Committee on Cruelty to Wild Animals*, Home Office, HMSO, June 1951.
8 Ministry of Agriculture, Fisheries and Food survey, published 1979.
9 *Animal Revolution*, Richard D. Ryder, Basil Blackwell, 1989.

**2 Rebels with a cause: Dave Wetton and the Hunt Saboteurs**
Interview with Dave Wetton, December 1996.

**3 The hunt is up**
1 *The Hunt and the Anti-Hunt*, Phil Windeatt, Pluto Press, 1982.

**4 Hunting, shooting and the royal family**
1 *All Heaven in a Rage*, E. S. Turner, The Kinship Library, Centaur Press, 1992.
2 *The Life and Times of George V*, Denis Judd, Weidenfeld and Nicholson Ltd, 1973.
3 *The Sphere*, December 19, 1911, on display at Exeter City Museum.
4 *King George VI and Queen Elizabeth*, Christopher Warwick, Sidgwick and Jackson, 1985.
5 *All Heaven in a Rage*, E. S. Turner, The Kinship Library, Centaur Press, 1992.
6 Gallup Poll conducted in November 1991.
7 'Prince Charles is unfit to be King, says Labour MP', Joy Copley, *The Daily Telegraph*, 2 March 1996.
8 *The Times*, 9 September 1997.

# Chapter 4 — That's entertainment?

**1 The circus comes to town**
1 *The Rose Tinted Menagerie*, William Johnson, Heretic Books, 1990.
2 *All Heaven in a Rage*, E. S. Turner, The Kinship Library, Centaur Press, 1992.
3 *Wild Circus Animals*, Alfred Court, Burke Publishing, 1954.

**2 Circus Hassani and Coco the Clown**
Based on interview with Ali Hassani, May 1997.
1 Interview with Tamara Hassani, Polly

Toynbee, *The Guardian*, 11 August 1980.
2 *The Daily Mirror*, 14 September 1996.
3 'No animals', Liz Hodgkinson, *Daily Mail*, 17 December 1979.

**3 From King Kong to Babe**
1 'Who's Watching The Movies?', Tim Phillips, *Animals' Defender*, Oct/Nov/Dec 1994.
2 Ibid.
3 *Companion Animals*, Animal Aid Information Sheet, 1996.

**4 The unfortunate consequences of Flipper**
1 *The Rose Tinted Menagerie*, William Johnson, Heretic Books, 1990.
2 Ibid.

# Chapter 5 — Life down on the farm

**1 Over the seas to slaughter**
1 *Beyond Beef: The Rise And Fall Of The Cattle Culture*, Jeremy Rifkin, Dutton, 1992.
2 Ibid.
3 *All Heaven in a Rage*, E. S. Turner, The Kinship Library, Centaur Press, 1992.
4 Ibid.
5 *The Logic of Vegetarianism*, Henry S. Salt, George Bell and Sons, 1906.
6 *A Far Cry From Noah*, Peter Stevenson, Green Print, 1994.
7 *Who Cares For Animals, 150 Years Of The RSPCA*, Antony Brown, Heinemann, 1974.
8 Ibid.
9 Ibid.
10 *The Guardian*, 24 June 1994.
11 *The Independent*, 14 April 1995.
12 'An Echo of the 1960s', Naomi Marks, *The European*, 24 February 1995.

**2 Animal machines**
1 Ministry of Agriculture figures.
2 *Animal Machines*, Ruth Harrison, Vincent Stuart Ltd, 1964.

3    'Blood and bacteria on the abattoir floor',
     *New Scientist*, 2 October, 1986.
4    *The Price of Meat*, Danny Penman,
     Gollancz, 1996.
5    *Outrage, The Animal Aid Journal*,
     April/May 1996.


**3  Peter Roberts: from farmer to campaigner.**
Interview with Peter Roberts, February 1997.


**4  Assembly line animals**
1    *Animals' Rights, Considered in Relation to
     Social Progress*, Henry S. Salt, Centaur
     Press, 1980.
2    *Beyond Beef, The Rise And Fall Of The
     Cattle Culture*, Jeremy Rifkin, Dutton, 1992.
3    *A Cause For Celebration: 150 Years Of The
     Vegetarian Society*, The Vegetarian Society
     (UK), 1997.
4    *Seventy Five Years Ago*, Bronwen
     Humphreys, The Vegetarian Society
     (UK), Autumn 1995.
5    See 3.
6    'Fifty Years Ago', Bronwen Humphreys,
     *The Vegetarian*, Summer 1996.
7    Ibid.


**5  Kathleen Jannaway: visionary or crank?**
Based on an interview with Kathleen
     Jannaway, November 1996.
1    Eva Batt, *Selections from her writings and
     tributes from her friends*, The Movement for
     Compassionate Living, 1989.
2    The first British vegan cookbook seems to
     have been *No Animal Food* by Rupert H.
     Wheldon. It appeared as early as 1910.
     Long before the formation of The Vegan
     Society, some vegetarians adopted a diet
     free from animal products and debated its
     ethical basis in *The Vegetarian Messenger*,
     notably between 1909 and 1912. See *The
     Vegan*, Spring 1998.
3    T. A. B. Sanders, 'Vegetarian Diets',
     *Nutrition Bulletin*, 5 (1979).


**6  The vegetarian revolution**
1    *Report on the Welfare of Livestock (Red
     Meat Animals) at the Time of Slaughter*,
     The Farm Animal Welfare Council,
     Ministry of Agriculture, Fisheries And
     Food, 1984.
2    *The Realeat Survey 1984-1997, Changing
     Attitudes to Meat Consumption*, The
     Realeat Company, 1997.
3    *Food, Nutrition and the Prevention of
     Cancer: a global perspective*, World Cancer
     Research Fund/American Institute for
     Cancer Research, 1997.
4    See 2.
5    Figure supplied by Kim Stallwood and
     Heather Moore, *Animals Agenda* magazine
     (US), 1995.


## Chapter 7 — Animal experiments: 'Everything changes and everything remains the same'

**1  The shambles of science and the Brown Dog**
1    *The Dark Face of Science*, John Vyvyan,
     Michael Joseph, 1971.
2    *A Century of Vivisection and Anti-
     Vivisection*, E. Westacott, Daniel, 1949.
3    Ibid.
4    *The Daily News*, 19 November 1903,
     quoted in *The Dark Face of Science* (see 1).
5    *The Dark Face of Science*, John Vyvyan,
     Michael Joseph, 1971.
6    *The Brown Dog Affair, The story of a monu-
     ment that divided a nation*, Peter Mason,
     Two Sevens Publishing, 1997.
7    Ibid.
8    See 1.
9    See 2.
10   Ibid.
11   Ibid.
12   *Animal Revolution*, Richard D. Ryder, Basil
     Blackwell, 1989.
13   See 6.

**2 Silent suffering: Sarah Kite and Huntingdon Laboratories**
Based on Sarah Kite's account in *Silent Suffering*, and an interview with her in January 1998.
1 *Silent Suffering: Inside a British laboratory*, Sarah Kite, British Union for the Abolition of Vivisection, 1990.
2 *The Cruel Deception*, Dr Robert Sharpe, Thorsons, 1988.
3 See 1.

**3 Fifty years in the wilderness**
1 *Antivivisection and Medical Science*, Richard D. French, Princeton University Press, 1975.
2 *The Dark Face of Science*, John Vyvyan, Michael Joseph, 1971.
3 Ibid.
4 *The Cruel Deception*, Dr Robert Sharpe, Thorsons, 1988.
5 Ibid.
6 *A Century of Vivisection and Anti-Vivisection*, E. Westacott, Daniel, 1949.
7 'Dogs, ducks and rodents conquered the skies for mankind', Giles Coren, *The Times*, 30 November 1995.
8 See 2.
9 Ibid.

**4 Biting back**
1 The Mobilisation For Laboratory Animals consisted of Animal Aid, the British Union for the Abolition of Vivisection, the National Anti-Vivisection Society and the Scottish Anti-Vivisection Society.
2 *Caught in the Act: The Feldberg Investigation*, Melody MacDonald and the Animal Cruelty Investigation Group, Jon Carpenter, 1994.

## Chapter 8 — Animal rights revisited

**1 Peter Singer and *Animal Liberation***
Written interview with Peter Singer, October 1997.

**2 Irene Williams: The original Spice Girl**
Interview with Irene Williams, June 1997.

**3 Militancy**
1 *Against All Odds: Animal Liberation 1972-1986*, ARC Print, 1986.

**4 Ronnie Lee: 'A dangerous criminal'?**
Interview with Ronnie Lee, July 1997.
1 *Archangel Magazine*, 2.
2 Ibid.
3 *ALF Supporters Group Bulletin*, 17.
4 *Animal Liberation* (second edition), Thorsons, 1990
5 *The Observer*, 9 February 1997.
6 *Youth TGI Survey*, 1993.

## Chapter 9 — Animal world

**1 A nation of animal lovers**
1 'Farm Animals in Eastern Europe', Janice Cox. Lecture given at the conference, 'An Agriculture for The New Millennium — Animal Welfare, Poverty and Globalisation', organised by the Compassion in World Farming Trust, 2 April 1998.
2 Reported in *The Observer*, 9 February 1997.
3 'GATT and Developing Countries', Dr Vandana Shiva. Lecture given at the conference, 'An Agriculture for the New Millennium', etc, 2 April 1998.
4 'GATT Implications for Animal Welfare in the EU', Peter Stevenson. Lecture given at the conference, 'An Agriculture for the New Millennium,' etc, 2 April 1998.
5 Introduction to *The Universal Kinship*, J. Howard Moore, ed. Charles Magel, The Kinship Library, Centaur Press, 1992.
6 Ibid.
7 *Nature in Trust*, John Sheail, Blackie, 1976.
8 Personal correspondence from Peter Singer, October 1997.

9   Ibid.
10  *Food, Nutrition and the Prevention of Cancer: A Global Perspective*, World Cancer Research Fund/American Institute for Cancer Research.
11  Ibid.
12  *Flight to Extinction, The Wild-Caught Bird Trade*, report by the Animal Welfare Institute and the Environmental Investigation Agency, 1992.
13  'A Journey to China', Virginia McKenna, *Wildlife Times*, Autumn/Winter 1996.
14  Literature published by the World Society for the Protection of Animals, 1997.
15  Ibid.
16  Ibid.
17  Quoted in *The Extended Circle, An Anthology of Humane Thought*, Jon Wynne-Tyson, Cardinal, 1990.
18  Ibid.
19  Personal correspondence from Maneka Gandhi to Animal Aid, 27 July 1996.
20  Ibid.
21  *Food, Nutrition and the Prevention of Cancer: A Global Perspective*, World Cancer Research Fund, American Institute for Cancer Research, 1997.
22  Personal correspondence from Maneka Gandhi to Animal Aid, 27 July 1996.
23  See 17.

**2  Maneka's ark**
Interview with Maneka Gandhi, April 1998. Additional information from 'Ahimsa With Attitude', Mia MacDonald, *The Animals' Agenda*, Vol 16 No 1.

**3  Antony Thomas: *To Love Or Kill***
Interview conducted August 1997.

# Chapter 10 — Past, present and future

1   Co-operative Bank policy.
2   *Nationwide*, BBC Radio 5 Live, 3 February 1998.

3   *Man and the Natural World*, Keith Thomas, Penguin Books, 1984.
4   'The wolf also shall dwell with the lamb and the leopard shall lie down with the kid; and the calf and the young lion and the fatling together, and a little child shall lead them… They shall not hurt nor destroy in all my holy mountain.'
5   Quoted from *The Enforcers* by Lynne Wallis, *The Guardian Weekend*, 24 May 1997.
6   Anglican Society for Animal Welfare and the Catholic Study Circle for Animal Welfare.
7   Notably *Christianity and the Right of Animals*, Andrew Linzey, SPCK, 1987.
8   For example, 'he who does not seek to cause the sufferings of bonds and death to living creatures, but desires the good of all, obtains endless bliss', *The Laws of Manu* V.
9   See *Animals in Islam*, Al-Hafiz B. A. Masri, Athene Trust, 1989, and *Animals and the Liberation of Theology*, Andrew Linzey and Dan Cohn-Sheebok, Mowbray 1997.
10  Public audience by Pope Paul II, 19 January 1990, quoted in *Animal Pride*, Animal Aid, June 1998.
11  *Agscene*, magazine of Compassion in World Farming, Summer 1997.
12  *Scientific Procedures on Living Animals*, HMSO, 1993
13  *Daily Telegraph*, 10 June 1997.
14  Proposal by Eire at the International Whaling Commission annual conference, July 1997.

# Selected bibliography

David Attenborough, *Life On Earth*, Collins, 1980.
   *Zoo Quest to Guiana*, Lutterworth Press, 1956
Peter Ballard, *Celebrating One Hundred Years of the National Canine Defence League*, NCDL, 1990
M. Beddow Bayley, *The Futility of Experiments on Animals*, National Anti-Vivisection Society, 1954
Ted Benton, *Natural Relations*, Verso, 1993
Michael Brown and John May, *The Greenpeace Story*, Dorling Kindersley, 1988
Antony Brown, *Who Cares For Animals: 150 Years of the RSPCA*, Heinemann, 1974
Rachel Carson, *Silent Spring*, Penguin, 1990.
Stephen Clark, *The Moral Status of Animals*, Oxford University Press, 1977
Vernon Coleman, *Why Animal Experiments Must Stop*, European Medical Journal, 1994
Peter Cox, *The New Why You Don't Need Meat*, Bloomsbury, 1992
Charles Darwin, *The Origin of Species*, Penguin Classics, 1985
Clare Druce, *Chicken and Egg: Who Pays The Price?*, Green Print, 1989
Maureen Duffy, *Men and Beasts*, Granada, 1984.
Michael W. Fox, *Towards the New Eden: Animal Rights and Human Liberation*, Viking, 1979.
Richard D. French, *Antivivisection and Medical Science in Victorian Society*, Princeton University Press, 1975
Robert Garner, *Animals, Politics and Morality*, Manchester University Press, 1993
Juliet Gellatley, *The Silent Ark*, Thorsons, 1996
Stanley and Roslind Godlovitch (with John Harris) eds, *Animals, Men and Morals*, Gollancz, 1973
Mark Gold, *Assault and Battery*, Pluto Press, 1983
   *Living Without Cruelty*, Green Print, 1988
   *Animal Rights: Extending the Circle of Compassion*, Jon Carpenter, 1995
Jane Goodall, *In the Shadow of Man*, Collins, 1971
   *The Chimpanzees of Gombe: Patterns of Behaviour*, Bellnap Press of Harvard University, 1986
   *My Life With The Chimpanzees*, Minstrel Books, 1996
Louise Lind-Af-Hageby and Liesa Schartau, *The Shambles of Science*, 1903
Ruth Harrison, *Animal Machines*, Stuart, 1964
Harold Hayes, *The Dark Romance of Dian Fossey*, Chatto and Windus, 1991
George Hendrick and Willene Hendrick, *A Savour of Salt*, Centaur Press, 1989
Jeremy James, *Debt of Honour: The Story of the International League for the Protection of Horses*, Macmillan, 1994
William Johnson, *The Rose-Tinted Menagerie*, Heretic Books, 1990
Barry Kew, *The Pocket Book of Animal Facts and Figures*, Green Print, 1991
Sarah Kite, *Secret Suffering, Inside a British Laboratory*, BUAV, 1990
Peter Mason, *The Brown Dog Affair*, Two Sevens Publications, 1997
Mary Midgeley, *Beast and Man: The Roots of Human Nature*, Cornell University Press, 1978.
Francis Moore Lappé, *Diet for a Small Planet*, Ballantine Books, 1975
Gill Langley (ed), *Animal Experimentation, The Consensus Changes*, Macmillan, 1989

Andrew Linzey, *Christianity and the Rights of Animals*, SPCK, 1987
    *Animals and the Liberation of Theology* (with Dan Cohn-Sheebok), Mowbray, 1997
Melody MacDonald, *Caught In The Act*, Jon Carpenter, 1994
Virginia McKenna (ed), *Beyond the Bars: The Zoo Dilemma*, (with Will Travers and Jonathan Wray),
    1987
Jeffrey Masson (with Susan McCarthy) *When Elephants Weep*, Jonathan Cape, 1994
Al-Hafiz B. A. Masri, *Animals in Islam*, Athene Trust, 1989
John Howard Moore, *The Universal Kinship*, Centaur Press, 1992
Nina, Duchess of Hamilton, *The Chronicles of Ferne*, Ferne, 1951
Ingrid Newkirk, *Free the Animals: The Untold Story of The Animal Liberation Front (US)*, Noble Press,
    1994
John Page/Jane Holgate, *Against All Odds, Animal Liberation 1972-86*, ARC Print, 1986
Tony Page, *Vivisection Unveiled*, Jon Carpenter, 1997
Danny Penman, *The Price of Meat*, Gollancz, 1997
Tom Regan, *The Case For Animal Rights* (with Peter Singer), Routledge and Kegan Paul, 1984
    *Animal Rights and Human Obligations*, Prentice Hall, 1976
Jeremy Rifkin, *Beyond Beef*, Penguin, 1992
John Robbins, *Diet For a Small Planet*, Stillpoint, 1987
Hans Ruesch, *Slaughter of the Innocent*, Bantam, 1978
Richard D. Ryder, *Victims of Science*, NAVS (distributed by Centaur Press), 1983
    *Animal Revolution*, Blackwell, 1989
Henry Salt, *Animals' Rights Considered in Relation to Social Progress*, Centaur Press, 1983
    *Creed of Kinship*, Constable and Co, 1935
    *The Logic of Vegetarianism*, George Bell and Sons, 1906
Robert Sharpe, *The Cruel Deception*, Thorsons, 1988
    *Science On Trial*, Awareness Books, 1994
John Sheall, *Nature In Trust*, Blackie, 1976
Marion Shoard, *The Theft of the Countryside*, Temple Smith, 1980
Peter Singer, *Animal Liberation*, Thorsons, 1990
    *The Great Ape Project*, Fourth Estate, 1993 (with Paola Cavallieri)
    *Animal Factories*, Crown Publishers, 1980 (with Jim Mason)
Marjorie Spiegel, *The Dreaded Comparison, Human and Animal Slavery*, Heretic Books, 1989
Peter Stevenson, *A Far Cry From Noah*, Green Print, 1994
Ruth Tomalin, *W. H. Hudson: A Biography*, Oxford University Press, 1984
Keith Thomas, *Man and the Natural World*, Penguin Books, 1984
E. S. Turner, *All Heaven in a Rage*, Centaur Press, 1992
John Vidal, *McLibel – Burger Culture on Trial*, Macmillan, 1997
John Vynan, *The Dark Face of Science*, Michael Joseph, 1971
    *In Pity and in Anger*, Micah Publications, 1988
E. Westacott, *A Century of Vivisection and Anti-Vivisection*, C. W. Daniel, 1947
Peter Wheale and Ruth McNally eds, *Animal Genetic Engineering*, Pluto Press, 1995
Heathcote Williams, *Whale Nation*, Jonathan Cape, 1988
Philip Windeatt, *The Hunt and the Anti-Hunt*, Pluto Press, 1982
Esme Wynne-Tyson, *The Philosophy of Compassion*, Centaur Press, 1970
Jon Wynne-Tyson, *The Civilized Alternative*, Centaur Press, 1972
    *Food For A Future*, Thorsons, 1988
    *The Extended Circle – A Dictionary of Humane Thought*, Cardinal, 1990

# Organisations

## United Kingdom

Animal Aid, The Old Chapel, Bradford Street, Tonbridge, Kent TN9 1AW
Advocates for Animals, 10 Queensferry Street, Edinburgh, EH2 4PG
Animal Concern, 62 Dunbarton Street, Glasgow G3 8RE
Born Free Foundation, Cherry Tree Cottage, Coldharbour, Dorking, Surrey, RH5 6HA
British Union for the Abolition of Vivisection, 16a Crane Grove, London, N7 8LB
Captive Animals Protection Society, 171 Cherry Tree Road, Blackpool FY4 4PQ
Celia Hammond Animal Trust, High Street, Wadhurst, TN5 6AG
Compassion In World Farming, 5a Charles Street, Petersfield, GU32 3EW
Council for the Protection of Rural England, 25 Buckingham Palace Road, London SW1W 0PP
Dr Hadwen Trust for Humane Research, 22 Bancroft, Hitchin, SG5 1JW
Earthkind, Avenue Lodge, Bounds Green, London N22 4LU
Farm Animal Welfare Network, PO Box 40, Holmfirth, Huddersfield, HD7 1QY
The Fox Project, The Old Chapel, Bradford Street, Tonbridge, TN9 1AW
Friends of the Earth, 26-28 Underwood Street, London N1 7JQ
Friends of the Earth (Scotland), Bonnington Mill, 72 Newhaven Road, Edinburgh, EH6 5QG
Greenpeace, Canonbury Villas, London N1 2PN
Humane Research Trust, Brook House, 29 Bramhall Lane South, Bramhall, Stockport, SK7 2ND
Hunt Saboteurs Association, PO Box 2786, Brighton BN2 2AX
International Fund for Animal Welfare, Warren Court, Park Road, Crowborough, TN6 2GA
International League for the Protection of Horses, Anne Colvin House, Snetterton, Norfolk, NR16 2LR
Jane Goodall Institute (UK), 15 Clarendon Park, Lymington, SO41 8AX
League Against Cruel Sports, 83-87 Union Street, London, SE1 1SG
Lord Dowding Fund, 261 Goldhawk Road, London, W12 9PE
Movement for Compassionate Living, 47 Highlands Road, Leatherhead, KT22 8NQ
National Anti-Vivisection Society, 261 Goldhawk Road, London, W12 9PE
National Canine Defence League, 17 Wakley Street, London EC1V 7LT
People for the Ethical Treatment of Animals (PETA), PO Box 3169, London NW1 2JF
Respect For Animals, PO Box 500, Nottingham, NG1 3AS
RSPB, The Lodge, Sandy, SG19 2DL
RSPCA, The Causeway, Horsham, RH12 1HG
Uncaged, 14 Ridgeway Road, Sheffield, S12 2SS
Vegan Society, 7 Battle Road, St Leonards on Sea, TN37 7AA
Vegetarian Society, Parkdale, Dunham Road, Altrincham, WA14 4QG
Viva!, 12 Queens Square, Brighton, BN1 3FD
World Society for the Protection of Animals, 2 Langley Lane, London, SW8 1TJ
World Wide Fund For Nature, Panda House, Weyside Park, Godalming, Surrey, GU7 1XR

# USA

American Anti-Vivisection Society, Suite 204, Noble Plaza, 801 Old York Road, Jenkintown, Pennsylvania, 19046

American Fund For Alternatives To Animal Research, 175 West 12th Street, Suite 16g, New York, 10011

American Humane Association, 63 Inverness Drive, East Englewood, CO 80112

American Vegan Society, Box H, 501, Old Harding Highway, Malaga, California, CA 08328

Animal Rights Network Inc, PO Box 5234, Westport, Conn. 06881

Animals Agenda, PO Box 25881, Baltimore, MD 21224

Animals Voice, PO Box 16955, North Hollywood, CA 91615

Beauty Without Cruelty, 175 West 12th Street 16G, New York, NY 10011-8275

Farm Animal Reform Movement, PO Box 30654, Bethesda, Maryland 20817

Friends of Animals (New York), 1841, Broadway, Suite 212, New York, NY 10023

Friends of Animals (Washington DC), 1623 Connecticut Avenue, Washington DC 20009

Fund for Animals (California), 12548 Ventura Boulevard STC 141, Studio City, California, 91604

Fund for Animals (New York), 200 West 57th Street, New York 10019

Greenpeace, 1611 Connecticut Avenue, NW Washington, DC 20009

Humane Education Network, PO Box 7434, Menlo Park, California, 94026

Humane Farming Association, 1550 California Street, San Francisco, California, 94109

Humane Society of the US, 2100 L Street, NW Washington DC 20037

In Defense of Animals, 131 Camino Alto, Suite B, Mill Valley, California, CA 94941

International Fund for Animal Welfare, PO Box 193, Yarmouth Port, MA 02675

Jane Goodall Institute, PO Box 599, Ridgefield, Connecticut, 06877

National Anti-Vivisection Society, 53 West Jackson Boulevard, Suite 1550, Chicago, Il 60604

North American Vegetarian Society, PO Box 72, Dolgeville, New York, 13329

Performing Animal Welfare Society, PO Box 849, Galt CA 95632

People for the Ethical Treatment of Animals (PETA), PO Box 42516, Washington DC, 20015 501 Front Street, Norfolk, VA 23510

Vegetarian Society Inc, Po Box 34427, Los Angeles, California, CA 90034

*Vegetarian Times*, PO Box 570, Oak Park, Ill 60603

*Vegetarian Voice*, PO Box 72, Dolgeville, New York, 13329

World Society for the Protection of Animals (USA), PO Box 190, Perkins Street, Boston, Massachusetts 02130

## Australia

*Animal Liberation* Magazine, PO Box 221, Mitcham, Victoria, 3132 (can provide details of separate state offices)
Australia and New Zealand Federation of Animal Societies, PO Box 16, Barkar Centre, Capital Territory, 2603
Fund For Animals, PO Box 126, Terrey Hills, NSW, 2084
Great Ape Project, PO Box 1023, Collingwood, Victoria, 3066
Greenpeace Australia Ltd, 37 Nicholson Street, Balmain, NSW, 2401
Humane Society, PO Box 38, Elsternwick, Victoria, 3185
International League For Protection of Horses, Box C, 616 Claremont Street Post Office, Sydney, NSW, 2000
RSPCA, The Bay, 29 Benthan Street, Yarralumla, Capital Territory, 2600

## India

People For Animals, 48 Usha Kiran, Carmichael Road, Bombay 40026
People For Animals, A4 Maharani Bagh, New Delhi, 110065

## South Africa

Animal Voice, PO Box 843, Kuils River, 7580
Association Against Painful Experiments on Animals, PO Box 85228, Emmarentia, 2029, Johannesburg
Beauty Without Cruelty, PO Box 23321, Claremont, 7735
SAAV, PO Box 3018, Honeydew, 2040
Vegetarian Society, PO Box 15091, Lambton, 1414

# Picture credits

We are grateful to the following for permission to reproduce photographs in their possession. Copyright is acknowledged where known or appropriate.

Front cover: Left to right: top, British Union for the Abolition of Vivisection, National Canine Defence League, Compassion in World Farming; centre, Anti-Bont Committee (from Animal Aid), Iain Green (Animal Aid); bottom, Bill Travers, Irene Williams

# Index